*T*he Call to Adventure

*T*he Call to Adventure

Bringing the Hero's Journey to Daily Life

Paul Rebillot

with Melissa Kay

HarperSanFrancisco
A Division of HarperCollins*Publishers*

HarperCollins books may be purchased for educational, business, or sales promotional
use. For information, please call or write: Special Markets Department, HarperCollins
Publishers, Inc., 10 East 53rd Street, New York, NY 10022. Telephone: (212) 207-
7528; Fax: (212) 207-7222.

FIRST HARPERCOLLINS PAPERBACK EDITION PUBLISHED IN 1993

Library of Congress Cataloging-in-Publication Data
Rebillot, Paul.
      The call to adventure : living the hero's journey in daily life /
Paul Rebillot with Melissa Kay. — 1st HarperCollins pbk. ed.
         p.   cm.
      ISBN 0–06–250709–5
      1. Conduct of life.   2. Self-realization.   3. Heroes—Psychology.
4. Rites and ceremonies—Psychological aspects.   I. Title.
BF637.C5R425   1993
248.4—dc20   91-58898
                                                                  CIP

93   94   95   96   97   ❖   RRD(H)   10   9   8   7   6   5   4   3   2   1

This edition is printed on acid-free paper that meets the American National Standards
Institute Z39.48 Standard.

For Stanford

CONTENTS

ACKNOWLEDGMENTS

While I take full responsibility for the contents of this book, I wish, at the same time, to express my deep gratitude to those who have helped, inspired, and encouraged its long journey into manifestation.

My thanks go first to Laurance S. Rockefeller and to Jean and Sidney Lanier for the generous grant from the Fund for the Enhancement of the Human Spirit, which made it possible for me to stop traveling long enough to begin this book. I am indebted to the editors and staff of Harper San Francisco for the book's final production and appearance in the world.

But before the writing came the inspiration. For this I look back with gratitude to Joseph Campbell and to John Weir Perry, for their pioneer work in the fields of mythology and the psychology of those in the throes of spiritual crisis. A special word of thanks goes to my friend and colleague Pennel Rock, for introducing me to the tantric practice of meditation on the three centers, out of which much of my teaching theory has evolved.

It was Richard Price, my teacher of Gestalt, and Stan and Christina Grof who helped me to realize that my own experience had been one not of mental illness, but of spiritual emergence. This healing revelation, for which I am most profoundly grateful, encouraged me to develop the Hero's Journey process presented in this book in the hope of helping others toward their own emergence as spiritually creative individuals.

Finally, my gratitude widens to embrace all those hundreds of men and women in Europe and America who, over the years, have risked their status quo to follow the path of the Hero—and whose unique stories have contributed to the deepening and refinement of this process. They are indeed my co-creators, and I acknowledge them joyously with reverence and with love.

FOREWORD

On California's magnificent Big Sur Coast, about forty miles south of Monterey and Carmel, on a narrow strip of land between the mountains and the Pacific Ocean, lies the famous Esalen Institute. Since 1962, when it changed its identity from a motel to the world's first growth center, this small settlement, barely noticeable from the scenic highway, has become a Mecca of the human potential movement. The people living and working at Esalen, or closely associated with it, have made original contributions to psychology and psychotherapy that can easily match those of any university, research institute, hospital, or other mainstream facility.

I had the unique opportunity to live and work at Esalen for fourteen years. It was in this extraordinary and unconventional human laboratory that I met Paul Rebillot and have developed a personal friendship with him. My wife and I invited Paul repeatedly as guest faculty to our month-long seminars, and were able to experience and enjoy his work both as participants and as observers. We were very surprised and impressed by the profound impact this playful, unthreatening, and deceptively simple approach can have on participants. Many of them experienced the process as healing and transformative; and mental health professionals talked about deep, experiential learning and valuable theoretical insights.

Even in the unusually rich and stimulating context of Esalen, Paul's original process, the Hero's Journey, was in a category of its own. While the other workshops offered valuable, but usually rather specialized approaches, such as Gestalt practice, psychodrama, group process, various forms of body work, exploration of mythology, dance, or painting, Paul's approach represented a creative synthesis, merging many of these elements into a unique amalgam of therapy, theater, music and song, ritual, dance, celebration, and costume-making.

Since time immemorial healing was a spiritual matter and was always connected with art—instrumental music, singing, dance, and painting. In the industrial era therapy lost its connection with spirituality and art; it became dry and devitalized. Paul Rebillot has been able to rediscover these dimensions and reintroduce them into the healing process. In addition, the Hero's Journey is permeated with a healthy sense of humor and provides exquisite entertainment. This element deserves a special emphasis and appreciation, since the role of humor as an important instrument of healing can hardly be overestimated.

It might be useful to look at some of Paul Rebillot's most significant sources of inspiration that helped him to create this unique process. There is no doubt that his lifelong passion for the dramatic arts was a factor of paramount importance. He studied theater arts at the University of Michigan and had many years of practical experience in directing, acting, and designing. His military service took him for a year to Japan, where he worked at the U.S. Army's Far East Radio Network. His exposure to an esthetically refined culture with an ancient spiritual and cultural tradition had a profound impact on his professional life as well as on his personal life. He was particularly impressed and touched by the Japanese Kabuki and No theater, and later incorporated various elements of these Oriental dramatic arts into his work.

His understanding of the full potential of the theater at its best—its healing, ritual, magical, and spiritual power—developed during a deep personal crisis that became a turning point in his life. In the middle of a play in which he was performing the leading role, he was suddenly struck by serious doubts and questions concerning the meaning of his life and life in general, and felt an overwhelming need to embark on a journey of self-discovery. He left the dramatic arts and went into seclusion, where he practiced intensive meditation. This period culminated in a two-month episode during which he experienced dramatic nonordinary states of consciousness. It was this shattering personal experience that gave him a new appreciation of the roots of European theater in the Greek tragedy, with its deep, cathartic effects.

Another vital source of Paul's inspiration was the field of psychology and psychotherapy. After this personal crisis, he felt the need to explore the experiences that had so profoundly transformed his existence and to give them some expression in his life. His quest took him to Esalen, where he was exposed to a wide spectrum of innovative humanistic and transpersonal therapies. He was particularly deeply influenced by Gestalt therapy, an approach brought to and further developed at Esalen by South African psychiatrist Fritz Perls. Gestalt practice is a unique experiential method of psychotherapy that uses intense focus of awareness on the emotional and physical processes occurring in the here-and-now to psychologically complete various unfinished traumatic issues in one's life. Paul had the opportunity to learn Gestalt practice from Perls's most prominent disciple, Richard Price, the cofounder of Esalen.

In Esalen Paul Rebillot also met Joseph Campbell, a brilliant thinker and teacher, generally considered the greatest mythologist in the world. It was Campbell's work that provided the model and the name for the Hero's Journey. Analyzing a broad spectrum of myths from different parts of the world, Campbell discovered that they all contained variations on one universal theme, one archetypal formula. This "monomyth," as he called it, seemed to appear in all cultures and all historical periods. It was the story of the Hero, male or female, an individual who receives a superior call and embarks on a journey of dangerous adventures. After a series of difficult ordeals that often culminate in an experience of death and rebirth, the Hero returns to the culture empowered, healed, or transformed, and uses the new gifts for the benefit of others.

Campbell's inquisitive and incisive intellect was not satisfied with the recognition of the universality of this myth over time and place. His curiosity drove him to ask what makes this myth so universal. Why does the theme of the Hero's journey appeal to cultures of all times and countries, if they often differ in every other respect? His answer has the simplicity and unrelenting logic of all brilliant insights. He realized that these myths are not fictitious stories of imaginary characters in nonexistent countries. Rather, the monomyth of the Hero's journey is an accurate description of the experiential territories visited by people in visionary states during a transformative crisis. And as the psychospiritual crisis of transformation is a human experience that is universal, so is the myth.

The universal occurrence of the motif of the Hero's journey, and the fact that it addresses the innermost dynamics of the human psyche, can help us understand why so many people respond so deeply and enthusiastically to Paul Rebillot's process. It is important to realize that the Hero's Journey process is not a superficial product of Paul's fantasy, but something that grew out of his personal struggle and his profound emotional, philosophical, and spiritual crisis. Coping with the basic dilemmas of human existence, he had to connect with the deepest dynamics of his psyche and experience its universal archetypes. Traditional psychiatry would see the dramatic nonordinary state of consciousness that made this possible as a pathological process, as a manifestation of psychosis. In the context of transpersonal psychology, experiences of this kind appear to be crises of spiritual transformation or "spiritual emergencies." With the right understanding, guidance, and support, they can have very beneficial results for the people involved. Occasionally, an individual can reach a successful completion and integration of these states without external help. In Paul's case the final outcome of this process—the quality of his subsequent personal integration and the extraordinary fruit of this experience, the Hero's Journey—certainly suggest that this is what happened.

The Hero's Journey is a prime example of how a gifted and creative individual can transform a shattering experience of the "dark night of the soul" into something that not only catalyzes his own healing and transformation, but provides a useful context for the inner journey of thousands of others. Paul's original idea was to create a process that would make it possible for mental health professionals to get a taste of the experiences that some of their clients go through, so that they could free themselves from their pathological preconceptions and appreciate the creative and healing potential of these states. Although the Hero's Journey certainly can serve this purpose, its potential transcends this narrow framework. It is a process that can promote growth and self-understanding for thousands of those who suffer from the "psychopathology of everyday life," as well as those who are labeled as patients and those who treat them.

Paul Rebillot's process is without any doubt a vehicle for deep individual transformation. However, the fact that it developed as a group experience, and can best be experienced in a group context, offers some significant additional benefits. Anthropologists, particularly Victor Turner, have shown that performance of ritual events in a group context creates a sense of interpersonal and social cohesiveness, tribal bonding, and a sense of community. Anybody who has had an experience with Paul Rebillot will certainly be able to confirm this observation. Participatory events of this kind could thus become an important remedy against the dehumanization and alienation characteristic of the industrial world and—provided they could be conducted on a large enough scale—could contribute significantly to the alleviation of the global crisis we are all facing.

I find it very exciting that this book, which offers clear, practical guidelines for the experience of the Hero's Journey, will now become available to all those who can benefit from it. I recommend it to all serious students of consciousness, as well as all those interested in their own healing, personal growth, and transformation. I hope it will be widely used as a guide by individuals as well as group leaders. For the latter it will certainly be a big challenge to match Paul's unique combination of talents—his many abilities as an actor, director, singer, musician, therapist, and a human being. It will take all that to recreate the ritual healing drama of the Hero's Journey with the same degree of perfection, mastery, playfulness, and sense of humor as its originator.

Stanislav Grof, M.D.
Mill Valley, California
September 20, 1992

A NOTE TO THE READER:

This book is a step-by-step instruction manual for the Hero's Journey process. It was created as a group process, the natural outflow of a ritual drama structure, and that is how I have presented it in this book. However, if you wish to work with the process on your own, you can participate in Gestalt fashion by becoming your own guide on the journey, finding your own space, creating your own altar, discovering your own music, accompanying yourself as a friend. The individual journeyer will find special instructions throughout the book. Where a partner is called for, I recommend using a journal. You may want to work with a friend and read the guided meditations for each other. The book also offers suggestions to group leaders or facilitators who wish to guide the process for other people.

Hearing the Call

*I*n 1968 I was thirty-seven years old. I had a little theater company all my own. I was the director, the producer, and the leading man. The dream of my youth had been realized. On this night I was playing the prince in *The Sleeping Prince*, a play by Terence Rattigan. My leading lady had just delivered a laugh line, so I was doing what is called "holding for laughs" before an audience of two thousand people. Suddenly, a startling thought seized my mind: "What am I doing with my life?" This was not a propitious moment to have such a thought! Here I was, standing in front of two thousand people, waiting for a laugh—was this really what I wanted to do with my life? At that moment an essential part of me left the theater forever. I was professional enough to go on with the play, but something had changed irrevocably.

From that night on I embarked on a tumultuous journey of self-discovery. This journey was to lead me through a profoundly disturbing period—what, for want of a more accurate term, our society calls a nervous breakdown, and what my friend Stan Grof calls a "spiritual emergency." I was bombarded by emotional, psychological, and mythic material, thrown into a strange and sometimes terrifying world over which I had no control. But from this journey through madness, I was able to bring back a healing knowledge, and the kernel of the material that would become the Hero's Journey.

THEATER AS RITUAL

When I left the stage that night, I knew I would have to change my career. I felt the need to invest my life in healing or helping others, rather than merely entertaining them. I considered making a complete break and becoming a psychologist. Yet I felt that my fifteen years of experience in the theater must have some value. Perhaps, instead of going away from the theater, I needed to go more deeply into it, to discover the origin of the theatrical impulse that has been in the human species since its beginnings.

I was also teaching at the time. I decided to direct my students in a production of *The Bacchae* by Euripides in order to investigate the beginnings of Western theater. In ancient Greece people would walk or ride in donkey carts for miles and miles to get to the theater of Dionysus. Once there they would watch plays unfold in the heat of the sun, from morning until twilight. I wanted to know why. What made their theater experience so compelling, and different from the one we know?

First, the theater itself was a cosmic environment. Sitting in the theater at Delphi, for example, the audience could see the whole Bay of Corinth, before which is the valley the Greeks considered to be the navel of the world. An actor standing in the middle of that stage participated in a cosmic event; he was in relationship to the whole of the universe.

What's more, in that theater the audience was not held by suspense as in modern theater. The audience knew what was going to happen to the main character, because the plays were based on the myths. They came not to find out what would happen to Orestes, for example, but to identify with him, and through him to experience a *catharsis,* a cleansing of their own souls. Through the play the impulse to slay the mother could be experienced and released. And when Athena cast the deciding vote for Orestes to stop the cycle of murder and vengeance, the audience experienced something called *en theos,* "enthusiasm," "the god enters within." An element of the transpersonal permeated this ancient form of theater; something divine entered into the hearts of the people.

At that time the new patriarchal myths were replacing the old matriarchal ones, and so these plays were also a way of publicizing the new gods and goddesses. The community was sharing in the new mythology, and in the political atmosphere in this theater as well.

Finally, it was a communal event. The semicircular shape of the amphitheater brought people together in a celebration around the mythological theme. One saw not only the actors in their cosmic environment, but also one's neighbor and the fish peddler from down the street. The theater event was a form of communion among the people, and between the people and their gods.

These awarenesses awakened in me a longing to create a deeper experience of theater in our own day. Until this time I had been teaching in the theater departments at San Francisco State College and Stanford University. But now, in the turbulent atmosphere of the late 1960s, I decided to leave academic theater and form a new theater company with my colleagues and former students. We lived together, calling ourselves "The Gestalt Fool Theater Family." We were experimenting with all kinds of theater, from ritual to Dadaism, breaking all the rules. Like many people living in San Francisco at this time, we were also exploring psychedelic substances. It was out of this total experience of life change, theater experimentation, meditation, and psychedelics that my journey entered the mythic level and my Hero began to emerge.

MY MYTH

One night, in a guided meditation, I met my Hero. He was called "Septimus, the Reader of Akashic Records." Some time later I learned that psychic Edgar Casey had predicted the discovery of the planet Pluto, calling it "Septimus." Since Pluto was discovered in the year of my conception, this fact captured my imagination. And so my myth begins there, on the planet Pluto.

On this planet live conscious beings, just as here, only they are not embodied; they are beings of light. The male could be envisioned as a globe of orange light, and the female as a globe of purple light. When they came together, they would create a whole new being and at the same time retain their own identities, so it was possible for them to be together and separate at the same time.

They had two basic levels of consciousness. They had what I called in my vision experience at that time "the outblink" and "the inblink." In the outblink they all experienced themselves and each other as separate, individuated beings. In the inblink the creatures of the planet Pluto united in the same thought. They became one consciousness. This inblink could be extended to all the other planets in the solar system; in fact, this communication is the gravitational pull that holds the solar system together.

One day the conference of the elders on Pluto—that is, the inblink— had been looking at the planet Earth. We noticed that it had developed a wobble that unbalanced the solar community. This wobble resulted from what we called "the Lucifer experiment." In this experiment the conscious beings of the planet Earth decided to experience themselves as separate from each other, even on the inblink. Well, the experiment had gotten out of hand, and people actually believed this separation to be true. This had caused war, racism, greed, religious bigotry, and the wobble. In short, Earth had become a troublemaker. And so the planet Pluto decided to send two of its members to incarnate and discover what it is that made these Earth creatures feel so separate from one another.

My wife and I were chosen to separate ourselves from the planet Pluto, and from the rapture that we experienced in our communion with one another, and to travel to Earth. I began to learn something about separation in the process of leaving home and being torn away from my partner. However, the pain of this experience was mitigated by a strange fascination with the purposeful determination of a particular sperm swimming toward my Earth-mother's womb. I became so captivated by the enthusiasm of this sperm that, as it penetrated the egg, I entered into flesh—and completely forgot who I was, where I was going, what I was doing, what my purpose was.

MY JOURNEY THROUGH MADNESS

Meanwhile, my outer life fell into greater and greater disarray. I had separated myself from the academic system and was doing my own theater; but without money and technical support, it was not living up to my expectations. My situation felt even more unfortunate because my lover had recently left me, and it seemed that everything was falling apart. Yet here was I, with this great task: to discover the rules of separation so that one day I would find my partner and together we would discover the keys to human consciousness!

My injured ego grabbed onto the idea of this magnificent mission. The disproportion between my everyday experience and my mythic experience created an ego inflation that finally broke me—I entered into a state of consciousness in which every occurrence related to the mythic experience. No other world existed for me. I was beyond human contact; I was completely separate. And so I began what I would later identify as the Supreme Ordeal.

Confined in a psychiatric hospital, I repeatedly dreamed that I was alone in a room with two green doors. There were bars on the window, and I could hear the wind howling outside. I felt very alone. It was a nightmare! I would awaken with a start to find myself alone . . . in a room with two green doors, with bars on the window, and the wind howling outside. My dream reality and my waking state were indistinguishable. I had no memory of any previous existence. This was where I was born, this was where I lived, this was my life—the room with two green doors. I didn't know who Paul Rebillot was. I had even forgotten the Pluto story. I felt totally alone in my attempt to discover the rules of existence.

After a while I realized I had a keeper, a man who fed and cared for me. His name was Mr. Preebles. I concluded that I was one of Mr. Preebles's people, that he had several people around the place that he fed and cared for, and that we belonged to him. We were born in these rooms and this was where we lived out our lives. Mr. Preebles's people.

Occasionally, one of the green doors would be opened. I was placed in the room and the door was closed behind me. I would play with the faucets and flush the toilet. I had no idea what they were for. Later, when they had left me, I would piss on the floor. I remember one ecstatic moment when the sun shone through the golden liquid arcing out of my body and splashing on the floor and I thought, "How beautiful to be alive!"

I became very interested in the protuberance in the middle of my face. I didn't know what it was for. However, as I looked out the window, I saw what seemed to be little versions of me on the ground. And it appeared that this was how they decided where they were going— they were literally following their noses.

All of these things were going through my mind as I desperately tried to discover who I was. For a while I gave Mr. Preebles a lot of trouble. When he brought the food in, I would rush to get out the door. Gradually, I realized that if I sat quietly he would come in and visit with me. I made an important discovery at that time. I realized that I didn't have to change who I was, but only what I did to get what I needed: I could change my behavior without changing my being. I think that was one of the most important discoveries of the whole experience.

After a while I was allowed to leave the room. I was able to walk around the day room with all these other restless people following their noses. How amazing to discover that there were other people like me in this world! Strangely enough, the question that kept going through my mind all the while was, "What level of development is this planet on?" Born anew, knowing nothing, and yet questioning the level of development of the planet. Curious.

One day I noticed many people sitting and staring at a box in the middle of the day room. I didn't know what the box was. White points of light danced across the front of it. Others watched with great interest, and all I saw were the points of light. From time to time a picture would emerge. My mind was taking the light and dark spots and organizing them into an image. I realized that this picture was a kind of shadow image similar to the people around me. I saw all these conflicts, particularly between men and women. I couldn't actually distinguish men from women, but I saw that some wore dresses and some had beards, and there seemed to be a constant struggle between them about who was smarter and who was more powerful. Everyone seemed to be suffering from this conflict. It made me feel very sad. This was my experience of television.

Some time later I was looking at a *Time* magazine, searching for something specific that would trigger my memory. I didn't know what it was, but I knew that I could find it. I came upon a picture of a group of bearded men with motorcycles, drinking beer out of cans. The caption read, "Hell's Angels." Hell's angels. Hell. Pluto. Angels. Messengers. Messenger from Pluto. At that moment the Hell's Angels suddenly awakened my mythic memory. I was the messenger from Pluto. The myth of Pluto returned to memory before the story of Paul Rebillot.

Now I began to dream of a group of people doing a very beautiful, slow dance. I watched the dance in my imagination for a long time, until finally one day I decided to do the dance myself. The dance was a form of T'ai Chi, a moving meditation. As I began to do the dance, memories of Paul Rebillot came back to me, and at that moment I suddenly had a clear sense of who I was. It was as if the two parts of myself came back together. Finally, I found a coin and a telephone number, and I was back in contact.

THEATER AS HEALING

This episode was my chaotic passage into a new career. From it I discovered the tremendous power of the human psyche to seek its own evolution. Through it I moved from theater as entertainment to theater as healing. For that is what I consider the Hero's Journey process to be: healing theater; a modern rite of passage.

In premodern cultures and in tribal cultures today, when people move from one stage of life to another, or when a new task is to be taken up, they are led through rites of passage, initiations that provide them with a total experience of the passage they are undergoing. This total experience prepares the body and the heart as well as the mind for the new level of being. Even in the last century, a young couple intending to marry would have to go out and build their own house or do some physical task that functioned as a rite of passage from one family unit to the creation of a new one. Even though it may not have been put into a ritual format, the barn-raising brought the whole town together to support the young people in this new step.

Today, in our age of intellectual "enlightenment," we have lost this sense of ritual. Yet there is still a part of us that is less rational—or perhaps more than rational; a childlike part of us that needs to experience the magic of a rite of passage. Again and again, my work with people has shown me the suffering and confusion caused by our society's lack of significant rites of passage. Without shamans or ritual masters to guide them, modern women and men must find their own lonely and usually traumatic paths from one stage of life to another, whether it be a child's discovery that there is no Santa Claus, an adolescent's awkward approach to puberty, an adult's marriage or divorce, or a change of career or home. Every such change requires a movement from one level of being to another. At every threshold something dies and something comes to birth.

Today there is a deep spiritual void at the heart of our society. We see it in the self-destructive behavior that is all around us—in drug and alcohol abuse, in the epidemic of crime and teenage suicide. This void may reflect our culture's lack of threshold rituals. Rites of passage speak to the human spirit. Where there are no rites, spirit is denied. Ritual lifts us out of the purely personal dimension of our experience into the universal, thereby reconnecting us with the spiritual realities of existence, without which life becomes a wasteland.

The Buddhists say that one of the basic fears is the fear of unusual states of mind. We fear these in ourselves, and we fear them in others. One way to deal with that fundamental fear is to experience an unusual state of mind in a safe situation, in order to discover how to go into it and—most important—how to come out of it. Psychedelic substances are one way, psychotic breaks are another; but there are still other ways to acquaint ourselves with altered states. Trance-dancing, Holotropic breath meditation, certain forms of yoga, and dervish twirling techniques are some of the different means we can use to enter altered states voluntarily. For me, the most interesting and familiar way is through ritual drama. The value of such a form is that it allows people to realize that they can both enter into and come out of an extraordinary state with full consciousness.

To meet this need, I wanted to create in the Hero's Journey a rite of passage universal enough to allow people to recognize the pattern of change, whatever the change might be.

The process outlined in this book is not a new creation, but one with which I have been working for more than fifteen years, and through which I have guided thousands of people in Europe and the United States. It is the fruit of those fifteen years and of the experiences of the people with whom I have worked. The fact that the process has been experienced by so many different people from so many different walks of life, from so many different countries, and with such different interests has caused me to refine it over and over again so that it can have as broad an application as possible.

When I first began, I believed I was creating the Hero's Journey for doctors and nurses working with people in crisis. But I have discovered through its evolution that its application is much, much broader. A writer can unblock and open up her own creative process. An alcoholic can confront his addiction. People going through spiritual crises, and people simply interested in their own spiritual evolution, have found the process extremely enlightening and frequently life-changing.

The Hero's Journey is a chance to play out a story of transformation within the framework of ritual, where eternity and chronological time interpenetrate. When we take an archetypal structure and act it out in the here-and-now, our daily life is illuminated by the eternal. This creates the possibility of an interchange between the two dimensions; a doorway is opened through which the archetypal world can enter our life, thus bringing new energy and form into the everyday world. This interpenetration of the two worlds is the essential nature of ritual drama.

HEARING THE CALL

A Hero, whether in myth or modern day, is one who hears a call and follows it. This is difficult in our time, because we are constantly receiving pseudo-calls through advertising: to do something, to do it a different way, to buy something, or to go somewhere. If there is within us no natural response to these pseudo-calls, the advertiser's task is to create a feeling that will prompt us to answer it. TV commercials, magazine ads, and billboards are constantly creating calls in this false way. Unfortunately, this constant pressing of the "call button" makes it difficult for us to recognize an authentic call when it comes.

When an authentic call comes—a call that will lead us from one stage of life into another, from one career into another, from one love relationship into another—the response to that call trembles deep within the essential being. But if we are inundated with calls, it becomes easy not to hear the voice of our essential self.

It is crucial that we do hear and listen to this voice, for it calls us to our continuing evolution—not only as individual human beings, but as a planetary species. We are continually being called toward our evolutionary process. If the call mechanism is so muddied up with false calls that we cannot hear the authentic voice, we are in a very dangerous situation. If many human beings are convinced that satisfaction is going to come from soft toilet paper or the detergent that makes your hands soft enough to hold, then we are all in a sorry state. Preoccupation with these false calls can in fact become a shield against, an avoidance of, the authentic call.

If many of us began to listen to our true calls, however, our society would have to go through a total transformation: for we would realize that the way we are living does not satisfy the authentic call of the human being; we would realize that material things cannot substitute for spiritual evolution. If we, as a species, began to listen to the depths of our own calling, we would be less likely to be distracted by this effulgence of commercialism; the energy we put into consuming might then be redirected toward self-discovery and personal evolution.

We stand at the threshold of a new millennium. It is clear that we cannot go on in the same pattern as we have in the past, because the planet will not survive. If humankind cannot move to a higher level of self-consciousness and discover its true function in relationship to the evolution of the species and of the planet, our only goal will be self-destruction.

I believe that our function in relationship to the whole of the universe is far different from the destructive one we are acting out. We have been looking at life through a lens darkened by materialism and consumerism, and we need to clean our lenses so that we can more clearly see what that function is.

The Hero's Journey is one way we can begin to clean those lenses, and begin to come in contact with the deeper level of our personal evolution as well as our species evolution. The Hero is one who hears the call and answers it. The nature of the Hero's Journey is to give us a chance to come in contact with our own internal call for transformation and to go about discovering the steps that we need to take in order to accomplish this transformation, and thereby participate in the evolution of humanity.

PART ONE
The Preparation

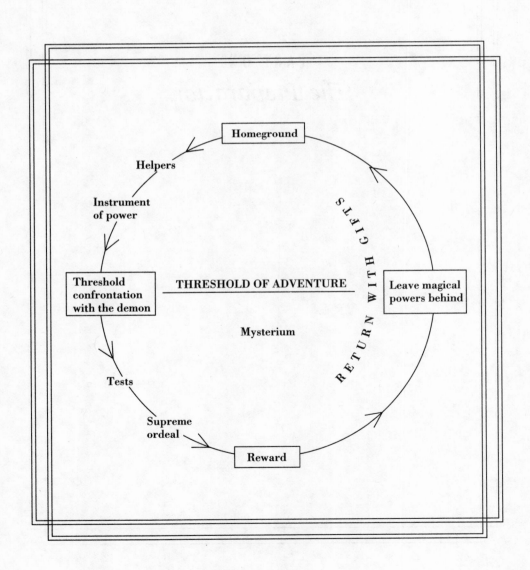

CHAPTER 1
The Hero's Journey: Where Are We Going?

*W*hen I began developing the material that would become the Hero's Journey process, my first step was to discover a pattern, a plot on which to construct the ritual drama. I was fortunate to encounter Joseph Campbell's landmark book, *The Hero with a Thousand Faces,* which outlines such a plot, exemplified in the myth of the Hero. Campbell found that all initiation rites have the same pattern: *separation* from the old way, from the community or group; *initiation* or movement into the new level; and *return* into the group with the gift of the journey. Using the plot line of this Hero monomyth, I designed a process to guide a group of people through the archetype of transformation so they can then make the application to their own lives. By experiencing the pattern of the Hero's Journey, many people have found that they know the form of transformation; then, as change inevitably occurs in their lives, it no longer threatens them. They know it will have a certain sequence. They have the map.

Before we begin our journey, I would like to give you this brief map. It will show you the terrain you will traverse and the characters you will become.

A BRIEF MAP OF THE TERRAIN

The main character of our drama is, of course, the *Hero.* Who is a Hero? For me this simple poem, written by a woman at the age of ninety-four, captures the essential heroic quality, "the sense to follow" when a call comes:

Something soft and gentle
Glides through your fingers

And it seems to grab your hand and lead you
On to something greater
If you only had the sense to follow it[1]

The Hero is neither an archaic structure from a paternalistic period nor a strictly masculine image, but an aspect of human nature, the aspect that hears the call from the deeper self and answers it. I use "Hero" to refer to women as well as men, because I consider "heroine" to be a diminutive form lacking in dignity. The Hero is the potential of every human being to follow the impulse to "something greater."

The story of the Hero's Journey follows a basic pattern. The Hero, as we have said, is someone who hears the call to adventure and follows it. Generally this person, man or woman, is reasonably well adapted to the sociocultural environment, but has a yearning, an inclination toward further evolution. At some point this inclination is intensified into an experience of a *call.* This call may come from outside in the form of an invitation or a suggestion from another, as when Jesus called his disciples, "Come, follow me"; or it may come in the form of an inner voice, as when Prince Siddhartha, beholding the suffering of life, felt compelled to leave his palace in search of wisdom and peace of heart. In either case it says, "There could be more to life than you are living." However it comes, the call sinks deeply into the person's being and remains there until it is either acted on by the Hero or killed by one who will not follow the striving of his or her own heart.

The call sets up the first level of resistance: whatever in the present life situation supports or depends on the status quo, such as one's job, one's home, one's responsibilities, or one's pattern of relationships. The Hero must recognize these and deal with them before he or she can begin the journey. In the Hero's Journey process, we discover the nature of our call through the *Homeground* exercises.

As the Hero continues along the path, helpers appear, people who give encouragement, guides or friends who point out the dangerous places. A *Spirit Guide* gives the Hero an *Instrument of Power* to use in the battles that must be fought and the tests that must be passed. For example, King Arthur is given a sword by Merlin; Athena gives Perseus her own shield; Cinderella receives the ball gown and entourage from her fairy godmother. In the process we will choose our own Spirit Guides and discover our own Instruments of Power.

1. Nadya Catalfano, in Kenneth Koch, *I Never Told Anybody: Teaching Poetry Writing in a Nursing Home* (New York: Random House, 1977).

Thus armed, the Hero proceeds to the point of no return, called the *Threshold of Adventure.* It generally appears as a gate, a cave mouth, the entrance to a forest—the passageway to another world. Here the Hero encounters a dragon, a castle guard, a three-headed dog—some threshold guardian that refuses admittance. This guardian is the second level of resistance, representing all the self-sabotaging forces within the personality. In the Hero's Journey process, we call this guardian the *Demon of Resistance.*

A *Confrontation* takes place between the Hero and the Demon, and it continues until a resolution is reached. The Demon does not die, but is reintegrated into the Hero's being. The Hero, sometimes accompanied by a transformed Demon, then proceeds into the *Mysterium,* a mysterious inner world.

The Mysterium is an extraordinary place, an enchanted forest of supernatural wonders. The Hero continues along the way, encountering the new and the strange. But armed now with the Instrument of Power and the knowledge gained in the Confrontation, he or she feels ready to deal with any situation. Soon the Hero will undergo the *Supreme Ordeal,* a monumental struggle with his or her basic fear.

Finally, having survived the Supreme Ordeal, the Hero has earned the *Reward* of the journey. It may be the Grail, the treasure, or the inner marriage for which this particular Hero has been searching. This is the gift of life that comes after the long night of death, the healing with which the Hero returns home. The magical aspects of the Mysterium are left behind when the Hero once again departs beyond the threshold, but the awareness and the fullness of the voyage remain to enhance or change the situation at home. With this *Return* to daily life, the journey is complete.

THE LEVELS OF THE HERO'S JOURNEY

The Hero's Journey takes place on several levels:

1. The *ritual:* This is the spiritual framing of the process, reinforced by the Ritual of the Vestal and the chanting of the Rams.
2. The *dramatic:* This is the mythological or archetypal story of the Hero, which we have just discussed.
3. The *Fool's Dance:* This movement meditation enables the participant to cross the threshold from ritual to drama by recapitulating, physically and through guided fantasy, the story thus far.

4. The *biographical:* This is our individual psychology, which arises out of our personal story.

5. The *didactic:* This is the theoretical explanation of the process, through which the guide tries to clarify what is going on rather than obfuscate or mystify the participants.

6. The *practical:* This is the coordination of the process with the demands of daily life (or, in the case of group leaders, with the demands of the schedules of the host organization and with the available natural environment).

Let's take a closer look at each of these elements.

The Ritual

Ritual is a doorway through which we move from the ordinary world into another dimension. It is a crossing of time and eternity—an event in which the universal patterns penetrate and fertilize everyday life. A ritual, then, is a threshold of consciousness. We can experience an expansion of consciousness through such a mundane event as breathing. For example, meditation on the rising and falling of breath, as in yoga, can transform this simple, everyday action into a profound contact with the pulse at the center of the universe.

Ancient myths the world over recognize that human beings who confront the power of the divine face to face, without protection, risk madness or death. The orderly form of the ritual, in which experience is measured out in "human proportions," protects us from experiencing this archetypal power directly.

The Ritual Circle

Ritual is the point of departure and the point of return for the daily session, as well as for the beginning and the end of the group. The Hero's Journey effects this movement over the threshold by creating a sacred space, a space set apart, a safe space. The ritual circle defines a protected area that people create with their bodies and their consciousness in order to safely experience altered states of being. This circle becomes a temple into which we invite the divine. The ritual circle says, "Here is where the mystery takes place."

In our society the most common experiences of altered realities are accomplished through taking drugs, or through "madness." In the drug experience, we cannot withdraw from the altered states of consciousness until the drug has run its course. In madness, we cannot escape until the madness somehow runs its course. In the ritual circle, however, we learn how to enter into and depart from expanded levels of consciousness by an act of will. It is very important to recognize that when we leave the ritual space, we also leave the realities and laws of the ritual space. For example, the person who discovers complete trust in the universe within the ritual circle will be supremely vulnerable to thieves and con artists if she fails to distinguish between the realms. The Arabs have a saying: "Trust in God and tie up your camel." The person who does not tie up her camel loses more than her camel to the con artist—she loses her faith in God and her ability even to believe in the mystery.

When we enter the ritual space, we have to leave behind the limitations of the mundane. We have to be able to fly. We have to be able to transform ourselves into peacocks or pollywogs if necessary. We have to be able to sustain what is called in the theater "a willing suspension of disbelief." This willing suspension of disbelief is a doorway through which we can enter other levels of consciousness.

Therefore, we must be able to leave the world of limitations and enter into the world where everything is possible, and then to leave the world where everything is possible and reenter the world of limitation. Only then do we understand both sides of the threshold. This comprehension of both sides of the threshold allows us to realize our visions in the world of flesh, and to offer our passion and our vulnerability to the world of spirit. This is one of the major teachings of the Hero's Journey process: the ability to move back and forth across that threshold voluntarily.

To the Guide:

The ritual circle is the core of the group process. Your location will determine whether what is going on in the group can go out into the outside world. If it is a protected environment and there is no other group there, and the host organization knows what is going on, the ritual circle can be expanded to include a greater space. When the outside environment is not compatible with the process, you will need to enforce respect for the boundaries. Transgression of these boundaries frequently creates misunderstandings and conflicts because people are communicating with each other from dramatically different perspectives—one might even say from different dimensions. If you are learning how to express your power by shouting and stamping your feet, for example, you don't do that at dinner. You do that in the circle.

The Candle

Lighting a candle serves several purposes. It changes both the environment and the mood of the people involved, it unifies the group, and it takes the focus away from the leader, placing it in the center of the room. It is said that black magicians sit in the center of the room and take all the focus to themselves, whereas white magicians put a candle in the center so that the energy is focused on the light and not on the magician. The light becomes the guide, illuminating the individual journeys. Meditation on the candle is a ritual that begins each day's session.

To the Guide:

As will be clear in the next chapter, I do not begin the ritual until I have talked about the process and we have had a chance to sing a little and play a little music and get to know each other a bit. I wait until everyone is present before lighting the candle in the center of the room, because this act says, "Now we together, all of us, are moving into another dimension."

The Drama

The ancient Greek city of Epidaurus was the healing center dedicated to the God Aesculapius. The Greeks recognized the relationship between mind, heart, and body, and included in their healing center not only a hospital, but a gymnasium, a temple, and a theater. Certain plays that dealt with a psychological reflection of the illness would be prescribed as part of a person's healing. In the plays the person saw the mortal human being in confrontation with the eternal archetypes. The Greek audience so identified with the actor that they could experience through him the healing power of the conflict, crisis, and transformation of the Hero.

The cosmic setting of the open amphitheater embraced actors and audience in a common world shared by mortals and immortals. Over the centuries, however, as the mysteries were lost to human consciousness, the drama withdrew from its cosmic setting and the audience was separated from the play. Today we sit isolated in the darkness, observing the lonely struggles of ordinary people on a proscenium stage transcribed by its little square of light. As the actors are plucked from their relationship to nature and the audience is separated from the play, the drama loses its cosmic dimension and therefore its capacity to heal. In order to recover the therapeutic magic of the theater, we must enter the theater of our own soul and become the leading actor in our own cosmic drama, allowing the eternity of the mythological structure to penetrate the chronology of everyday life.

In the ritual drama format, the individual becomes an actor and experiences these relationships directly. We enter the ritual circle and listen for the call toward a deeper experience of the essential self. This call is the universal archetype. What is it to us, as individual human beings? How do we picture it? What is the vision? What image does it present to us? What kind of heroic personality do we need to accentuate or build in ourselves in order to be able to go out on the quest in response to that call? What obstacles do we put in front of ourselves—obstacles in relationship to our environment, to our own psychological structure? What is our Demon of Resistance?

Rather than viewing the drama from a distance, as an ancient Greek might have, in the Hero's Journey we become the leading actors in our own stories. Every myth, every story, every drama is a picture of consciousness—a picture of how different aspects of consciousness interact with each other. When we enter into the drama of the Hero's Journey, we play all the roles. Not only do our minds and psyches absorb the meaning, we can experience and integrate the drama in our bodies as well.

The Fool's Dance

The Fool's Dance leads us from the ritual into the drama. Our passage from the everyday world into the ritual world begins with the ritual lighting of the candle. We focus on light, on consciousness. Then we move from the world of consciousness to the world of archetypes, of the drama, by way of a very slow, meditative dance that physicalizes the images of the story. In Hindu meditation practice, it is said that by taking on the physical position of the *mudra* (the symbolic hand gesture), you open your consciousness to the experience expressed by the posture. The Fool's Dance is a series of mudras, a series of postures that come from the relationship between the eternal and the individual process. We translate our images of the Hero, of the call, of our reactions to the present life situation, into body postures that move us from the quiet, meditative state of the ritual into the feeling for the drama. Each day the Fool's Dance recapitulates the story to the point we have reached in the drama; at that point the drama comes to life.

The idea of the Fool's Dance comes from the highly stylized No theater tradition of Japan. In the No theater, the actor begins by meditating on his mask. He walks very slowly toward the stage, and with each step of the walk, he enters more profoundly into the character he is playing. By the time he steps onto the stage, that character steps onto the stage—not the actor playing that role, but that character.

The actor begins from a state in which he is essentially a void—void of feeling, of personality; he is pure being. He begins to do the gesture, and as the gesture approaches its apex, he fills himself with the experience of that gesture—perhaps deep compassion for the world, Buddha-compassion. As he reaches the apex of the gesture, his whole being—his body, his soul, his mind—is filled with that compassion, so that when he reaches the high point, he *is* the experience of that compassion. The gestures of the actor at the high point of the play are accompanied by drum and other rhythmic sounds.

Similarly, in the Fool's Dance, as we stand and take on the *zero position*—which is the beginning and the end of the Fool's Dance—we are in the position of void. As the body takes on the posture, it moves from the void into the drama, into the feeling experience of the story. If you really learn what is in the zero position, you will have gotten more than the workshop. The Buddhists speak of "the fertile void" from which all things can move. I think of "zero" as the point in the void that has begun to individuate. It is the point of center. And what is a point? A point is something that has unlimited possibilities of movement, but is taking none; it is just being. As soon as it moves in one direction, it has limited itself in that direction, but it has also manifested its uniqueness. And that is what the movement from zero into the first position of the Fool's Dance is. And what is the first position? Me—ordinary, everyday-life me. The question then becomes, "How do I move myself from universal wholeness into whatever kind of lopsided self I have created? And how does that being continually transform into all the variations of the dance of my soul?" The movement from "zero" to "me" and back is the whole drama.

The Biography

The next level of the process is the psychological level. If the Fool's Dance goes from "zero" to "me," and the question of the workshop is how to get back to zero, the answer is through the Hero drama. In order to get through this drama, then, how do we prepare the roles? How do we prepare the characters? How do we find out what kind of Demon each of us has? what kind of Hero?

In the theater there are basically two theories of how the actor works best. According to Diderot the actor takes on the posture of the emotion or of the character, remains objective to it, and simply imitates nature. The other concept, that of Stanislavski, is that the actor must evolve the character from his or her own personal experience, through the doorway of the "as if." In the Hero's Journey process, we find our characters by Stanislavski's method. We examine our personal life situation and habits, our psychology, our persona, the way we deal with issues.

So the third level of the process is that in which we discover how we go about accomplishing our goals, how we deal with relationships, how we feel about our work and about ourself. This begins in the examination of the Homeground situation. By examining four aspects of the life process, we seek to discover our personal psychological structure. How do I deal with problems? What are my resistances, my pain, my suffering? These are "the rehearsal materials" for the drama. In the rehearsal period, using the Stanislavski approach, we take our own psychology, our own personal process and psychological structure, and suit it to the play.

That is what we do to prepare the drama. To create the Demon of Resistance, for example, we discover our resistances by looking at our body armor, at the way we habitually hold our body, at our tensions, and at what those tensions might suggest in terms of feelings that we are holding back. A person who is always holding his shoulders up, for example, may be chronically resisting the desire to reach out and touch people. That is the person's psychology. In the Hero's Journey process, we don't focus on the psychology in order to work through the psychological problem. Rather, the psychology becomes the key to the creation of the character. Frequently, participants deal with psychological problems through the characters of the Hero and the Demon. The Hero, for example, may be reaching out for love, and the Demon may be saying, "Stay away! Don't touch! Don't go near anyone!" In this way the psychological material is being worked out on the fantasy or drama level.

In many cathartic disciplines, such as Gestalt, Bioenergetics, Primal therapy, and Reichian therapy, primary emotional process is most important. In the Hero's Journey, however, while it is important, it is grist for the drama. The media of art and creativity lift raw emotion to a new level: the transpersonal level of drama and ritual. Most people come to psychological workshops to work out a problem or a particular conflict, but that is not the main focus of the Hero's Journey. It is not designed to help people work out a specific relationship problem, for example, although the issue may be resolved at a much deeper level in the course of the journey.

When the personal psychological work is placed into the temple through the enactment of the ritual circle, every human being, healing himself or herself, heals something of the human species. And when this is done as a conscious intention to heal the human species, that is another level of consciousness—a step even closer to the truth. It means that we are devoted not only to ourselves in our own healing, but to something greater than self. Devotion to something greater is a quality of the Hero, according to Joseph Campbell. So if I am going to a therapy session to deal with my individual problems just because I want to feel better, that's fine. If I go to heal myself with the awareness that as I heal myself, I am also healing the consciousness of this planet—then I am a Hero.

The Didactic

During the journey, in order to provide as complete an experience as possible, the leader makes intermittent explanations of the basis for the various steps of the process and its connection with Gestalt theory.

The Practical

The practical level involves balancing the needs of the outer reality with the material of the journey. As a participant you should try to set aside a particular time and space for your journey work. As a group leader, you will need to consider the institution and environment where the journey is taking place.

To the Guide:

For example, the Hero's Journey generally includes a Heroes' Banquet. The supporting institution may enjoy participating in the creation of the celebration. Guides, however, should be attentive both to the potentials for enrichment and to the limitations of the host organization. It is important to take full advantage of the environment, both external and internal, in programming the process. The Heroes' Banquet might be a picnic by a river, a garden party, or a catered affair in the great hall of the facility. You might take the opportunity to work outdoors at other moments in the process as well. The relationship to nature—such as a sudden shower or a beautiful sunset—can be a magical enhancement of the scope of the mythological voyage.

Clarifying the Levels of the Psyche

The levels of the Hero's Journey actually reflect the levels of the psyche. Experience of the process can teach us how to move consciously from one level to the other, from the mythic to the personal, for example, while at the same time keeping them ordered and distinct. With this awareness we will not be inclined to act out one level of our psyche in another level of somebody else's reality. For example, some years ago, when LSD was fashionable, some people who were tripping would believe that they could stop cars with their eyes. Acting on this level of consciousness, they would then rush out onto the highway and attempt to stop cars with the power of their eyes. But the drivers of the cars were operating on another level of consciousness, which they expressed with honking horns, screeching brakes, and telephone calls to the police. Instead of experiencing their power to express themselves through their eyes, car-stoppers ended up in the hospital or in jail.

It is not absolutely necessary for journeyers to distinguish these levels of the process. Still, if they do (and guides help to keep them clear), this will also serve to order and clarify the levels or dimensions of the psyche. To make this conscious is another way to demystify the process. Remember: In the Hero's Journey process, we have the freedom to choose to enter or not to enter. To ensure that choice, the process must be as clear as possible.

CHAPTER 2
Finding Your Way

*W*hen I guide the Hero's Journey, I give participants a certain formula, and then they are completely free to do with it as they like. I may not always be satisfied with what they do, but that is for me to deal with. However, I am tougher with some people than with others. If I see people spending all their time playing games and resisting, I will call them on it. I am respectful but not permissive; I have certain standards. So if in writing this book I say, "Do it exactly this way," then I become a fascist, and have not allowed you your creative process. If I say, "Just do it some way or another," I betray the possibility of quality control over the material. We will, therefore, need to find a middle ground.

An important aspect of the Hero's Journey process is the excitement and creativity of finding your own way through the material. My aim in this book is to offer a creative atmosphere in which you can grow in your own direction based on the material, and to provide tools that will enable you to create alternative ways of doing the Hero's Journey. I would like you to study this structure and then be able to decide how to work with it, rather than feeling that you have to follow it "chapter and verse." Nonetheless, you will need to be aware of certain considerations.

A FEW CONSIDERATIONS BEFORE YOU BEGIN

1. Do I need a theater background? The Hero's Journey process is certainly theatrical, and some theater or psychodrama experience will give the guide tools to encourage the people to express themselves dramatically and to create events with a sense of theatrical flair. A theater background also makes it easier to do ritual. However, there is a danger. People with a theatrical background often believe that "the performance is all," and that is not the case in a ritual. The depth of the experience is all. So if you have a theatrical background, you must realize that the play is not the thing; it is the depth of the experience, the significance of the ritual, and respect for individual process that are essential.

2. What about music? Although the process can be done without music, I find that music is very important and a great help in unifying the group. It is not necessary that the guide be a musician. Some people select music from tapes to create mood and atmosphere, others have found musicians to work along with them. Live music is ideal. It pulses with the rhythm of the group as it is happening, whereas recorded music demands that the group pulse to the rhythm of another time. It is also possible, however, to do the process without music. It could be very powerful done in silence, or with the sounds of nature.

3. How far can I push myself and the group? The cardinal rule is never to push yourself beyond the level of your own resistance. The most intensive push technique I use in the Hero's Journey is the breathing process given in the Supreme Ordeal, and even that is done in such a way as to respect the individual's resistance. You must decide how much resistance you can work through, and how much is essential to your sense of safety. It is a very delicate balance. For example, when we explore our body's defense system to develop the Demon, we do this in a gentle way by lying on the floor and examining the body's resistances to gravity. By intensifying tensions, we can discover all the ways the body has defended itself since birth. This is in contrast to groups in which individuals are put into the center of a circle and threatened, hit, pushed, and poked at, making them so defensive that the body is as constricted as possible. This sort of method is unconscionable, and should never be a part of the Hero's Journey.

4. What about personal freedom? It is *essential* in the Hero's Journey process that, at every step of the way, the individual is free to decide whether or not and to what depth he or she will participate in each exercise. This is what distinguishes the process from madness. In madness we are not free; we are swept away by the outpouring of unconscious material, and are unable to distinguish between reality and dream. In the Hero's Journey, however, we are always able to make that distinction and to enter into the fantasy by an act of will. That is what makes it a ritual, and that is what makes it, for me, a holy form and a self-responsible form. So if as a guide you intrude on a journeyer's freedom, push-ing, insulting, hurting, using fascistic techniques—or if you as an individual do this to yourself—you are abusing the process. Fascists may create heroes, but they create heroes who are slaves. The Hero's Journey is not about slavery; it is about individuation, about courage, about finding one's own way.

5. *What about participants for whom the process is inappropriate?* Whether you are working with this material as an individual, or you intend to guide others through it, it is important that you have some sense of how to identify a fragile person. If a person is not able to make eye contact or to complete a clear sen-tence; if a person is always talking in highly symbolic language without the ability to enter into the here-and-now in simple contact; if a person is unable to focus on other people's issues; if the person is constantly directing everything back to himself or herself—then you might be suspicious about the capacity of such a person to sustain the process.

If you suspect that a participant is not very stable, call that person out before the group starts (or even after the group has begun), talk to the person, and find out if he or she has a history of mental instability. Although it is not impossible for a person who has had an emotional breakdown to do the process, it is important that the person has reintegrated, has come to some sort of clo-sure, and is able to be self-sustaining. The nature of a ritual is that people take responsibility for entering into another state. A person who does not have a good solid ego structure may be able to enter into another state, but may not be able to come back—or may be unwilling to come back because the altered state seems so much more interesting. This is often what keeps people in chronic psychological stalemates: they are more interested in altered states than in the gray level of everyday life. Guides must be sensitive to these issues.

THE LIVING RITUAL

Before you embark on the Hero's Journey, whether as a guide or on your own, it's a good idea to have some familiarity with ritual structures, and to have some sense of the difference between a dead or bloodless ritual and a rit-ual that has life and depth to it. A bloodless ritual has no substance to it; it simply repeats archaic phrases and gestures. A living ritual is apparent by its sense of vitality and relevance. It touches the core and has a clear application to everyday life.

Whatever your feelings about Catholicism, one of the great things it has done is to sustain a certain sense of ritual. The church is a repository of old forms; and when someone truly alive performs the ritual, the same old words, sounds, music, and movements suddenly spring to life and have meaning, not only for the mind, but for the soul and for the spirit. Some religious traditions—Jewish, Catholic, Buddhist, Hindu—have kept ritual alive, although in our times it is often experienced as diluted. In the 1960s many people began the trek to India to experience the power of the ritual life there. Tribal cultures such as those of the native peoples of North and South America, the Africans, and the aborigines of Australia are ripe with a passionate sense of ritual. So anyone who has had experience of those cultural traditions knows the value and power of living ritual. If you have ever walked into a church or synagogue or other sacred space and have participated there in a ritual and felt a sense of awe, of entrance into another level, another reality, you know in your soul what ritual is and are able to encourage other people to find it. This respect for ritual is important if you are to guide either yourself or others through the Hero's Journey.

It is certainly helpful to have at least an interest in and a comfort with mythology and fairy tales, but it is not necessary to be an expert. Because you are dealing with archetypal levels, it is good to have some sense of the myths. Once when I was doing the journey in Ireland, I was reading a collection of Irish fairy tales and myths. Reading them lifted my sense of what Ireland is. When I mentioned the names of the Irish mythological heroes in the group, it created a deep sense of familiarity with the participants.

So, it is helpful to both individual journeyers and guides to have a comfort with mythology, not necessarily an expertise in mythology; a comfort with ritual, not an expertise in ritual; and a feeling of comfort with emotional and psychological process. Acquaintance with the works of C. G. Jung, Joseph Campbell, John Weir Perry, Mircea Eliade, Esther Harding, and Robert Graves is also very helpful.

WHO CAN BE A GUIDE?

It is not essential to experience the process as a participant in order to be a guide. It is not a question of having done it, but a question of selfhood, of personhood and authenticity. As a guide you must understand who you are, and what this kind of process can evoke. You must also be in contact with what you want for yourself. That is, do you want to have everybody look at you as the wonderful guide of this process? That's okay, there's nothing wrong with that, but that can't be the only reason for doing it. Nor can the only reason for doing the process be to make a lot of money. At some level you have to be devoted to the human spirit, to have a sense of investment in the evolution of the human spirit. If you do not have that, do not attempt to guide the process. Nor can the Hero's Journey be led by people who do not have a healthy respect for practical, everyday reality. A guide must have a sense of spirit, a sense of ground, and respect for the individual human being.

In Gestalt process the facilitator or guide is there to hold the ground while those who are working fly—upward toward heaven, downward toward hell, through the past or into the future—into whatever level of their psyches they need to explore. The people who are working need to know that there is a place they are coming from and a place to come back to, and the facilitator holds that place. This gives people the freedom to follow their inner experience. That is one of the functions of the guide in the Hero's Journey as well: to hold the ground—to know the time limits, to know the sequence, to know where the group is going and where it has come from and what it needs to do, what is possible and what is not possible, when the meal hours are, and so forth. The guide is the one who has the overall picture constantly in mind and the specific moment always in hand.

As the guide you do not have to know exactly what is going on with each individual; but you do have to have some sense of how people are following the process. Are they in it or out of it? Are they getting lost in a detail? Since the material is very sensitive, from the beginning the guide must be aware of each person in the group— keeping track of their stability and capacity to take responsibility for their psychic material as it emerges. When people open themselves to deep feeling states, the guide has to be particularly sensitive to the fragility of individual members. As the material deepens, a person who does not have a sufficiently solid ego structure runs the risk of entering an altered state and not returning. Although this is rare, it has happened.

If you are going to lead the process as I detail it in the following section, it is very important to have done sufficient psychological work on yourself that you feel capable of being with people who are in powerful emotional states. You cannot be frightened by deep feelings. For this it is best that you have experienced your own emotions through some experiential therapy, such as Bioenergetics, Gestalt process, or Primal therapy.

In any kind of psychological or spiritual work, any growth work, it is important that the person in a leadership position continue to work on his or her own growth process. That is absolutely essential. For a leader or guide to think of himself or herself as a finished product is gross personal inflation. Gestalt process, as I understand it, does not have a beginning or an end; you do not come in sick and go out well. It is *process,* ongoing. Therefore, whenever material comes up, you work it through, and go on living until the next time. It is a life process, an ideal way for a group leader to stay in contact with himself or herself. This is important because what goes on in group can easily touch off individual process, and where the guide is blocked, the group will stop; the level to which the guide has evolved is the level to which the group will evolve. Some people in the group may have evolved beyond the guide; they will find their own way. But people who have not evolved beyond the guide will stop their evolution at the place where the guide has stopped. Therefore, the continuing evolution of the guide is important for the group. For example, a guide who has not yet learned self-acceptance will not be able to accept members of the group. A guide who has not experienced his or her anger and become comfortable with it may become frightened of a group member's anger and try to stop or repress it.

The Hero's Journey is an initiatory process in which each step builds on the one before it. The work is so concentrated that a person who leaves even for an hour may be lost. Thus, as a guide, you must avoid at all costs becoming what I call the "cruise director." This type of guide is so far removed from the material that he or she allows people to miss sessions without either catching them up or telling them they have to leave because they have not followed the sequence. This guide says casually, "We'll be doing these entertainments . . . you can come when you want, and stay away if you have something more interesting to do." The cruise director guide, for example, wouldn't be concerned if participants had missed the sessions in which the Hero is created, yet returned for the discovery of the Demon. Of course, these participants would have no idea what the Demon is all about, or why they are looking for resistance when they haven't even found the source of that resistance. This is not what the Hero's Journey is about.

In sum, the only prerequisite to guiding the Hero's Journey is a sense of responsibility for process and for the people whom you as guide are taking under your direction. You have a responsibility for what takes place. You must have respect for the process itself, and a commitment to the people who are entering into it: responsibility, commitment, and devotion to the evolving human spirit.

CHAPTER 3
Entering the Mystery

*T*he purpose of preparation is twofold: to make yourself ready for the ritual, and to make the space ready for the ritual. In the celebration of ancient rituals, or in the production of a play, the preparation period is an important time. This preparation serves as a metamorphosis from the everyday into another level. This chapter is addressed primarily to group leaders. However, as an individual journeyer you will also need to prepare yourself and your space, and you may find some of the following recommendations helpful.

As a leader you must have taken the first step to the new level through your own transformation before you can lead others into it. In the Japanese No theater, as well as in ancient Greek theater, the actor would spend a long period of time meditating on the mask of the character he was going to play before even putting it on. This meditation was a kind of prayer intended to move his soul into another reality. You are also moving yourself into another dimension, another world, in order to begin your journey or be able to assist others across the threshold. Like the shaman in a society that acknowledges such thresholds, you have to know what it is like on both sides. Healers and shamans in these cultures often take on an illness, experiencing it spiritually, discovering how to heal themselves before they can work with the person who is ill.

Shamans know that people must heal themselves; the shaman is not the source of healing, only the guide. The same is true of the guide of the Hero's Journey. You must know what it is like on both sides of the threshold to adequately help the participants. You recognize that, whatever problem the person presents, its resolution lies beyond the threshold of the everyday.

PREPARING THE SPACE

Preparing the space is an essential part of preparing yourself. The simple act of transforming the space can lead us from one dimension into another. Native Americans, for example, when preparing for a celebration of sacred rites, would spend days, weeks, even months in clearing away, building, cooking, weaving, carefully creating and organizing the place and the implements of the ritual. Familiar objects take on a numinosity, enhanced by the slow transformation of consciousness. So when you are preparing the space, you are entering into a kind of meditation. Ordinary things arranged with care become extraordinary, the space becomes consecrated, a place apart, because you have taken the care to make it special. Beauty is a kind of magic. Care is a kind of magic. So consecrated, a ritual space is one in which an action that has consequence at many levels of the psyche can take place. When people walk into such a space, they immediately feel, "Something unusual is going to happen here!" They are not just coming into a room with a lot of strange people about whom they feel uncomfortable. They are entering into an ambiance of beauty and care. That's important!

I like to create an altar in the center of the room: a piece of colorful, attractive cloth, a candle, some leaves or flowers or other objects from the outdoor environment made into an arrangement in the center of the room to give it focus. Since I like to use spontaneous group music, I place around the altar a circle of simple musical instruments such as claves, tambourines, castanets, maracas—rhythm instruments that anyone can play. Sometimes, if the situation is right, I might hang a flag or a wall hanging to suggest heroic endeavor, to create a setting. But for me the basic structure in the room is an altar with the group candle. Setting an attractive piece of cloth on the floor raises that space in consciousness. That is what an altar is: a place that is set aside, elevated in awareness, at which special things take place. For a group it is also a common center. It creates a point of focus beyond the guide and the other participants.

PREPARING THE MUSIC

You can create a meditative mood when people arrive by playing appropriate music. Through such preparations you are already settling into your new function. You have finished doing what needs to be done in the ordinary world and now, through the action of gathering flowers, setting out the altar and creating an ambiance, you are focusing your attention on the journey into the extraordinary.

PREPARING YOURSELF

I have always found it necessary to take some time for myself before the group begins. I dedicate myself, my work, and the group itself to some higher power, to some aspect of God. My way has always been to choose one of the names of the gods or goddesses of any civilization, any period of history that I find myself in rapport with, and to use that as my dedication. "I dedicate this group to Avalokiteshvara, to Jesus Christ, to Hermes. I give myself over to you that my personal problems may be set aside, so that you may work through me and give these people what they need for their own evolution in the great work of the human spirit."

Whether you are the guide or an individual journeyer, it is important that you spend a moment giving yourself over to something higher than yourself, to something archetypal, before entering into the ritual. There is a great danger in taking too much responsibility for the growth that people experience in the group. Then you no longer think of yourself as a guide to the source, but as the source itself. That is a very unhealthy frame of mind, both for the group and for the leader. Working with archetypes is always very powerful and some step—such as the dedication I have suggested—is necessary to protect the guide from overidentification with the archetype, which is a form of psychological inflation. When such inflation occurs, the archetype no longer works as a healing force for the group, but as an instrument of tyranny for the leader. If you approach the gods with the wrong disposition, they become destructive; therefore, it is necessary to cultivate an attitude of humility and respect. The dedication is an effective way to do this.

When I offer myself up in dedication, I become a participant, taking the group from that god or goddess. Each unusual event that takes place in the process becomes a revelation through which I learn more of the particular nature of that god or goddess, who are the true guides of the groups. And since they are also the guides of our existence, when I dedicate myself to them, I am simply allowing myself to become aware of that truth.

Whatever issues you may be dealing with have to be put aside for this special time so that you can be totally present for the others. When I am working with a team of guides, we spend a few moments together in meditation, releasing any kind of tension that might be going on between us—or making a pact not to allow that tension to infect the group—so that we can devote our full attention to the process. That doesn't mean that you forget your personal problems. You know what they are, you know they are there, you may even at some point talk about them in the group in order to dispel any mystery about yourself. If you are in the middle of a difficult situation, it is worthwhile to acknowledge what it is so that the group does not waste its time trying to explain what they may sense. Groups have a tendency to place the leader on a pedestal, and such a revelation can demystify and humanize the image of the guide, who is after all only another person like the rest of the group. This is especially true when the context is archetypal and exultant by its nature, as the Hero's Journey is. A human leader presents a good indication that it is possible for group members to make the journey, warts and all.

Dressing for the first session of the group is also very important. I am very careful about color. On the one hand, I want to look attractive and special, but on the other hand, I don't want to look extraordinary. I don't want to walk in dressed in a robe, for example, because unless such dress is recognized as comfortable for the group I am addressing, it risks setting me aside too much. When I dress in preparation for the group, I always balance two factors: wearing something comfortable that keeps me in harmony with the group, and at the same time sets me aside as the ritual master. I never want to err in the direction of specialness, so that people say, "Who does this guy think he is?" Nor do I begin the group in old torn-up blue jeans so that they ask, "Where is the leader of the group?" I have known group leaders who deliberately underdress, and I think that is a failing, especially for the opening session. I will also clothe myself with respect to the season, not only in relationship to the temperature, but also in terms of color. However, such color decisions are unique and personal. What is and is not appropriate will depend on you and your relationship to the group in question.

After all the preparations have been made, it is a good idea to be there to greet the participants and give them a sense of welcome. People are usually shy and uncomfortable at the opening of a new group, and a human touch can aid in the transition. It is a matter of balance between ordinary and transcendent. Always maintain that balance; especially since the focus of the group is ultimately transpersonal, it is very important to keep it grounded in the ordinary. In this way it becomes a step-by-step passage into the other dimension. Greeting the group members also releases my own feelings of timidity and nervousness. It puts me in contact with individuals, rather than the more foreboding concept of "group."

A WORD ABOUT THE FORMAT

I have divided the Hero's Journey process into a seven-day format (see Appendix II, Daily Structure), which is by far my favorite length for the Hero's Journey; however, I have also provided a three-day format. In the seven-day format, the first day begins in the afternoon, at three o'clock, and consists of two sessions with dinner between. The plan for each following day will depend on how far the group has progressed. Generally, the day is divided into three sessions of about three hours each, with comfortable breaks. It is not advisable for group members to distract themselves with additional activities extraneous to the process. The process is a consciousness intensive, and people who are unwilling to commit themselves to it are advised to leave so that the group energy can be preserved and maintained at peak intensity.

MATERIALS FOR THE PROCESS

Following is a list of recommended supplies for the journey:

- simple musical instruments
- altar cloth
- candles: one seven-day, one small votive
- workbooks: one per participant (see Appendix III)
- art paper (18 × 24): six sheets per participant
- crayons
- pencils
- Tarot cards (Waite deck or other that pictures all the cards)
- pocket mirrors: one per three participants
- costumes
- blindfolds: one per two participants
- scented oil
- wine or grape juice
- wine goblet (two or three if large group)
- incense
- small bowls: one for water, one for earth
- music cassettes
- tape recorder

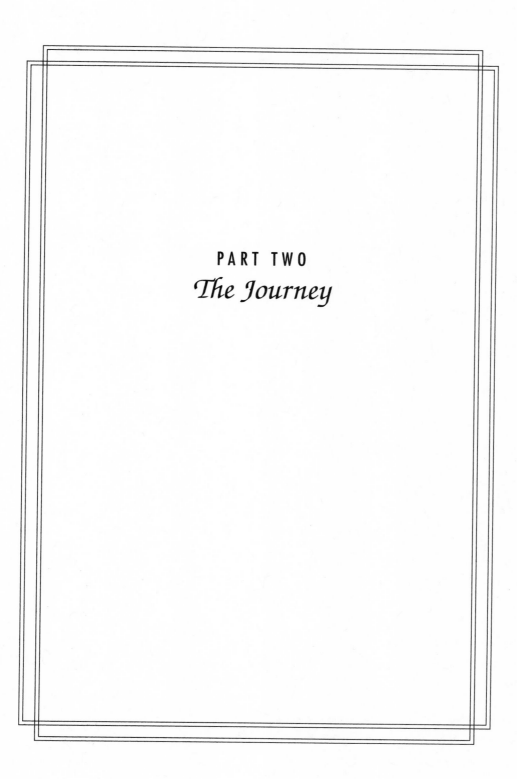

PART TWO
The Journey

CHAPTER 4
Gathering

*T*here was once a Chinese sage who awakened from sleep with a curious expression on his face. His companion noticed this and asked, "My friend, what is the matter? You have such a look of consternation on your face. Is something troubling you?" The sage replied, "Well I'm not sure if I have just awakened from a dream in which I was a butterfly, or if a butterfly is just now dreaming that he is me."[1]

I sometimes awaken in the dark of night, and for a brief moment I am not sure of where I am. Is this my childhood home, my San Francisco house? Am I in France, England, or still visiting friends in Big Sur? Where is the window, the door? How do I get to the bathroom? Such confusion can be easily explained by the fact that I travel a lot. But it is also that I am in a certain altered state, that threshold between sleep and wakefulness called the hypnagogic state. It is here that the Hero's Journey takes place, in that twilight zone between waking and dreaming where the boundaries are not too clear, and one dimension seems every bit as real as the other. So much is possible here that can only be hinted at in ordinary consciousness.

BEGINNING

To the Guide:

The opening is often one of the most difficult moments in the group. Rather than beginning with a lecture, which consists of people listening while

1. *The Wisdom of Laotse,* translated and edited by Lin Yutang (New York: Random House, 1948), p. 238.

I talk, or introductions, during which we all pretend to listen while uncomfortably waiting our turn, I prefer to have us all make noise together, rhythmic noise, rather like music, through which we can all speak and listen to each other at the same time. To this end, as I mentioned in the last chapter, I provide the group with simple rhythm instruments, rather like toys that they can play with—fun and not too challenging. People singing together, stamping their feet together, making rhythm together—doing something that they can all do at the same time—establishes a tribal sense, a sense of belonging together.

It is also possible to get some sense of the participants by watching how they deal with the instruments. Note the difference between a person who chooses a tiny noisemaker and shakes it distractedly, and another who chooses the loudest, most ostentatious one and beats it savagely on the floor. You can learn a lot about how people are approaching the process simply by watching them play with the instruments. Do they play harmoniously with the rhythm of the group, or do they ignore the others and try to either take a leading role or play quite out of rhythm, listening to the sound of another drum? It is not necessary to make judgments or draw hard, fast conclusions: that could be dangerous and lead you to respond to the judgment and not to the person. Just observe and take note. Such observations may be helpful later.

Not everyone will want to begin in this way. It is not the device that is important, but its purpose: to facilitate the transition from separate individuals to a group, and from ordinary reality to the realm of mystery and myth.

I like to follow the music with a story and a song.

WHY NOT?

Gestalt psychologist Fritz Perls claimed that there was only one response to the question "Why?" And that is "Because . . . "

"Why?"

"Because . . . "

"Why?"

"Because . . . "

"Why?"

"Because . . . " And everything following, Fritz said, "is bullshit."

Of course, Fritz's approach was in reaction to the Freudian analytic mode, and he saw the endless quest for explanations as a fruitless search for justification of present neurotic habits. Instead of "Why?" he preferred to ask the question "How?" which directs our investigation to the operation of the psyche in the here-and-now.

However, the philosophers of old knew that there was another response to the question "Why?" And that is, "Why not?"

I offer this phrase as a kind of Instrument of Power—the power to free you to take a chance and do something that might seem a little risky. Let it resonate through your head over and over again, "Why not? Why not?" If there is good reason not to do something, your being will tell you so. Exploring new modes of behavior may open the door to more life experience and give you the chance to explore unknown aspects of yourself that have gone unnoticed till now. "Why not?"

When a seed is planted in the soil, it drinks in the nourishment of the earth and the warmth of the sun. These energies set up a kind of pulse that beats in the heart of the seed. The pulse grows stronger and stronger until the husk can no longer contain it. Suddenly, the seed throws out a shoot and growth begins. We are much the same in our growing process. When we are greeted by a new experience, we can feel the pulse quicken in our chests. Blood filled with adrenaline floods the skeletal muscles so that we will be ready either to run away from the experience or stay and confront it. This flight or fight mechanism is shared by all animals. If, when we notice this beating in our chests, this deepening of breath, we call the emotion "fear," we will back away and flee. The pulse will gradually calm down and we will come back to the comfortable norm. However, if we can alchemically call this increased vitality "excitement," we will be more likely to stay, face the new experience, and grow, just like the seed in the earth. The phrase "Why not?" is meant to give us the permission to do just that—to stay beyond our limits so that we can discover what is on the other side of our fear.

Before entering into the mythic land of the Hero's Journey, I like to challenge myself and the participants by singing this song:

"Why Not?"[2]

Have you ever noticed
How the question "Why?"
Is a way to clip your wings
When you want to fly?

2. © Paul Rebillot

"Why should I live something new?"
"Should I even try?"
And you're trapped in the labyrinth
Of the question "Why?"

"Why?" Because, Because, Because . . . "
It goes on and on,
Tangled up in a web of reasons
While your life flows by.

Well, we've got an alternative
One we've all forgot.
When you ask yourself, "Why should I . . . ?
" . . . Why not?"

Why not live something new?
Why not climb a tree?
Why not live a mystery?
Why not let yourself be?

(Chorus:) You are free to fly!
Free to live, free to die!
You are free to be who you are
Who you are is free, that's who you really are.
Why not? Why not?
Why not? Why not?
Why not? Why not?
Why not? Why not?

If you've got a good reason
Not to swim or fly,
Trust your body to tell you so
Without asking "Why?"

Simply look around you,
Is there danger there?
Or are all those monsters
Merely made up out of air?

(Chorus)

THE THREE AGREEMENTS

To the Guide:

At this point I tell the history of the process, how I came to develop it, and the story of the journey, as presented in the Introduction and chapter 1. I then discuss the following agreements, which I ask each of the participants to make.

To the Journeyers:

The point of the Hero's Journey process is to incarnate, to dramatize the story with your whole being: body, heart, and mind. By experiencing your own story as fully as possible, you imprint on your soul the process of transformation. That is what the Hero's Journey is: it is the way the human organism transforms itself. Every time you make a change, whether of worldview or career, love relationship, or stage in life, you polarize yourself into Hero and Demon. You confront these aspects of yourself, resolve the conflict, and move into a new level of awareness and experience. You receive the reward of your transformation and then return to your life situation illuminated by a new sense of self. Every time we make a change in our lives, no matter how great or how small, we go through this process.

The journey consists of a series of calibrated challenges to help you discover this process. You might think of yourself as being in Heroes' cadet school. The challenges that you are given deliberately call up your resistance. Only in meeting resistance can you develop courage. Slowly, little by little, each challenge becomes more frightening, more threatening, more shocking than the one before.

We can relate to a new experience in four different ways. We can look at it and say, "This is frightening to me and yet I am going to go ahead and do it anyway." That is courage. It is what I call the melting technique. You melt away the resistance by admitting it and then going ahead and doing it anyway. It is very important that you express it; you cannot pretend that you are not afraid when you are. Admitting it to someone else lightens the weight of the resistance and makes it more possible to go ahead to do whatever it is that you are called upon to do to the best of your capacity. This is courage; this is the action of a Hero.

If you have done Bioenergetics, Primal therapy, or any of the emotionally cathartic therapies, you know there is another way of dealing with resistance. It is what I call "the stick of dynamite in the stomach" approach. By intensifying the breath or putting the body in certain stress positions, emotions are released, thereby freeing the body of the physical blockage that accompanies resistance. I prefer not to use this process, although I use something approaching it in the Supreme Ordeal.

The third way of dealing with resistance is to allow the resistance to win. This is just as important as any of the others. If I give you an exercise that you do not want to do, don't do it. However, you must say, loudly and clearly, "I do not want to do this exercise." And you do not have to say this at the beginning of the exercise; you can say it right in the middle if you want. But if that is true, if you find yourself out there fighting and fighting and not being able to get through the resistance, simply say, "I do not want to do this exercise," and you are clear. You have made a heroic statement; you have said no. If you are working in a group, you have said no to a whole group of people and to the leader, and that in itself is a heroic gesture. You are then free to join in the next exercise without a problem.

However, there is one other way that people deal with resistance that is antiheroic; it is called passive resistance. This is when you pretend to be doing what is called for, but you are not doing it at all. It is the way of adolescents. Mother says, "Go to the store and get something for dinner," and the adolescent says, "Okay, as soon as I'm finished with this, Mom; I'm on my way; I'm going, in five minutes, I'm going . . . " A half hour later, he has still not gone. When I give an exercise, a passive resister pretends to do it just long enough to get across the room and sneak out the door. I would prefer that you not do that. If you are going to participate in an exercise, participate; if you choose not to, make that statement. But do not do it and not do it at the same time. This is a ritual format, and that means you take responsibility for entering into it or not. This is one of the major themes of the process, self-responsibility.

So there are certain things I would like you to agree on before beginning the process. First, agree that you will not passively resist. The second agreement has to do with violence. Violent urges may be released in the course of the journey, particularly when dealing with the Demon of Resistance. Therefore, I would like you to agree to act out violence only on appropriate objects, such as cushions and mattresses, and never on people. Finally, if two people are interacting physically and one feels afraid of violence, honor the word "stop." If someone says this word to you, it means, "Hands off."

These are the three agreements I would like you to make: no passive resistance, act out violence only on cushions and mattresses, and honor the word "stop." (*I go around the room and ask for each person's agreement.*)

THE OPENING RITUAL

Individual journeyers should create a simple ritual, such as lighting a candle followed by a meditation or brief meditative reading, to begin each working session (see Appendix I, Ram Meditations).

To the Guide:

At the beginning of each workshop, I like to focus the group's attention by the lighting of a candle. It creates a meditative atmosphere and begins the movement inward. Choose a large, seven-day candle (available in most supermarkets). The candle is a symbol that represents the group as a unit, a gestalt of beings who have come together to do the process. The flame is the everlasting flame that burns, if the situation allows, throughout the period of the group. Each day we elect a vestal who attends to the candle for the day, protects it through the night, and then returns it to the center of the group in the morning, when she or he selects a new vestal for the task.

The lighting of the group candle is followed by a meditation to prepare the people for the drama. (See Appendix I, Ram Meditations, Day One. I move directly from this meditation into Homeground Exercise 1: Movement Meditation, in chapter 5.)

Beginning each day with a meditation brings the group together with a common purpose after a time of separation. The vestal has guarded the candle through the night. If the vestal has taken it out of the room, he or she now brings it back and sets up the altar cloth with the candle in the center. Recommend that the vestal take a moment to set the altar in order for the entrance of the group. Perhaps he or she can pick some flowers or greens or set some rocks and stones from the environment around the candle to prepare for the moment when the group enters. During this time of preparation, the vestal can meditate on some brief ritual he or she might want to do to pass the light on to another vestal for the day.

When you are about to meditate and perform a ritual, it is not necessary to remain solemn as the group enters. So many people have been wounded by the somber traditional religious approach to ritual, that a friendly, even joking atmosphere can help relieve the tension of such unfortunate early programming. As a matter of fact, it is not a bad idea to include a bit of humor, especially in the more serious rituals, to allow any tension to release itself. I'll say more of this when we come to the dedication of the Instruments of Power.

After the meditation ask the vestal to choose someone else in the room to pass the candle to as the new vestal. Invite the vestal to create a brief ritual of the passing of the candle. Let each one do it spontaneously, in his or her own way. It may just be calling the other person to the center of the room and passing on the candle. Or the person may do some movements or circle the room with the candle: whatever gesture that person chooses to create a ritual of the passing on of the flame.

CHAPTER 5
The Departure

*B*efore you can begin your journey, you will need to establish your Homeground: the point of departure. It is here that we discover the individual nature of each journey.

To do this we look at four aspects of life: *home, lifework, beloved,* and *self.* I deliberately chose these words because they have many levels of meaning. One could as easily change them to more specific terms, such as home, job, love life, and self. However, the possibility of a more transpersonal journey may be deflected by words such as job and love life. The broader term allows us to include the more limiting concept as well as its greater meaning within the meditation. For example, when we use the word "home," we may have the image of our childhood home, indicating that our sense of home is so shaped by childhood that we have difficulty identifying where we are living now as home. This may be an important revelation, one to be dealt with.

The concept of "lifework" allows the question: Does what I am doing to earn my living have anything to do with my lifework? If not, why not?

The word "beloved" opens the door to a great many possibilities, from our life-partners or children to God. It allows the possibility of discovering who it is that we really value, and in what way. Sometimes people, in considering this aspect of their Homeground, discover an empty space. This can suggest a number of possibilities. They may be ready to allow someone into their lives. They may be afraid of contact. They may have just lost an important loved one and want to keep that space empty for the present.

I combine the discovery of Homeground with the Call to Adventure. It is this call that actually begins the journey. We are constantly receiving calls that try to motivate us toward some action. Advertisements, television commercials, even family and friends try to convince us to do something we may or may not want to do. They are all pressing our "call button." In the Hero's Journey, we are listening for a deeper call.

The guided meditation that follows uses the concept of the magic wish or Miracle to discover the call for the individual journey. After looking at the four aspects of Homeground, you will have some idea of what needs attention in your garden. If you have been honest with yourself, you will know what is necessary for your journey. I used to have people decide for themselves what they would like to "wish for" as their Miracle. However, I have come to prefer that the impulse arise more spontaneously from the subconscious. In this way we both bypass our internal censor and reach beyond what we think we need so that a deeper, more authentic call can emerge, one that may surprise us.

The call is one of the most important aspects of the journey. It is from this image that all else proceeds. The nature of both the Hero and the Demon of Resistance follow from the quality of the call. Certainly, the impulse to take a difficult math class in college will call forth an entirely different set of images from those evoked by a call to surrender to love and relationship.

HOMEGROUND EXERCISE 1: MOVEMENT MEDITATION[1]

The first exercise following the Opening Ritual is designed to define the space called Homeground. To prepare for this meditation, participants must first become centered in their bodies.

To the Journeyers:

Everyone stand. Quietly, without disturbing the feeling of the meditation, find a place in the room. The Homeground fantasy is done as a movement meditation with the eyes closed. Swing your arms around to make sure that you don't bump into anything, that you have sufficient space to be able to move without disturbing your meditation. You do not have to move from your space. You can create a whole world in a little space if you make movements like dancing or running or walking but keep your feet in the same position on the ground.

1. I wish to gratefully acknowledge Jean Houston's guided fantasy to a "room with four walls" as the inspiration of my own Homeground Fantasy of the "room with four doors." See the report in chapter 4 ("Games for Expanding Your Consciousness") of Howard R. Lewis and Dr. Harold S. Streitfeld, *Growth Games: How to Tune In Yourself, Your Family, Your Friends* (New York: Harcourt Brace Jovanovich, 1970).

First, situate your feet on the ground a comfortable distance apart, directly under the hip joints, so the space is not too wide or too narrow, but just the right position for you in relationship to your bone structure. The feet should be tracking straight ahead, neither turned out in the ballet position, nor turned in to the Bioenergetics pigeon-toed position. The knees are slightly flexed. You can see 360 degrees around you when the knees are flexed and you are not constraining yourself. Recall the three globes of light and balance them, one on top of the other.

To the Guide:

If you are not using the Ram Meditations (see Appendix I), teach the group now about balancing the belly, the chest, and the head centers of the body, one on top of the other.

When you have the three centers stacked one on top of the other, displace your weight slightly over the right foot so that you experience the feeling of being off-balance to the right. Feel the tensions that the muscles have to hold in order to maintain that disequilibrium, and also feel the limitation of your movement. You can now move only your left foot; your movement has been limited by that displacement to the right. Also, you have to move with your left foot when you are displaced to the right, so it makes the left movement possible, but it also limits your potential. Now, moving through center, let your weight displace itself to the left. Following the image of the pendulum, let your body swing right to left, with the radius of the pendulum gradually becoming smaller and smaller until finally the pendulum lands at the point of perfect center that is neither right nor left. Find that position, take a deep breath, and allow your body to relax into it.

Now let your weight come forward over your toes slightly. Feel what it is like with your nose pointing into the future, rushing ahead toward some goal. Feel the displacement, the tensions in your body, and the potential for movement in this position. Now let your weight shift itself back over your heels with your body behind the center of balance, displaced into the past. "Ah, yesterday!" Once again, let the pendulum swing between forward and back, back and forward, diminishing its radius, until finally you find that point of perfect center between the two. When you have achieved that point of center, take a deep breath, let your body relax into it, and call this position the *zero position:*

neither forward nor back, neither right nor left, just being present in the here and now—zero position.

Take a little time to let yourself feel centered. Let your hands hang quietly at your sides. Breathe into your belly. I'm going to play a little music (*slow, rhythmic walking music*). Just let your body move to that music, dance your here-and-now.

Now imagine yourself walking. Let your dance transform into a walking movement. You find yourself walking . . . down the stairs . . . in the dark. At the bottom of the stairway, in front of you, you see a light. Move down the stairs toward the light.

You've reached the bottom of the stairs and you find yourself entering a huge room filled with light. As you look around the room, you notice that each of the walls has a door right in the center of it, and over each door is written a word. You go up to the first door (*light, melodic music*). Over the top of that door you see written the word "Home." Behind that door are images of home . . . they will be whatever that word means to you. Open the door and go inside. Behold the images of home. What colors do you find behind the door marked "Home"? What smells and tastes? Home. What shapes do you find there? Are they sharp and hard-edged, or soft, warm, and round? What are the textures that mean home to you? What images or pictures do you see? Let your body move with these images. If they're sharp and hard, let your body move in sharp and hard ways. If they're soft and round, let your body move in response to the soft and round images of home.

Pay attention to any kind of tension in your body, and explore that tension with movement. If your body is relaxed, let your body move with that sensation. Each person is unique. Each person has his or her own reactions to the word "home." Let your body move according to your feelings. Take a deep breath and let some sound come out that expresses your feelings about home. (*Allow some time for movement; then bring the music to an end.*)

Sense into the way your body feels right now. If you are still standing in a posture from your dance, keep that posture. If not, create a statue or sculpture with your body right now that expresses your feelings about home. What does that sculpture look like? Pay attention to how it relates to the ground, how it feels in your feet, in your pelvis, your buttocks, your abdomen and stomach, your shoulders and arms, your breath, the tilt of your head, the expression of your face. Call this sculpture "Home."

Imagine now that you leave the room marked "Home." As you do, the sculpture melts away. Take a deep breath, and blow away all the images of home. Blow them away and let them go, like so much smoke. The door is closed, and you are back in the room with the four doors. Move to the second door (*music with strong rhythm*). Over that door you see written the word "Lifework." Behind that door are images of work, whatever lifework means to you. Open the door, go in, and find out what is behind the door marked "Lifework."

What colors do you find here, behind the door marked "Lifework"? What kinds of smells and sounds? Lifework. What kinds of shapes do you find here, behind the door marked "Lifework"? The shapes of your work. Let your body begin to move with those shapes. Let the shapes take on pictures and images. Images of work. Move your body the way you do at work. Let your voice express the way you feel about your work—your own sounds to express your own feelings, whatever they are. . . . Lifework. Your work. (*Again, allow time for movement, then bring the music to an end.*)

Now take on a posture that expresses your feelings about work, about your lifework. Find a posture that expresses your feelings about your work. What would the sculpture look like? How does that sculpture relate to the ground? Feel that posture with your legs, pelvis, stomach and chest, shoulders and arms and hands, the expression of your head, your facial expression. Lifework. Feel that posture. Experience it totally—the posture called "Lifework." Then gradually let it come back down to zero. And as you relax the posture, take a deep breath and blow away the images of work. Walk through the door again and let go of the images.

Shake out your body a little bit to release any tensions you might be holding.

Now imagine yourself walking up to the third door (*nonvocal romantic music*). On that door you see written the word "Beloved." Behind that door are images of love. Open the door and go inside: the room of the beloved. Images of love. Again, what colors do you find here? What tastes and smells in the room of the beloved? What shapes do you find here? Allow your body to move in relationship to the beloved. Let your voice express whatever your feelings are in the room of the beloved. (*Music to finish.*) Once more, let your body take on a posture that expresses your reaction to the word and to the images of the beloved. Feel that posture, in the way that it relates to the ground, with your feet and your legs. Feel your genitals and your rectum, any sensations you have there; how you breathe in the posture of the beloved, what you find in your shoulders and arms, the expression of your face, the tilt of your head. Call this sculpture "The Beloved."

Once more, it is time to leave this room. As you leave it, let the posture melt and soften, take a deep breath and blow away the images of the beloved.

You come to the fourth and final door (*nonvocal spiritual music, such as flute or harp*). Over that door you find written the word "Self." Behind that door are images and symbols of your self. Open the door, go inside, and behold what you experience behind the door marked "Self." Again, what kinds of shapes and colors do you find here? What kinds of symbols, images, pictures do you find in the room of the self? Let your body dance and move with those images. Let your voice express the way you feel about your self. (*Music to finish.*) Once more, take on a posture, a sculpture that expresses all of the feelings that you have about your self. Experience that in your legs, your pelvis, your stomach, chest, shoulders and arms. "This is the way I feel about myself." The tilt of your head, your facial expression. "This is the way I feel about myself."

Now once again leave the room, close the door behind you, let the posture melt down, and as you do so take a deep breath and blow away the images of self.

You find yourself back in the room with four doors. But a strange and miraculous thing has happened. In the center of the room, you see a golden throne. And over that throne you see written the words "Throne of Miracles." As in a fairy tale, you are to be granted one wish, one miracle that will come true. Now that you have had a chance to look at the four corners of your life, you can allow yourself to dream, to envision a miracle—the miracle that will fulfill your life.

But before you sit down on the throne, review the four areas of your life by taking the postures you have created. Take the posture called Home. Is this the way home feels to you? Or have you idealized it in some way? If you have, what is the truth? Lifework. Feel this posture and think about your work. Is this the way it feels to you? If not, what is the truth? Do the same with the Beloved, and the Self.

Now sit down on the throne and take a few moments to breathe (*uplifting music, such as Pachelbel's "Canon in D."*) You are going to allow your deeper self to send up a vision of what could fulfill your life and integrate the four rooms. Allow a color to arise, a sensation, a feeling. Perhaps a few other colors swirl into it. Gradually, these colors take form and an image emerges. The image is the symbol of what could integrate the four rooms and illuminate your life. Spend some time with that picture without necessarily understanding its meaning. Just be with it. . . . Now allow some words to emerge from your depths to tell you what the meaning of this Miracle is. Let your body respond to the image with movement, even as you sit there. Breathe it, taste it, participate in it as fully as possible. Give it voice, sound, song. . . .

Your Miracle. Your Call to Adventure that inspires you to leave your Homeground and begin your journey.

Imagine yourself leaving the Throne of Miracles, and return back up those stairs into this room. Your Hero's Journey has begun.

To the Guide:

After people have gone through the vision of their life situation and have envisioned their Miracle, they are usually in a significantly different mood from when they entered the room. So it is very important that the instruction and the material that comes now is given with delicacy and respect for this atmosphere. Allow them sufficient time to reintegrate in the here and now. To enable them to stay in the experience without distracting themselves, I recommend that they not interact with each other. At this point it is a good idea to put on some quiet, meditative music to maintain the feeling of peaceful internal investigation.

HOMEGROUND EXERCISE 2: ARTWORK

To the Journeyers:

The Huichol Indians of Mexico use peyote to enter into altered states. When they return from their journey, rather than talking about it, they create beautiful artworks out of colored yarns to express the soul of their experience. With these artworks they can integrate the material and communicate it at another, more emotional level than the verbal. That is what I would like you to do now. (*I provide good quality drawing paper and several boxes of oil pastel crayons.*)

Now, take a piece of art paper and some crayons. Recapitulate what your experience has been in going through each of the four doors, with the vision of the Miracle in the center of the page. If you haven't had very strong visual images, allow this work with color and shape to augment your experience. Not everyone perceives the inner world visually. Some experience it more kinetically, and others experience it more aurally. One of the goals of this process is to round out the way each person perceives, to facilitate the possibility of greater sensual contact with both the internal and the external world. So the use of color, shape, and design on paper is a way of adding the visual to the emotional and the kinetic. It is not necessary to draw pictures, although you can if you want. If you feel inhibited by the idea of doing an artwork and drawing pictures, simply use colors. Choose a color or a series of colors that expresses what your experience of home was. Were the shapes sharp and linear, or were they soft and rolling? Express the feeling level of the experience without necessarily trying to depict it. Often people trouble themselves with the difference between what they see inside their heads and what they are capable of putting down on paper. They occupy their time focusing on the difficulty rather than simply allowing the expression to take place. I recommend that you use this design for the artwork (*see the Workbook in Appendix III*).

The purpose of this exercise is to bring that other world into this one, to make the transition between where you have just been internally and the here and now. It is also a way to document the story in ways other than just talking about it, and it gives you a meditation mandala to work with after you have completed the process. You can meditate on your drawings and recall some of the psychic level of the story. I encourage you to make artworks for most of the major stations of the journey.

To the Guide:

Pass out paper and colors and let the people spend some time drawing their Homeground. I would allow half an hour for this drawing.

When you begin to notice that enough people have finished, it is time to pass around copies of the Hero's Journey Workbook provided in Appendix III. This allows the people who are finished drawing to be occupied with something and gives the others a chance to complete their artwork, leaving leeway for the different rhythms in the group.

HOMEGROUND EXERCISE 3: THE WORKBOOK

The Workbook is another way to document your story. It is also designed to help you step back from the process a bit. The nature of the process is to get deeply involved by becoming the image, fully experiencing the archetype, and then afterwards to take distance from it, seeing it objectively. Therefore, there is a constant dialogue between implication and separation from the archetype. The Workbook gives a chance for that separation to take place. It is written as a fill-in-the-blanks story. Keep it as simple as possible—as if the story were being told to children. This simplicity will enable the psyche to integrate the story as it would a fairy tale.

When you finish your drawing, take the Workbook and begin to fill in the blanks up to the beginning of the work on the Hero.

HOMEGROUND EXERCISE 4: FINDING THE SPIRIT GUIDE

To the Guide:

In another part of the room, as the participants are working on their drawings and their workbooks, spread out in a circle either Tarot cards or other picture cards of archetypal images. If you are using Tarot cards, I recommend the Waite deck or any other that includes pictures for all the cards. Spread out the whole deck. You may want to have duplicates of the Major Arcana, since these cards are especially popular. The participants will keep their cards throughout the journey and return them on the last day, unless you choose to make a gift of them. I encourage those who choose the same image to find a chance to work together in the course of the journey. When everyone has chosen a Spirit Guide, have the group come back together in a circle.

One of the most important images in the cast of characters of the Hero's Journey is the Spirit Guide. This being is able to see beyond the Hero and the Demon to the integrated self. The Spirit Guide is interested in helping the Hero reach the goal, but is also interested in the Demon. The Demon is an essential part of the whole person and cannot be simply done away with or ignored in order to satisfy the aspirations of the Hero. The Spirit Guide is the representative of the individuated self and is there to help in the accomplishment of that individuation. That is why the Spirit Guide does not try to destroy the Demon, but rather to transform it into something that can be useful for the accomplishment of the heroic quest. In some of the Hero stories, the Demon is killed or destroyed in the guise of a dragon or ogre. However, if the Spirit Guide can be presented in a way that is sympathetic to both Hero and Demon, the likelihood of simply destroying the Demon, who is after all a part of the full self, is averted. The old idea, "If thine eye offends thee, pluck it out," tends to leave us half blind in the world.

When you finish your drawing and writing, look at the images (*the Tarot cards or other archetypal images*) and choose the picture of someone to help you accomplish your Miracle, a spiritual or other-worldly entity, a friend. You are looking for your Spirit Guide, that being who can see deeply into your psyche, who knows the whole story and, as a matter of fact, has in some way brought you to the journey in order to further your evolution. You may not understand now the full significance of the image you choose, but it will probably reveal itself to you in the course of the journey.

HOMEGROUND EXERCISE 5: SHARING YOUR STORY

In a Group:

Find someone in the group you do not know. Make eye contact with that person and make a date, outside of group time, to sit down and share the details of your journey thus far. That means reading out of the workbook and showing another person your design and your Spirit Guide. This is a challenge because it means making some contact with another member of the group at a deeper level than "Hello, how are you? Where do you come from? What do you do?"

Now that you have begun the journey, everything that takes place in the course of this period of time is part of your journey. Every meeting, every interchange or confrontation becomes part of your journey. Once you have entered into the fantasy, you have put on the glasses, so to speak, and they stay on throughout the process. The journey continues even in your sleep. For example, tonight, just before you go to sleep, I would like you to spend about ten minutes looking at the image of the Spirit Guide you have chosen. Let your mind do what it wants to do. Simply look at the image, so that the last thing your eyes have seen before you turn off the lights and go to sleep is your Spirit Guide. You might have your workbook next to the bed so that you can write down any dreams you have during the night. The dream may not make sense immediately, but possibly the Guide is showing you something important that will clarify itself for you in the course of the workshop. So let your Guide take you to the other side of the threshold tonight.

THE RITUAL CLOSING

To the Guide:

Now the group comes together in a circle. You may invite the people to hold hands in order to feel that contact with the whole group. Look once again into the candle, go into a quiet space, and chant one Ram or your own variation to close the evening, so that every day begins and ends with chanting.

Group-Building Suggestions

Depending on the time of day the first session ends and the amount of time that you have, you can do various exercises to help the people get to know each other. Here I suggest two: Sharing in Families, and the Art Museum exercise.

Sharing in Families

Divide the group up into subgroups of five or six and have each individual share his or her story and artwork. Sometimes these smaller groups, from five to ten, can work very well as "little families" within the greater whole. If the group itself is very large, then it might be necessary to subdivide the group into smaller sections that can meet every day for a period of time so that people can process the material they have experienced with each other. This gives the participants a chance to develop intimacy with a small group of people rather than trying to get to know the whole group, especially if the group is larger than twenty.

After the experience of the Homeground (Homeground Exercise 1), and before the distribution of the Spirit Guides (or even with the Spirit Guides), it might be a good idea to subdivide the group and have them share their materials. One way I have found effective is to have each person go into the center and recapitulate the postures he or she has found for the four rooms, as well as a posture that represents the image of the Miracle. This is a challenge; it is a bit of a test to get up in front of a group of new people and show off your body, and at the same time it is a way for them to integrate more and more into their bodies the images they have found for these five aspects of the journey.

The Art Museum Exercise

This is another exercise aimed at helping build the group awareness. It also encourages participants to make contact with people they might not ordinarily contact, to begin to search out not only the people with whom they feel comfortable, but those who might be helpful to them precisely because of their differences.

After they have completed their Homeground drawings, have them put the drawings up on the wall as in an art museum. Then they walk about, as in an art museum, admiring the paintings and talking to each other about them.

To the Journeyers:

Walk among the various paintings. Look at them, look for things that other people may have in their paintings that you do not have in yours. Notice the different ways that the paintings are done. . . . Now look for a drawing that seems to have something that yours lacks, or look for a drawing that is very much the opposite of your own. If you have drawn stick figures with very little color, then look for one that is the opposite, one with lots of colors flowing into each other. Or if yours is all color and no structure, look for one with structure. Look for a drawing that you would say is complementary to yours in terms of completing what yours lacks. When you have found that drawing, find out whose it is and contact that person . . . (*Give them time to do this.*)

Now imagine that you are a group of art students and this is the first day of an art class. We are now looking at the paintings that the other artists have done. You are looking for somebody who can help teach you something you would like to learn about art. Maybe the sense of color, the sense of shape, the sense of order, of design. Get together and talk with that person about what you can teach each other, but speak only in terms of color, shape, or picture. For example, "I can teach you something about my sense of color if you can teach me something about shape." Or, "I can show you how to draw pictures if you can teach me something about this wonderful sense of color that you have." Take some time to talk about how you might be able to serve each other and teach each other as students in an art school . . . (*Give them time to do this.*)

Now I would like you to imagine that color has to do with sensation or the body center, and that shape and form have to do with the organization of that sensation, as the heart center organizes the rhythms of the body into feelings; and that symbol or picture has to do with the head center, which works with memory and meaning. Rather than talking about teaching each other a sense of color or a sense of order, talk about how you can teach each other about sensation or about emotions or about the working of the mind. See what you have to offer each other in terms of these levels of human experience.

Now that you have reviewed your present life situation, envisioned your Miracle, and found the image of the spirit-being who is guiding you, you are ready to awaken your Hero. Allow the images you have discovered to work in you through the night. Even though the meaning of your Miracle and your Spirit Guide may be unclear to you, trust that the Hero within you understands them and is already stirring in your heart.

CHAPTER 6
The Hero

*I*n this session we will call upon memory and imagination in order to discover, in a playful way, the Hero: the protagonist of our ritual drama, the part of us that wants to change, that wants to experience something new.

To the Journeyers:

The Hero is the aspect of the personality that says "Yes!" to life and adventure, the part of us that sets or perceives a goal and goes about trying to accomplish it. In order to come in contact with that aspect, you are going to spend the next period of time being very positive about yourself. You will look for the qualities that you need to develop in order to create this Hero, the one who is capable of accomplishing the Miracle in your life.

Now, what happens whenever we are having fun and being good to ourselves? Generally, it is followed by a period of depression. That is because, whenever we think well of ourselves, another part keeps tugging at us and saying, "You're lying to yourself, you don't believe that; you're conceited." I call this saboteur the Demon of Resistance, the one who gives us a difficult time whenever we feel good. Although I divide the process into the polarity of Hero and Demon, essentially we are developing the two at the same time because it is very difficult for us to feel really good about ourselves without hearing that negative voice saying, "Are you sure? This can't last forever. Everybody's looking at you. You're making fool of yourself"—and so on. That is the material for the Demon coming up.

So, as you are bringing out the positive aspects of your personality, I would also like you to begin to become aware of how you Demon yourself.

Become aware of the tricks you play on yourself in your mind, how you tell yourself you are silly, incompetent, too old, or whatever you tell yourself. Clearly identify that as the Demon. Acknowledge that role; let the Demon express itself, and then go ahead and act—so that you can recognize the voice of the Demon within you sabotaging your good feelings about yourself. Do not ignore it. Do not pretend it isn't there. Do not try to hide it. Let it be—and also continue to act on your own heroic challenge.

A child running out to catch a butterfly is a very heroic being because she is exploring the unknown. She is on an adventure, chasing that butterfly into the woods. That is what a Hero does. We all have that heroic quality in our bodies, in our presence, in our being, and it is there from childhood. The problem is that we then develop images of ourselves that cover up the child until we feel we have lost it. We haven't lost it, however; it is still there in us. To get in touch with our heroic self, we have to regain the ability to play like a child.

Archetypes are images of the energetic aspects of the human being that all human beings have in common. When I say "Mother," for instance, everybody knows what I mean. They may have different personal images, but they are all based on the same archetype. If I say "Hero" or "Demon," most everyone has a sense of what that might mean. Children live in those archetypal forms because they are practicing how to be human beings. They try on this role and that until finally they take a little bit from this and a little bit from that to shape their own individuality. We need to return to that sense of play, that free flow of life in imagination before the ego gets fixed in the "me" of us. We will enter into various roles and play them out—allowing ourselves to recover as much as possible that freedom. The difference between a child and an adult is that a child plays the game of life for fun, while the adult makes it a matter of life and death. It is the same game, just different stakes. I would like to encourage participation in these games, not as a matter of life or death, but simply to have fun.

To the Guide:

This is the most difficult part of the workshop. I have often described it as pulling a huge barge upstream. I need to take care of myself during this time: sometimes to take a break away from the group; sometimes to do some quiet meditation, to spend time examining my own resistance, which invariably comes up along with the group's. Basically, the creation of the Hero is a struggle with resistance. It is important for the guide to know that. After all, the

Hero is the one who hears the call, recognizes it, and—despite all obstacles—decides to follow it wherever it may lead.

Follow the opening ritual and meditation with some warmup exercises with music, exercises that both prepare the body for movement and give the people in the group a chance to get a little more comfortable with each other.

Ritual: Ram Meditation, Day 2 (see Appendix I)

FOOL'S DANCE

Each person should begin by recalling his or her Fool's Dance, which recapitulates the ritual-drama thus far and brings the participant to the experiential threshold. The postures are those learned in Homeground Exercise 1 in chapter 5. To these now add postures for the Miracle and the Spirit Guide. The Spirit Guide is the only posture that comes from an outer image, the Tarot card. The sequence for today is: Zero-Me-Home-Lifework-Beloved-Self-Miracle-Spirit Guide.

HERO EXERCISE 1: IMAGES OF HEROES

To the Journeyers:

Now that you have reviewed your Fool's Dance, close your eyes and find your zero position. Take a deep breath and relax into it . . . I will now guide you through your Fool's Dance in the form of a story.

Once upon a time, there was a person named Me. (*Take the posture.*) I went down a long flight of stairs into a room with four doors. I opened the first door, which was marked "Home." (*Take the posture.*) Behind that door I saw images that made me feel like this. When I left that room, I came to a second door that had the legend "Lifework" written above it. (*Take the posture.*) And this is the way I felt about the images I saw behind that door. The third door was marked "Beloved." (*Posture.*) And the fourth was the room marked "Self." (*Posture.*) When I came out of the fourth and final door, a strange occurrence had taken place. There, in the center of the room, was a golden throne. It was called "the Throne of Miracles." I sat down on that throne and I imagined this Miracle. (*Take the posture.*) Along came a Spirit Guide. (*Take the posture.*)

Stay in the posture of the Spirit Guide for a moment and let yourself take on that quality of being. As the Spirit Guide, look at yourself sitting on the throne and invite yourself to discover your own Heroic Self. As the Spirit Guide, begin a kind of movement or dance to invite yourself to leave the throne and set out on the path that leads to your own Heroic Self. Then gradually come back into yourself again. Imagine leaving the Throne of Miracles and gradually begin to move, very slowly, with the feeling of a walk; see the Spirit Guide in front of you, beckoning you, calling you to follow. The Spirit Guide is going to lead you through a series of images, a series of events, that will ultimately coalesce into the feeling, the image, the personality of your own Heroic Self.

Continue the walking movement. As you do, little by little, let your eyes crack open a bit. The image of the Spirit Guide stays in that other dimension, but as your eyes open, the colors of this dimension mingle with the colors of the other. When your eyes are open enough so that you can see to move, walk around the room. Experience your walk. Stay inside yourself and pay attention to the way you walk, to the way your feet touch the ground, to how you experience balance as you move, how you breathe. Try different rhythms of movement, too. But stay in your own space, being aware of how you move, how you hold your spinal column, how you relate to the ground.

In a Group:

Gradually begin to look around at other people. How does that influence your walk? See if you feel a compulsion, when you look at other people's eyes, to put on a big smile, or if you can just look without a mask. Look at other people and discover what you do. Greet each other, say hello, make contact. After a time come back into awareness of yourself, without looking at other people, and experience what happens to your walk when you return to yourself.

Keep walking, and as you are walking meditate on your Miracle. Take a little time, allowing the image of the Miracle to appear before you, to guide you. Now we are going to begin to play different roles.

Childhood Hero

When you were a kid, who did you admire or want to be like? It may have been a person; it may have been a character out of the funny papers or out of a fairy tale. Think of some hero that you had as a child. Take the first one who comes to mind and imagine how that person would walk. See if you can take on that walk. If it was a real person, imitate the person. If it was a cartoon character, let your body walk like that cartoon character might walk, influenced by the costume and the terrain. How would that person hold his or her spinal column? How would that person swing his or her arms as he or she walks? And imagine the expression on that person's face. Let your face take on the expression of that person, put on that face.

In a Group:

Now look around at the other people; imagine how that childhood hero would respond to the other people in the room and respond to each other that way. Greet each other in the voice of that childhood hero. Introduce yourself to someone. Make contact with someone and describe your life to that person. Talk about yourself. Stay in the character of that childhood hero and describe yourself.

(*After a pause:*) I would like you to stop what you are doing right now and close your eyes. Pay attention to the posture of your body and see if you are still in the posture of that childhood hero or if you have come back into the posture that feels more like your own. If you have come back into your own posture, return to the posture of that childhood hero. Really feel that spinal column, that lung capacity, that expression of your face, of your shoulders and arms. Be that hero in your body for a moment. Feel that. And ask yourself, what are the qualities that you like the most about this hero, this person? Allow yourself to think of two or three qualities that you like best about this childhood hero. And then write down those qualities; or, if in a group, tell them to the partner you are with right now: "As this person I am beautiful, strong," whatever.

Body and mind are one, and the way the body is, so is the mind. If the body posture is powerful, that will influence the way you feel. If you cannot maintain the body posture for more than a few minutes, it is likely that you will have a difficult time adapting yourself to a new point of view. If you have slipped back into a familiar posture, return to the posture of the image so you can experience that point of view in relationship to the world. You are changing your point of view. Search for the positive qualities of the character you are playing. Even a negative character can become positive if you look deeply enough. For instance, if you find yourself playing Hitler, find the positive, affirmative qualities that exist in that image. Hitler was powerful, he was charismatic—those characteristics are very positive to a habitually timid person. Thus, it is possible to find positive qualities even in this madman. So search for the positive qualities.

To the Guide:

We are going to do a whole series of images like this. Provide large art paper and bright colors. Instruct the group to draw a line about three inches down from the top of the page, and then to write boldly two or three qualities that they like best about this character. They will add to the list after each image.

Each time you do one of these games, you will give them a signal at a certain point to stop what they are doing. It can be a bell or a call. They will stop in exactly the posture they are in so they can discover whether they have fallen back into their familiar posture or whether they have been able to maintain the posture of the image they are playing. When you call "Stop!" ask them to meditate on the most positive qualities that they find in that role.

Movie Star

I would like you to start walking around again. Recall your Miracle. After a few moments, let it go. This time, think of a movie star, a superstar. Think of how that movie star might walk, what kind of costumes that movie star frequently wears, what kinds of roles you most like to see that movie star play. How does that movie star walk in relationship to the earth? Bouncy, or smooth, seductive? Let your body take on that walk. How would that movie star hold his or her spinal column? That is a very important key—the holding of the spinal column. Imagine that movie star's face—lips, eyes, tilt of the head. Put on that face, using your mouth, your eyes, the muscles of your face. Become that movie star.

In a Group:

How would that movie star look at the other movie stars in the room? Remember, we have got a roomful of movie stars. Greet each other, using the voice of that movie star. Look around now. Choose someone to star with you in your next movie. Go to that person, introduce yourself, and create the movie now. Act it out. (*Allow time for this.*) . . . Bring the movie to its grand finale.

Stop what you are doing and hold your posture. Close your eyes. If you have slipped back into your own posture, take on the posture of the movie star again and feel that body; feel the difference in the body of the movie star, in your breathing, in the use of your legs and arms. Meditate on the qualities that you like best in this movie star, the most positive, powerful qualities. When you have them, open your eyes and express them to a partner. Then go write them on your paper.

Animal

Now find a place in the room and lie down on the floor. Just take a rest for a moment. Let your body sink down into the floor and feel how you can let yourself surrender to the force of gravity. You do not have to worry about falling in this position; you are as safe as you can be, so just let yourself be. Feel how you can give yourself over to the forces of gravity. The next image has to do with the instincts, with the natural ability, the instincts that are necessary to you as the Hero of this particular journey. Before we go into the image, take a moment to recall your Miracle. If you can, visualize it in front of you. Take a few breaths. Remember, the Miracle is leading you to find the qualities you need in all these heroic images, the qualities that will ultimately come together to form your Heroic Self. Take a deep breath, blow away the image of the Miracle, and once again sink down into the earth.

Imagine an animal, the first animal that comes to mind. Even if it surprises or amuses you, choose the first one that appears. If you can visualize the animal, imagine it standing there in front of you. See it, or recall the look of that animal. What kind of expression might you read on its face? How does the animal hold its body? Is it male or female? Let the animal begin to move in front of you. Watch the way it moves, or recall the way you have seen the animal move, the way it uses its spinal column, its legs, its tail, its ears, its nose. Just observe it. Imagine the animal in its environment. Is it a day animal or a night animal? Does it stay close to the ground, or does it swing through the trees? Does it swim? fly? What kind of food does it eat? See the animal getting its food. Does it eat herbs? grain? bark? flowers? insects, or other animals? How does it go about getting that food? How does the animal defend itself against predators? When the animal is in trouble, what does it do? What are its instinctive responses to danger? If you do not know what they are, just imagine what they could be. Let your imagination create. This is an animal inside of you, so it can do whatever you imagine it can do. How does it mate? Either remember, or if you do not remember, imagine how this animal relates to the opposite of its own sex in the mating dance. What about the home life of this animal? How does it give birth to its young? How does it nurture them? teach them? How does the male of the species relate to the young? How does the female of the species relate to the young? And which is it that you are imagining as your animal? Is this animal a herd animal? Does it stay with its group? Or is it a loner? What is its home life like, its nest or lair?

Imagine this animal now in its home. It is during this animal's resting time. Imagine the animal asleep. How would this animal sleep? Would it sleep curled up, standing up, legs curled under? How would the animal sleep? If you do not know, imagine. When you get a bit of an image of it, allow yourself to apply that to your own body and put your body in a position as close as possible to the position of that animal asleep. And little by little, with your consciousness, become, as best you can, that animal sleeping.

In a few moments, when I give the command, all the sleeping animals will awaken. Meditate for a moment on how your animal awakens, or you as this animal will awaken. Do you wake up alert, or do you come slowly into consciousness? Are you ready to defend yourself? Are you on the run? What kind of awakening process might your animal have? When I give the command, you will awaken. You will begin to move about and experience your body as the body of that animal—without interacting with the other animals until I tell you. So now, let the animals awaken!

Stretch your body. Feel your body. Feel yourself as that animal. Move about as that animal might move. Try the sounds that it might make. Fill the air with the sound. Again, if you do not know what that sound is, imagine what it might be. Create it. Now move about the room as best you can so that you can feel your body as that animal in movement, with the power and excitement, the energy and beauty, as well as the instinctive capacities of that animal.

In a Group:

Begin to look around you and notice the other animals. Whom do you want to make contact with? Whom do you want to stay away from? Whom do you want to make love with? Whom do you want to eat? Do you see any animals of your species? Do you want to make contact with them? Move about the room and interact with each other as these animals. If the animals are violent, act it out without hurting each other. Interact with each other.

Now I am going to put on some drum music. When you hear the music, gradually let yourself evolve from that four-legged beast to a human being with all of the characteristics and all of the qualities of that animal. And dance with the other animal-people, preserving the quality of your animal. (*Put on some rhythmic music, and let them begin to interact with each other.*)

Stop what you are doing and hold the posture. If you have slipped back into your own posture, reassume the posture of the animal-turned-human being, and meditate on the three or four most positive, affirmative qualities that you find in this animal. Three or four positive, affirmative qualities. If you find yourself coming up with negative qualities, look through the negative until you find the affirmative aspect. A killer can be a very powerful being who knows how to get what she needs. When you have found the qualities, again open your eyes and say them to a partner. Then write them down on your paper.

Adventurer

For the next image, we are going to play a little game that you may have played as children. It is called "statues." You and your partner curl your fingers so that your hands hook into each other's, and then you begin to spin around in a circle. At a certain point you let go of each other, and however you end up when you fall out of the spin, you freeze. That is your statue. Do you remember that game? Well, that's the game we are going to play now.

If you are alone, you can simply spin around three times. In a group, choose a partner and hook your hands together. Now, before you begin to turn, just take a moment to recall your Miracle. Do not say it to each other. Keep your eyes closed, stay inside yourself, and take a moment to meditate on your Miracle. The Miracle is always the guiding element that leads you to the characters that you need to find. Just breathe, and meditate on the Miracle . . . Gradually, let go of the image of the Miracle, take a deep breath and blow it away; then open your eyes and slowly begin spinning around.

▬▬▬▬

To the Guide:

(If you are in a small room and there is not enough space, you may want to make sure that the people do not spin too fast.)

▬▬▬▬

Let your spin become a little faster, a little faster, and then, at the count of three, let go. One, two, three, let go! Form your statue. Now hold your statue and feel the posture that your body has fallen into. Stay in the posture. Experience it. I would like you to imagine that you are in an adventure story, that your body's posture is a picture of the hero of that adventure story doing something. What are you doing? What is it that you are doing in this magnificent adventure story? How are you dressed? What is the great adventure that you are on? And how did you arrive at this scene, this place? What led up to this moment? Are you alone on this adventure, or are there others with you? Where are you going? What are you searching for? What is your goal? If you need to adjust your body to be a little more comfortable, do so. See if you can relax as much as possible. Stay in the posture as long as you can to maintain the sense of this moment. What is your name as an adventurer? What period in time might this be? Or is it beyond time and place?

Now just let your body relax. Find your partner, who might be in another part of the room. (*If you are alone, take a notebook.*) Sit down together back to back, relax against each other. Describe yourself as this adventurer, and tell your story. Partners, spend some time telling your stories to each other. (*Pause*) Now, stop your dialogue. Get up from your seated positions and take again, as closely as you can recall it, the posture of the adventurer, and recall three or four qualities that are the most positive, affirmative qualities that you found in this character. When you have them, share them with your partner and then write them down on your paper.

To the Guide:

There is not always time to do seven heroic images. When I decide to do only five, I do the childhood hero, the movie star, the animal, the important person, and the god. I let go of the adventurer and the lover. However, I like to include these two because they give a broader scope to the whole picture. The important person is very personal in relationship to the individual's life, and the childhood hero has an element of childishness or innocence about it. The adventurer gives a mythic dimension to it. And the lover provides a sensuous quality, which may or may not be included in the animal and the movie star. I like to allow for that possibility.

The Lover

In a Group:

Let's make a big bed in the middle of the room. (*The individual journeyer should make a comfortable bed with as many pillows as possible.*) Throw all the pillows into the center of the room, and without crushing each other, everybody lie down together. Cuddle up. Make sure that you are close enough to somebody so that you can whisper into an ear. And not everybody into the same ear! You will have to work it out so that you can find someone you can talk to and who can talk back to you. Maybe make some contact, some slight, delicate physical contact, but only what feels comfortable. Just let your bodies sink into the cushions and into the contact. Be aware of the warmth of the other human being near you. Lie there, sensuously, touching somebody's arm or stroking somebody's cheek. And while you are luxuriating in this comfort, once again recall the image of your Miracle. Take a few moments to meditate on this image, breathe it in, then let go of the image, take a deep breath and blow it away.

Become aware of the warmth around you. Be aware also of your own body posture as you lie there, maybe stretching a bit. Imagine that you are one of the great lovers of literature or history or myth—one of the great lovers who is celebrated in song and story! Which lover might you be? And who is your great love? Once again, if you do not recall the details, make them up. Imagine that you are in a scene with that great love right now. What is the setting? Are you in a bedroom? Are you out in the countryside, by a stream? Is there moonlight? Is it night? Is it day? What are the colors? the clothing? the draperies? the bedding? the decor of the room? Just imagine it. And how are you dressed, or not dressed, in this situation? What is the scene of your love story, right now? Are you together? Are you waiting for each other? Have you just come together? Have you just met? Or are you about to part? What is the scene of this love story? And what is it about this person whom you love that makes him or her so special? Just let yourself become that great lover. Turn to the ear closest to you and whisper your love story. Tell it. (*If you are alone, write a letter to your beloved or to a friend, telling your story.*)

(*Give the group about ten minutes to do this.*) Stop what you are doing. Once again, imagine yourself as this great lover and ask yourself what qualities you found in this role. And when you have found them, express them to your partner and then write them on your paper.

The Important Person

In a Group:

Choose a partner and sit down together facing each other. Before you come into too much contact, close your eyes, and once again, hold the image of the Miracle in your awareness . . . Take a deep breath, blow away the image of the Miracle, and let yourself relax.

Call to mind some person in your life who has been very important to you, important enough to have in some way changed the course of your life. It may have been a teacher, a lover, a relative, or a friend—somebody the contact with whom has influenced the course of your life irrevocably. Let it be a real person, not somebody you read about in a book. Spend a few minutes meditating on that person. What was the context of your relationship? Was it student-teacher, friend, lover? Imagine that person. How is that person in his home situation? What kind of home does that person have? If you don't know exactly, then imagine. What kind of work does that person do? How does that person feel about his or her work? How capable and talented is he or she? How does that person relate to the people that he or she works with? What is that person's emotional life and love life like? How does that person make love? Once again, if you do not know, imagine. Is he or she tender, powerful, sensuous and exotic? How does that person behave in a love relationship? What is that person's relationship with himself or herself? How does that person feel about himself or herself? And what is that person's relationship to you?

Now spend a few moments meditating on that person's body. For example, if that person were sitting in the room where you are sitting, how would that person use his or her body? Would that person sit in the same position, or would it be different? Adjust your body. Let that person take over your body for a bit of time. Allow that person to use your back, your arms and legs. Let that person be sitting here in this room. What kind of expression might that person have on his or her face? Take on that expression. Subtly. Feel it inside of your face, feel the quality of being that exists behind that expression. And gradually, when you are ready, let your eyes come open and present yourself as that person to your partner. (*If you are alone, write as that person in your notebook.*)

You are now that important person! Introduce yourself and talk about yourself to your partner . . . After you have talked about yourself for a while, talk about your relationship, as that person, to you. For example, if I become Joseph Campbell, who was a very important person in my life, I would talk to my partner about this man, Paul Rebillot, whom I met at Esalen, and what my relationship to him is. So after you have talked about yourself as this important person, talk about your relationship to you from that perspective.

To the Guide:

(Sometimes, since we have been working for a while, I like to give the group a break at this point, while they are in the role, and invite them to continue to play this role but to go out and have a cup of tea or coffee together and chat in the quality of this character. It gives a little relief from the process, yet, at the same time, they stay in the process.)

━━━━━━

Let go of words, stop what you are doing, take the posture of the character, and once again think of three or four qualities that you found in playing this person. When you have found them, express them to a partner and then add them to your list.

The God

I call this last image "the awakening of the gods and goddesses." I would like you to come back into the center of the room, put down some mattresses, and once again lie down and just rest for a moment more, meditating on the image of your Miracle . . . Take a deep breath and let it go.

Imagine that this place, right now, is the home of the gods and goddesses. It might be Olympus, Valhalla, Heaven. All of you here in the room are gods and goddesses, and just now it is resting time; the god or goddess that you are is asleep, at rest. And since you are asleep, the universe is quiet and dark and resting as well. However, because you are a god or goddess, each movement, even the stirring of breath, is the birth of a star. So be aware of the least little movement within your body as light being born into a universe of darkness. Each little movement you make begins to create the universe. With each stirring of breath, stars are born . . . planets, solar systems, nebulae blink alive into a universe of darkness.

It is the time of the awakening. Very slowly, aware of your body, stretch your arms and your legs; and as you do so, imagine all the lights that come into being with your stretching. Keep stretching; keep your eyes closed, but gradually let yourself come awake as this god or goddess, rising slowly from your couch, beginning to move and to dance (*triumphant, spiritual music is playing at this point*). Dance the universe into creation with whatever quality of being that you as god or goddess bequeath to that universe. After a little time, let your eyelids begin to crack open so that you can see the other gods and goddesses moving around you. The gods and goddesses dance together and participate in the act of creation. When you are ready, let your eyes come open fully, and dance the universe into being. (*The music should gradually come to some kind of climax; after a while bring the music down . . .*)

Now you have created the universe. Look at it. Imagine it there in front of you with all its lights and colors. What kind of universe is it? Is it a universe of beauty and glory? of passion? of violence and power? What kind of universe is it that you, as this god or goddess in relationship to your brothers and sisters, your fellow gods and goddesses, have created? And what particular quality have you imparted to that universe? Give that universe your benediction. Bless it and then turn it free to multiply and reproduce itself. Let it go . . .

Now, once again, it is the time of rest. Very slowly, very easily, come back down to your couch, to your bed, stretch and yawn. The gods and goddesses once again go to sleep and, one by one, the stars dim. The universe grows quiet, and the gods and goddesses gradually fall asleep once again . . . (*After a little time . . .*) Become aware of yourself once again in the room; with your eyes closed, listen to the sounds of the here-and-now, the sounds of the world around you, the sounds in the room. Feel the mattress beneath you. If you are in contact with somebody, feel that contact. And meditate for a moment on the universe you created, on the particular quality of your universe. How similar or different was that from the universe you create in your daily life? Did you allow yourself more here, when you could play it as a game? Or, perhaps, did you create the same universe that you create in your daily life? Meditate on the similarity or the differences . . . And then, once again, recall the image of the god or goddess, take on something of the quality of that being and think of three or four qualities that describe that god or goddess. When you are ready, share them with a partner, and then write those qualities on your paper.

HERO EXERCISE 2: OWNING THE HEROIC QUALITIES

To the Guide:

For this exercise you will need several pocket mirrors, one for every three participants.

To the Journeyers:

After you have written the last three qualities on the paper, go to the top of the page and above the line at the top write, "I AM." Now look at what you are! Look at the whole list of your qualities!

In a Group:

Sit down with a partner and read your whole list to each other: "I am wonderful, powerful, spontaneous, beautiful, sexy, adorable"—whatever it happens to be. Read them to each other and just revel in that moment. (*Allow a little time for this.*)

In playing these various roles, you have given yourself a chance to act out certain qualities that you may not think of yourself as having. The role you have identified as yourself may be far more limiting than what you give your-self permission to play when you put on a mask, the mask of the characteriza-tion or the personification.

Actors and actresses can be very interesting people to observe. An actor may enter the theater timidly, a kind of Caspar Milquetoast—quiet, with-drawn, mousy. He goes up to his makeup table and begins to put on his makeup in his quiet, timid sort of way. Gradually, his expression takes on au-thority. His costume gives him broad shoulders. His hat gives him an addi-tional foot of height. As he walks to the entrance to the stage, he has gradually taken on power, force, and nobility. He steps out on the stage, and, *voila!* He is the king—magnificent, noble, powerful! Then, as soon as he is again off stage, he collapses down into himself, creeps quietly to his makeup table, takes off his makeup, and goes off into the night the same Caspar Milquetoast who en-tered the theater.

It always seemed curious to me that an actor could assume such com-pletely different personalities and not recognize that he was the same person who crossed that frontier onto the stage, somehow not recognize that the nobil-ity, beauty, and power—all the qualities of kingship that he was able to mani-fest on stage—were, in fact, him! As Caspar Milquetoast he lacked those qualities; but as Agamemnon or Hamlet, he could manifest them. The actor who does not make the connection between his on-stage self and his off-stage self gradually loses more and more of his essence with each role he plays, and consequently becomes superficial in his daily interchanges with people. He loses contact with himself because he separates himself from the roles he plays on stage. Whereas the actor who can recognize that the person on stage is merely an extension of the person off stage grows with each role. With each new character he finds more of himself. Similarly, when in a new situation, you explore a different, perhaps risky form of behavior, you expand yourself and become a fuller personality.

Now you are going to give yourself a chance to find out if, when you come back to who you think you are, you are able to own the qualities you gave yourself permission to own when you were playing a role. Can you say honestly and completely, from the center of your being, for example, "I am sexy," "I am beautiful," "I am powerful"? Can you say that? Well, we have a way of finding out. That way is to look someone in the eyes and to say to that person, "I am powerful." Then listen inside yourself and feel how your body responds. Your body will not let you lie. If you are lying, if you are saying something that you don't accept or don't believe, your body response can make that clear to you.

It is not a question of whether you *have* that quality, it is a question of whether you *own* that quality. Whatever you can imagine yourself being, you are. After all, who is imagining it? It isn't somebody else imagining it in you; you are imagining it. So if you can imagine it, you are it. The problem is that you will not allow yourself to own that aspect of yourself because of things that may have happened in childhood or in the process of growing up; you will not allow yourself to experience your natural beauty, your natural power, your instinctive loyalty. Perhaps you were told, "If you say you are beautiful, that's conceited," or "If you act powerful, you scare the people around you"; you were told not to do that. So instead of being able to be the powerful, creative, beautiful, spontaneous person that you are, you have a tendency to program yourself out of experiencing these qualities.

This exercise will give you a chance to discover which of the qualities that you have listed you can own and which you do not own.

In a Group:

Divide up into groups of three. Sit across from the two people you are with. Learn their names so you can say to them, by name, each one of the qualities on your list. For example, "John, I am powerful." You look John in the eye and you say, "John, I am powerful." Listen to what your body says. Does your body accept this? Does your body remain comfortable, maybe even pleasurable when you say that? Or do you feel your body tensing up, your jaws tightening? Do you feel yourself wanting to burst into laughter or tears when you say, "I am powerful"? Try it with the other person: "Joan, I am powerful." Do you stop breathing? Is a voice in your head saying, "This is silly; you know you're not"? Do you feel a tensing of your spine? Or can you say it and breathe naturally and easily and feel comfortable doing it? The function of the partners is simply to give the working person your eyes, your awareness, your presence to say the words to. You are not going to attempt to throw the person off, make her laugh, or argue with her; let the person who is working discover for herself whether she is able to own each quality. Do not try to test her. Afterward, you can help in discerning the theme or finding the most important word.

The person it is most difficult to express these qualities to is yourself. Take a mirror, look into your own eyes, and say, "(*Say your name*), I am powerful." Once again, listen to your body. If your body does not give you a response that says it is not true, then simply leave that quality as it is. When you come to a quality that you find your body resisting or your mind arguing about, or if you find a quality that makes you burst into tears or laughter, then take a crayon and underline that word. That is a quality you have trouble accepting as your own; it is not a quality you do not have, it is a quality that you do not own. Go through your entire list. Each person goes all the way through his or her own list at one time, so that you can get an overall sense, a gestalt, of the qualities that your being has found necessary to help you in the creation of your heroic figure. If you are in some confusion about a quality, ask yourself: Is this something for which I would like more support? If it is, then underline it. If it is a quality that doesn't matter much to you one way or the other, then it doesn't matter much one way or the other, so don't worry about it. If it is a quality that you feel sometimes, and other times, not, and right at the moment you don't, then underline it.

When you have underlined all the qualities that you do not own, spend a little time looking through the list and see if there is a theme. For instance, if do you not own qualities like "beautiful," "attractive," "interesting," you might say that the theme is self-confidence. Do you underline qualities like "powerful" and "convincing" that might come under the overall heading of strength? Is the theme physical attractiveness? Or is it freedom? Find the word that expresses your theme, and then behind the "I AM" at the top of the page, write that word. For instance, if all the qualities have to do with confidence, then behind the "I AM" at the top of the page write "confident": "I AM CONFIDENT." That is the word you will use in the next phase of the process. If you are not able to discern a theme, look for the quality that you would most like to have support for, the quality that you do not own and would like to have group support in owning for yourself. Write that quality behind the "I AM."

HERO EXERCISE 3: LITANY OF LOVE

The following material is for a group process, but individual journeyers are encouraged to create and dance out your own Litany of Love. In this dance you will affirm all the qualities you have written on your list, building energy to enter into the Support Process.

To the Guide:

This is a very active process, and people may need an energy perk. If you are working with musical instruments, this is a good time to pass them out and get a rhythm going. This will bring the group back together and lift the excitement to an appropriate level. If you prefer, you can play some recorded music and get people moving together, clapping hands or doing something to participate in a group rhythm. At a given moment, introduce a rhythm that can generally accommodate the qualities they have been developing. It is a good idea to keep abreast of the work that the group has been doing so that you can use what you notice going on in your examples. You may have to lower the volume of the sound for them to hear and follow you, or you can write the instruction on a blackboard. Tell them to create a litany of love out of their qualities. It goes something like this:

> *I am powerful!*
> *I am spontaneous!*
> *I am charming!*
> *I am free!*
> *I am sensuous!*
> *I am loving!*
> *I am passionate!*
> *I am me!*

All of the qualities come from their own lists except the two end phrases, "I am free!" and "I am me!" and are improvised and sung all at the same time. Give them a little time to get into it and sufficient time to go through their lists. Then, when you feel ready, climax and bring it to a close. By this time the excitement should be up and you can begin the next process.

HERO EXERCISE 4: SUPPORT PROCESS

To the Journeyers:

The Support Process is perhaps the most tribal and ancient of all the processes that we do in the journey. It is based on methods of support observed in primitive cultures. When someone is preparing to confront an out-of-the-ordinary task like hunting or fighting or the first sexual encounter, the tribe comes together in a festive mood and creates a circle. The candidates, those who are about to enter into the new activity, go into the center of the circle. They may not feel ready for the task at hand. They may be frightened, sleepy, or in some way out of sorts. The tribe appreciates that, and with rhythmic drumming and chanting, it pours into the group in the center all the encouragement it can, imitating as well as possible the feeling that is needed for the forthcoming confrontation. The sounds and rhythms for a young couple are decidedly different from those for a warrior.

Meanwhile, in the center of the circle, the candidates experience their fears, their resistances, and their excitement, allowing their condition to be as it is without immediately trying to change it. They may express their feelings ritualistically, giving vent to them in order to release them. The tribe continues supporting with rhythm until, little by little, the central group responds. The excitement builds until the central group is ready to go out and attend to the task at hand.

This is much the same principle as a healing circle. The encircling group sends support to the center, and the person in the center, whether actually present or not, is given the option to use the energy as she or he likes. The difference here is the addition of sound, rhythm and chanting, to more clearly manifest that support.

The purpose of this process is to give resistance a chance to release itself and to build both individual feelings of support and self-worth as well as group trust.

One person enters into the center of the group. It is important at this point to clarify the affirmation. The best affirmations are those that can be put into an "I am" or existential framework: rather than a possessive ("I have power"), a future ("I will be powerful"), or a negative ("I am not afraid") framework. The affirmation should be simple, direct, and have some feeling of action. If the statement is too long or complicated, the leader may have to question the person to find the right word. When the guide makes a suggestion and the person's eyes fill with tears, or a thrill goes through the person, then you know you have hit the right one. But it is the person in the center who makes the decision; if the person chooses to be supported in something that does not follow any of these rules, you must respect that; it is that person's choice, and somewhere deep down the person knows the reason, even if it is seemingly a negative quality. However, if the person chooses something the group cannot support, the person will have to find something else. It is more important that the person feel supported by the group than that the person defeat the group by asking for something the group cannot support (for example, "I am a killer").

It is important that the group reflect the energy of the person in the center. If, for example, the person is asking to be supported in power and is maintaining a rather weak, quiet state, the group will have a tendency to push at her. But if the group reflects rather than pushes at the person, she will be more likely to discover what she is doing on her own.

(If you are an individual journeyer, you might put on some strong rhythmic music and create a dance of support for yourself. Imagine all the people who love you around you, singing their support as you create a dance that expresses the important quality you want to own. Don't be afraid to express the resistance, but dance through it until you can own the quality.)

To the Guide:

Sometimes, if this is being done in a more limited time period, I will have the small groups make a circle around the person and then simply touch her and support her with the words. The person in the center just receives it. This takes it back to a simple form of healing circle, and the physical contact takes the place of the rhythms.

Put a cushion or mattress in the center of the circle to be available for expression of anger, negation, or rejection. The person in the center says what she would like the group to support her in. She might say, for example, "I am powerful." The group begins—with music, with instruments, and with their voices—to make a kind of rhythmic structure and song, a repetition of the words, "You are powerful." It can go into harmonies, depending on the spontaneity, the excitement, and the creativity of the group. The person in the center listens to this support, this affirmation. She also pays attention to her body. If, for example, she feels a tension in her shoulders, she exaggerates that tension and releases it. If she feels some anger or sadness coming out, she can express that on the cushion by hitting it or squeezing it. Meanwhile, the group is still supporting—not contradicting. For instance, if the person in the center starts saying "No!" and the group is saying, "You are powerful," it could easily seem to get into a dialogue of conflict. The person in the center can say, "No, no, no!" as much as she wants; the group is supporting and affirming, not arguing and debating. Keeping the affirmation as a rhythmic chant retains the quality of support. The person in the center goes through whatever reactions and feelings she might have. When she has exhausted this, there is nothing left for her to do except be present with the music. She begins to listen to the music and the rhythm and gradually lets her body respond to that rhythm rather than the rhythm of her resistance. She responds to the rhythm of the group without thought, just taking in the affirmation. Hopefully, the movements will become more expressive of that quality. As the person begins to dance with the rhythm, she allows herself to experience what it is like to feel the group's support for that quality; and as a result of that support, to feel her own power, for example. As she begins to feel more powerful, she can return that gift to the group—with her eyes, with her looks, with her hands, with her gestures and her dance—until finally she is able to sing, "I am powerful!" What was poured into her is now pouring back out into the group. "I am powerful!" She receives; she experiences her resistance; she responds, and then she allows herself to express; she lets the energy of the group support her and give her this experience, and then she returns it to the group. "I am powerful!" That is the sequence.

The person in the center makes the decision about when the group stops, with a gesture that says that's enough—unless, of course, it goes on too long, and then the group will make the decision.

To the Guide:

Sometimes you might encourage the person to go a little further if she seems to be on the verge of making some breakthrough, but ordinarily I would respect the person's decision as to when to stop. Give the person the responsibility of making that decision. Then that person selects the next person to go in the center. This continues until everyone has finished. Allow about fifteen to twenty minutes per person.

HERO EXERCISE 5: HERO FANTASY (GUIDED MEDITATION)

To the Journeyers:

You are about to meet your Hero in a guided meditation. Sometimes people worry if they do not have visual images. If that happens to you, do not spend your guided fantasy time criticizing yourself. Your experience of the fantasy depends on the way you perceive the universe—through your eyes, through your ears, or through your kinetic sense. If visual images do not come up for you, let yourself hear the fantasy. Let yourself sense the fantasy in your body. Let your body move a little bit to give yourself a kinetic picture of the fantasy. If you want to get up and move, that is fine too. Let your body move to help you incarnate the fantasy. Accept what comes and elaborate on it with your imagination. Although generally a guided fantasy is given in a visual format, it does not have to be experienced visually.

Lie down and let yourself sink into the earth. After the dance of support, when you allowed yourself to receive the affirmation of the group, imagine that you went outside in the sun, found a warm spot, and lay down to rest. Now it is a little while later. You have been out here on the lawn resting, sleeping. You are just beginning to awaken from that deep sleep. You fill your lungs with air, you feel the sun on you, the breeze, the grass beneath you. You stretch your body and let yourself awaken from that deep and restful sleep. Imagine that you sit up, open your eyes, and look around you—and find yourself in a completely different place.

You are in a strange and beautiful meadow somewhere, another place. Imagine that you get up and look around that strange and beautiful meadow. Be aware of the texture of the grass, the smells, the sun, the breeze. Are there any flowers around? Do you hear any insects or birds in that strange meadow? Walk around that meadow, explore it. Perhaps there are some animals there. Allow yourself to move around and explore the meadow. In the middle you come upon a pathway, a lane that seems to go out of the meadow and into the forest. You take that path, and in the middle of it you see a sign that says, "This way to the House of the Hero."

This is the path that leads you up to the house of your own Heroic Self. So as you are walking along the path, you remember the images that you played earlier—first, the image of the childhood hero. As you are walking along the path, you walk like that childhood hero walks, feeling the qualities of that childhood hero in your body. You remember the movie star that you played, and you begin to walk like that movie star. Remember the qualities that you felt in yourself as that movie star. Remember the animal that you played, the feeling of the animal in your body. You begin to walk through the woods as that animal. That important person in your life, the one who influenced your life. You begin to feel that person and walk like that person. The lover. You begin to move like the lover along your path. The god. You recall with your body all of the qualities of all these various heroic people that you created this morning.

Now, up ahead of you there, appearing in front of you, is the house of your own Heroic Self. In what kind of house does your Heroic Self live? What color is that house? How is it set? What are the grounds like? Somewhere inside that house resides the Hero who is the synthesis of all those heroic images that you have been exploring, the synthesis—your own Heroic Self.

So you go up to the front door and you knock. Somewhere deep inside the house you hear footsteps, footsteps approaching, coming closer to the door. It is your own Heroic Self, coming closer and closer. The door swings slowly open, and there, standing in front of you is your own Heroic Self!

Look deeply into the eyes of the Hero, standing there in front of you, looking back at you. Look at the expression on your Hero's face. Reach out and take the hands of your Heroic Self. Feel the strength, the love as that Hero makes contact with you. Now the Hero invites you to come into the house. So together you walk through the front door into the house of your own Heroic Self.

Be aware of how the light falls in that house, what colors your Hero has used in its decoration, the sounds in the house, the feeling of the house. The Hero invites you into the favorite room. Enter with the Hero and discover what room that is—your Heroic Self's favorite room in the house.

Once in that room, the two of you sit down together and have a little chat. Once more you look into each other's eyes. And you ask the Hero, "Tell me, what is your secret name?" And the Hero will tell you that name, a name to be shared only with other Heroes. "What is your secret name?" (*Pause*)

And ask your Heroic Self, "What is your quest?" Your Miracle will now reveal itself in symbolic form, as an object or a person. Ask your Heroic Self to tell you what it is. "What is it after which you seek?" And your Hero will tell you that. "What is it after which you seek?" (*Pause*)

And ask your Hero, "What do you want of me?" And your Hero will tell you that as well. (*Pause*)

Anything else that you would like to ask of your Heroic Self, ask it now. (*Pause*)

It is time to leave the house of the Hero. So together you rise and begin to move toward the front door. You come to the door. The Hero opens the door and the room suddenly floods with sunlight. The two of you stand together in that brilliant light. You reach out to embrace each other goodbye. You gather the Hero to your chest and the Hero gathers you as well. You can feel the Hero's heart beating against your heart. You feel the Hero's cheek against your cheek. Chest against your chest. You feel the Hero's strength against your body as you embrace each other to say goodbye. And suddenly a magical event occurs. Warmed by the sunlight, it is as if the pores of your body open slowly and, little by little, the Hero and you melt into each other, merge into one. That heartbeat that you feel inside of you now is the heartbeat of the Hero. That breath that you are taking now is the breath of the Hero. All the bones and muscles of your body have become the bones and muscles of the Hero. You have become your own Heroic Self!

You, your own Heroic Self, standing in your doorway, looking out over the path that you must take to fulfill your quest. Suddenly, off to the left, you see a rider approaching on a horse. He is a messenger. The messenger gallops closer and closer and finally stops in front of you and gives you a message:

"You are cordially invited to the first annual Conference of Heroes, this evening at (*read the time and place of the Heroes' Banquet*). (*See Hero Exercise 8, below, for more detail.*) Please come." (*Pause*)

Take a few moments to breathe. Allow yourself to come back into this room, gently.

HERO EXERCISE 6: COAT OF ARMS

To the Guide:

The group will need a moment to mentally and emotionally return to the room. Allow time, but do something subtly to bring them back. When you see many of them have returned, begin organizing the paper for the next process, so that they realize that you are about to begin.

To the Journeyers:

In the Middle Ages, whenever a knight or lady approached a castle, the people in the castle could tell who was coming by the colors that the person displayed or wore or carried on a banner. This was the coat of arms that the person carried. A coat of arms proclaimed to the world from what family, from what heritage, from what land this knight or this lady had come. We are about to create a coat of arms for our Heroes. This is not a coat of arms of a family or a heritage; it is a coat of arms of the soul.

Whatever you want to put down on your paper as a statement of your Heroic Self, do so now. You can create a design with pictures or just colors; it can be whatever you like as a statement of this Heroic Self in the depths of your soul. If you want to recapitulate something from the meditation that you just went through, you can do that, but you do not have to do that. It is not important that you recapitulate anything; it is not important that you depict anything. What is important is that you use color and shape and form to create something that represents a coat of arms that is a manifestation for you of the Hero. You might even consider this process as an extension of the meditation that you just went through. If, for instance, you did not have many visual images during the meditation, your use of color and form and shape on paper can augment that aspect of your sensual awareness so that you now create some visual images. Colors, forms, and shapes help augment your sensual experience of the Hero. One thing I would like you to incorporate into the design is your heroic name. Even though it is the secret name, the name the Hero hides from the rest of the world, this name can be shared among other Heroes. So proclaim yourself! Make your blazonry, your coat of arms, a proclamation of your Heroic Self.

HERO EXERCISE 7: DRESSING THE HERO

The following material is addressed to those working in groups, but individual journeyers should also find ways to manifest and express the heroic image you have discovered. Create a costume. Prepare a festive meal. Write a speech as this Hero, declaring your mission and your quest and asking for support. To whom do you feel you are speaking as your own Heroic Self?

To the Guide:

If you have pieces of cloth or other costume materials for the group to use in dressing their Heroes, set them out now while they are making their coats of arms. If you do not have anything, you might suggest to the group, when they have finished working, that they bring to the group room anything they might have and be willing to share with each other to help each other dress the part of the Hero. If you are out in the country, people might want to deck themselves with vines, leaves, and flowers. They might even take the sheets off their beds and wrap them around themselves—something to help them manifest the heroic aspect of their being.

To the Journeyers:

In the Bible it is said that God took clay, and out of that clay he shaped the first human being. Well, right now you are going to have a chance to do that in terms of your own self. With a costume and with the rough clay of your own body, you are going to create the image of the Hero you have envisioned in your deeper self. As you are putting your costume pieces together, gradually let yourself take on some of the quality of the Hero. Let yourself shape yourself into the manifestation of the vision that you have had in your guided fantasy. This is a little like children playing dress up. When we were kids and Mom and Dad had gone away, we could go into their room and take out interesting things from their closet and put them on. It is another "as if" situation in which we are costuming ourselves as if we were these Heroes we have seen inside of ourselves—which, in fact, we are. So give yourself some time to look around, to help each other, to dress. Dress the Heroes now and later on we will have the heroic presentations. *(Allow some time for this.)*

HERO EXERCISE 8: HEROES' BANQUET

To the Guide:

If you are in a place where meals are being served, determine early on when the banquet for the Heroes is going to take place and ask the cook to do something special for this meal. If this is not possible, I recommend that on the morning of the day of the Hero, people bring a special food, something that they particularly like, to share for dinner, enough for three people. That way you will have a rather luxurious table and everybody can share something with somebody. Sometime while the participants are designing their coats of arms and creating their costumes, you and your assistants can prepare the banquet table, or you can ask the group to do it.

When the banquet is ready, you might have a little parade or dance, bringing the Heroes to the banquet table. I frequently lead them on a walk around the environment, carrying my harp and playing it. You could have the Heroes playing musical instruments, or put on some processional music to give them the feeling of entering into this banquet chamber as heroic beings. Then invite them to sit down.

To the Journeyers:

Just look around the table at each other and see that special quality, the glow that seems to be on all the faces here. Oh, sure, we have unusual clothes on, we have makeup on, we have fixed our hair, we have done something different—but that is not where the glow comes from. Those are all external signs. The glow is coming from within, and all of these little additions that we have put on are simply ways of enhancing that glow—the glow that is something of our Heroic Self shining out and making itself present for the world to see. And you know, you don't have to act like a Hero; you don't have to do anything special or put on a funny voice or talk about strange and unusual things. You are a Hero. Anything you talk about, and anything you do now is what a Hero talks about and what a Hero does. So, enjoy yourselves! Eat, drink, laugh, have a good time, and realize that at this moment in time we are our own Heroic Selves. And I would like to propose a toast, to the Land of Dreams, which is the land that Heroes come from!

HERO EXERCISE 9: HERO PRESENTATIONS

To the Guide:

When the meal is finished, prepare the group for the Hero presentations. It is best to have an area in the room or at the head of the table in which a chair has been set up as a kind of throne, maybe with some drapery behind it or something to create a feeling of specialness. It is best situated so that people can see clearly—on a dais if there is one. Place a table in front of it with the group candle, some scented oil, and two loving cups—one with wine, the other with grape juice.

The purpose of this presentation is to give the group members a chance to get up and express themselves as Heroes; to synthesize all the aspects they have been working with—the body, which is the physical aspect of the Hero; the emotions, which are the feeling aspect of the Hero; and the image that they saw in their mind's eye, which they now manifest as best they can through their costumes. They are going to improvise around the theme of the Hero and get up in front of the group to present themselves. This is a challenge because it means they are going to have to get up in front of the group and talk. At the same time, there is a sacred aspect to it because the anointing of the Hero consecrates the quest, making whatever it is the person is looking for or envisioning a holy quest. If they are not approaching what they are doing with a certain amount of reverence, the anointing will suddenly make them look at what they are doing, make them more aware of what they are asking for themselves. The passing of the loving cup is also a way of bringing the group together. The exercise calls for them to ask for something of the group. It is an adult who can ask something of somebody; it is a child who waits for somebody to give him what he needs. An adult is able to say, "I would like you to do this for me; I would like this from you." That in itself is challenging and maturing.

To the Journeyers:

Now we are about to experience the Hero presentations. In medieval times, when a knight approached the court of the king, before going out on his quest, he would frequently get up and talk about himself, boast about his origins, his powers, and his adventures. Then he would reveal his quest. He would say, "I need your help," asking for money, companionship, or support. The court would decide whether or not they would support him. If they decided they would, then the queen would bring to him a loving cup, a cup of wine poured by the king, and she would say: "This is a cup of good cheer, of good friendship; from our heart to your heart. With this cup we enter into communion with you." The drinking of the cup was a way of sealing the relationship. The knight would then keep watch in the chapel, meditating on the rightness of his quest through the night. In the morning the first Mass was said for him. As part of the Mass, the priest consecrated the quest. Now it was not just an individual quest, it was a quest made holy, giving it significance for the whole human spirit. This consecration of the quest was a very important aspect of the knight's preparation for his mission.

The Buddhists talk about the five basic fears of the human being: the fear of death, of loss of livelihood, of altered states of mind, of loss of reputation, and the fear of speaking in front of an assembly. Well, ladies and gentlemen, you are going to confront one of those five basic fears right now. You are going to get up, here in this special place, and speak in front of the assembly as your Heroic Self. You will come up, take your place, and talk about yourself: your name and something about your background; let your imagination create where you come from as this heroic person and tell us what your quest is. The quest is a symbolic expression of your Miracle, the Call that began your journey. So, tell us what your quest is and then ask something from us— perhaps to come up and touch your hand, to applaud you, or sing to you, to lift you up into the air or embrace you, whatever you would like to ask of the group as support for your quest. The group members will do the best they can to satisfy your request.

As you come up, decide who you would like to anoint you and who you would like to give you the loving cup at the end of the process. When you have received what you asked of the group, then the person you have chosen anoints you. The anointing can be given on the feet, on the hands, on the heart, and on the head. You can ask for it wherever you like. The priest or priestess doing the anointing can draw a circle, a cross, or create some personal ritual with the idea that your quest is being consecrated to God, to the vital force of evolution, to nature and all creation. Words may be spoken or it can be done in silence. However, you should approach it with a sense of sacredness, because this is a consecration. Then the cup bearer passes the loving cup to the Hero. He or she may wish to make a statement pledging the goodwill of the group. The Hero drinks a toast to the group. I encourage applause or some expression of appreciation and support. The Hero then selects the next person, and the process continues until all have presented themselves.

To the Guide:

Allow about fifteen minutes per person. If the group is large, you may want to do this exercise in smaller subgroups. That concludes the process of the Hero. At the completion of the presentations, you might encourage a little party or dance. However, at the very end of the session, bring everyone together in a circle for the ritual closing. (The day of the Hero can be abbreviated by cutting down on the number of heroic images to four or five. Then, rather than creating a poster with all the qualities, at the end of each image the participants can close their eyes, become aware of the qualities, and then simply express those qualities to another person. After all the images have been completed, either do an abbreviated "Litany of Love" or go directly into the Hero fantasy. End the Hero fantasy by taking on a posture of the Hero that can be incorporated into the Fool's Dance.)

Although at the beginning of the day of the Hero people may have incredible resistance, by the end of the day they frequently feel uplifted because of all the aspirations that have been expressed and all the support they have felt from each other. *It is very important that people not drop out of the process at this point, because there is also the element of inflation that is being encouraged. To leave the workshop at this point could be a bit dangerous.* The Demon balances out this material so that there is a stronger feeling of grounding. If someone should decide to drop out at this point, I recommend a strong warning about the danger of leaving the workshop ungrounded.

CHAPTER 7
The Demon

By now you may be feeling a little uncomfortable, a little uneasy. You have been focusing on positive, affirmative things, acting out and becoming a Hero; if you are working in a group, you have been supporting each other, being warm and friendly and learning how to trust each other. As a result of all this, the other side of the coin begins to make itself felt. People generally begin to feel that they do not deserve all those good spirits. You may feel depressed; you may even experience nausea or body aches. But this is *not* the time to give up. The Demon of Resistance is beginning to make itself known.

━━━━

To the Guide:

Participants may complain or come late to this session: accept that as part of the process. Complaints or criticisms can be accepted as part of the process and taken as clues to how people resist their own good feelings about themselves. Often, as the participants are developing their own Demons, my Demon shows up. So if you begin to feel depressed or somehow uncomfortable, it is important to ask, "Is it possible that while I am guiding these people to find their Demons, my own Demon is making itself known?" Bringing it to the light is one of the best ways of dealing with it. Once it is in the light, it is not as potent any more. It becomes easier to deal with when you can see it in relationship to the group. It is always helpful to have an assistant or coleader in this particular structure because it is so powerful and absorbing. If it becomes too much, the other person can take over, or the two of you can process your own material away from the group by expressing yourselves or talking about it.

━━━━

RITUAL: RAM MEDITATION 3

Once again, the day begins with the balancing of the three centers and the chanting of the Ram (see Appendix I). After the meditation, do some exercises with the people to help them get into their bodies a bit; then have them do the Fool's Dance and add the image of the Hero.

FOOL'S DANCE

To the Journeyers:

Find your zero position. Recall for yourself the Hero you found, the name and the qualities of the Hero. Get a sense of that Hero as the one who is able to accomplish your Miracle. Create with your body a sculpture of the Hero reaching for the object of the quest, moving toward the Miracle. How would your Hero's arms and legs look? How would your Hero use his or her torso, chest, expressing reaching for or going after the quest? Let yourself experience how your Hero's posture relates to the ground. What happens in your pelvis and your abdomen? What do you feel in your stomach, chest and back, shoulders and arms, neck and head? What is your facial expression? Experience this posture as the image of your Hero expressed by your body. This is the way your Heroic Self expresses itself. Take a deep breath, and melt down to zero.

Now we will go through the Fool's Dance, adding this image of the Hero: Zero-Me-Home-Lifework-Beloved-Self-Miracle-Spirit Guide-Hero-Zero. Breathe.

This time as you are going through it, see if you can allow yourself to go from one posture to the other with as flowing a movement as possible, so that you are not stopping in each posture so much as flowing through one posture into the next.

To the Guide:

Repeat the Fool's Dance with slow, meditative music. Repeat again two times, once flowing, and the second time taking a breath with each posture. When they finish, have them sit down.

The point of the Fool's Dance is to learn to take new perspectives easily, so that your point of view in relationship to the world can become more fluid. That is what the whole Hero's Journey is about—the ability to take new points of view. Hopefully, at one point or another, you will tumble from any fixed position so that you can break down some old barriers and allow for the possibility of something new. That is what happens when someone goes through a change of consciousness. All the old structures fall away and a new structure emerges. But a new structure cannot emerge unless an old structure falls away.

FINDING THE DEMON

To the Guide:

Invite the group to sit down and have a few moments of sharing about what has happened, where they find themselves today in their bodies, anything they may have to say about yesterday; take some time to process whatever has come up from the night before and as a result of the Fool's Dance this morning.

To the Journeyers:

With the Demon we go in the opposite direction from the Hero. The Hero is built from the top down, and the Demon is built from the bottom up. The three centers of the body—the body center, the heart center, and the head center—are centers of certain kinds of activity within the body.

First we have the balance center, the center of gravity, the *chi*, located about two inches below the navel. This has to do with our balance and our relationship to the earth. If I am in balance, I am in my chi. When we are in real danger, the head gets out of the way and we are right down there in the survival center. The expression of that center, the body center, is movement. The body center is the balance center, the survival center; it is the most ancient center of the body. This is something we have in common with the animals and the reptiles as well, with anything that has to survive.

The heart center has two pulses. It is the rhythmic center of the body. Here we have the rhythm of breath, which is like the musical phrase, and we also have the pulse of the heartbeat, which is the measure. It measures out our experience. That is what music comes from: the rhythm of the heartbeat and the phrasing of the breath. When you add the melody of the voice, you have an expression of emotion. The heart center is the center of relationship, the center of emotional expression. You could say that the heart center organizes the sensations and the experience of the body center into emotional expression. Pure sound is the expression of emotions, the language of the heart center.

Then we have the head center, in which we organize material and create meanings out of what is going on in the world. We are the meaning-makers of the world. We are the ones who create the meaning of the universe. We create it in our minds, in our head center. That is the center of abstraction. You can verbalize and you can also get a sense of relationship and proportion. That is the action of the head center. The language of this center is symbol, word or picture.

All three centers working together bespeak an organized human being. Words and symbols are the expression of the head center. Sound is the expression of the heart center. And gesture or movement is the expression of the body center. So when the word that I am saying, the sound or tone that I am making to say it, and the gesture or movement that I am making to express it all say the same thing, I am organized. In the workshop we are continually attempting to bring these three centers into harmony so that they are all expressing the same thing at the same time. When that happens, you have begun to organize your being, you have begun to be whole.

To develop the Hero, we started with the images in our heads, went down into our feelings, and finally into our bodies, integrating all three at the Heroes' Banquet. Now we are going to proceed to the Demon. We proceed to the Demon in the opposite direction. We start with the body, move into the feelings, the heart, and afterward we create a fantasy with our heads; we integrate the three with the Demon Dance.

"Satan" means "adversary," or "obstacle." The Demon is the one who stands in the way of the Hero, who prevents the Hero from accomplishing the quest. So the character of the Demon depends entirely on the nature of the goal. The Demon is not merely control. It is the part that is totally inappropriate to the situation. For example, if I am at a sophisticated dinner party and I want to make an impression on my host, the Demon is the one who exhorts me to take off all my clothes and piss in the soup tureen: completely inappropriate and absolutely opposed to my goal of impressing my host. However, if I am making love to my wife, am about to have an orgasm, and I stop myself, then the Demon is control. The Demon is not always the same thing. I cannot say the Demon is just control, or just the child who wants full expression here and now. It is more like a combination of the two. It is that which prevents you from attaining full realization of yourself.

BODY ARMOR

The first step in finding the Demon is to find out what kind of muscular armor we are walking around with in our bodies. We have to distinguish two aspects of that armor and find out what the Demon aspect is. One aspect is spontaneous, and the other is control. We need to discover these parts and out of that material create a Demon.

So we are going to develop both the Controller and the Spontaneous Child. The following exercises will help us discover the muscular armor within the body.

Demon Exercise 1: Experiencing Retroflection: How Body Armor Develops

Imagine that you are a little kid, and standing in front of you is a parent. I am going to give you two instructions. The first instruction is to do something that comes spontaneously out of you. That instruction is to reach for the parent. Then I am going to give you a second instruction, which is what comes from the parent at that point. That instruction is to stop, do not reach. And I would like you to attempt with your body to obey both instructions fully.

Imagine now a parent there in front of you. Let your arms and your whole body reach out for that parent. Reach out right from your center. Stop! Feel what happens in your body. Breathe and reach again. Stop! Breathe. Reach again, with your fingers, your face, your shoulders. Stop! Reach. Stop! Reach. Stop! Now reach and stop at the same time. Experience in your body what it feels like to reach and stop at the same time. Feel what happens in your shoulders, your arms, your jaws, your facial expression, your stomach, your chest. Let go. Most of us hold back the desire to reach out in the shoulders, but you may feel it somewhere else.

That drama generally takes place over a period of time, perhaps about five years in our childhood. The question is, who stopped you? *It is you who stopped yourself.* That is the first step in realization, in growth, to realize that I am the one who stopped myself. My mother may have struck me or rushed away from my arms. That stopped me the first couple of times. But after a while, I began to stop myself. By taking responsibility for the fact that I am the one who stops myself from reaching out, I begin to be able to change the pattern. Until then, I can continually blame mother or blame somebody else. And as long as I can blame somebody else, I do not have to do anything about it; I can remain stuck. Mother is not to blame. No one is to blame. This is the way it happened. I stopped myself from reaching out.

Holding back is a very natural process that is called *retroflection* in gestalt theory. It is a very simple survival process that allows us to hold back something that wants to come out. Without it we would not be able to hold back our need to urinate or defecate long enough to get to the toilet. Animals can do that; they can hold back these needs long enough to get out of the nest so it will not stink up the nest and alert predators. The process of retroflection is essentially a process that saves the animal's life, a mechanism of defense. We also have the capacity of retroflection.

Retroflection is a problem when it has become habitual, for example, when the desire to reach out is continually held back. At first the holding back is a conscious decision acted out in the body. Imagine walking around most of the day squeezing your shoulders up to your ears. It's painful! However, the body is a magnificent equilibrating machine; it constantly attempts to do what the mind asks it to do. If I have to hold my shoulders up consciously, that is going to take a lot of my attention. So the body takes over the job. Over each muscle we have an envelope of tissue called fascia, which is a bit like plastic wrap. It sticks to itself. If I hold my shoulders up all the time, the fascia around that muscle begins to stick to itself. Now the fascia is holding the muscles up so that they cannot relax and my shoulders can no longer hang properly in relationship to gravity. I do not have to hold them up consciously any more. However, now the three body blocks will be off balance, so I will have to throw my head forward and my pelvis forward in order to balance the disequilibrium in my chest. So here I am, my head and my pelvis thrust forward into the world and my heart and shoulders held back, safe from harm—and I am real cool! I got my act together! This is my character armor. My character armor is in my body's structure.

And when I say I am cool, what do I feel? I do not feel anything, because the body has found another way to deal with all these issues. I have cut off my head. I do not feel anything from the neck down. It is like a twilight zone down there. Experimenters have planted electrodes in animals' brains, in either the pain center or the pleasure center. When they increase the amount of energy going into these electrodes, the animal becomes more and more agitated until the agitation stops and the animal goes into a hypnotic trance. Something similar happens to the human being. In order to deal with the pain of all these clashing energies that people are experiencing in their bodies, the mind obliterates these sensations. That is why people often have difficulty identifying their feelings; they do not know what is going on below the neck. I believe that is what is meant by the unconscious or subconscious mind: feelings and sensations have gone into the automatic survival system and are no longer part of conscious awareness. In order to bring the body back into consciousness, we have to intensify some of the feelings and impulses beneath the surface.

If I am walking around with my shoulders up, my chin thrust forward, and my pelvis forward, there is a lot of pain in my body. When I cut off my head so as not to feel that pain, I am probably going to talk a lot, to make a lot of noise, because I have got to deal with that pain in some way. The only way I can deal with it is through excessive verbalization.

Wherever there is a holding back of something that wants to come out, you begin to get a fix in the body, a tightening of the muscle structure. Muscles are for movement. Bones are for balance. Muscles are what we use to move our bones from one balanced position to another. However, when my fascia is holding my muscles in a rigid, unnatural fix, those muscles try desperately to be bones. Sometimes the muscles in a person's body are so hard that you cannot even touch the bones. When the muscles are soft and organized, you can reach right in and touch a bone any place on the body. Any place you cannot reach in and touch a bone there is blocked energy.

And any energy that desires to release itself and is held back in the system too long becomes poisonous. When the retroflected desire to reach out is held back too long, it becomes self-critical and self-destructive.

Point of view is not just a mental state. It is the point from which I view the world, a physical relationship to the world as described by the synthesizing center of the mind. If I walk around the world with my head down, looking up from under my eyebrows, I look and feel frightened. I see the world as a menacing place. There is a law of physics that says nature abhors a vacuum. If I am walking around the world with this point of view, I am creating a vacuum, because this attitude is not appropriate everywhere I go. However, pretty soon somebody is going to come along to fill in this vacuum. I call a person with the opposite point of view to fill in the vacuum of my own. A fearful person seeks a terrorist. A masochist seeks a sadist. Then I marry him or her and I have an excuse. I can say it is my wife's fault, or my husband's fault, the blacks' fault, the

Jews' fault, the whites' fault—somebody's fault, not mine! I am just a poor innocent thing. When I attract somebody to come victimize me, then it is safe for me to blame that person. I no longer have to do anything about myself.

Now as the body does all these equilibrating processes, it will become fixed. The body is a manifestation of the whole being. As in the earlier exercise, the first "stop" came from outside the body, from the parent. Consequently, the person is identified with the victim of that "stop." We are identified more with the one who is receiving the pain of the headache than with the constricted muscles and blood vessels that create it. We are identified with the recipient of the pain rather than with the giver of the pain, and yet we are both. In order to regain our power, we have to own that we are the creators of our own pain. That is why in gestalt language we say, "I am giving myself a headache," or "I am choking myself." In order to gain back that power, we have to own the power of the retroflected action—the power of the "stop" rather than the incapacity to reach out. That is the process we are going to go through now, step by step: transferring our identification from the victim to the victimizer, the Controller.

We begin by looking into the body to discover what kinds of armor, what kinds of controls, are there. Having spent a full day focusing on the Hero, our resistances should be intensified.

We will put our bodies in the safest relationship to gravity, that is, flat down on the ground. Any part of the bone structure that is not touching the ground is being held up by muscles, except for the arch in the neck, a small arch in the lower back, and the backs of the knees and ankles. Those may not be touching. Any other bone that is not touching the ground is being held up by some retroflection within the body. By discovering this pattern of retroflection, we can also discover our point of view.

In effect, we are going to make a caricature of our own points of view. It will look extraordinary, a little bit like a madhouse. One of the ways of reattaching the body to the head, or reawakening the consciousness of the tensions within the body, is by exaggerating what we are doing in the body. We can then feel how it is that we are doing what we are doing. That is why in Gestalt one of the major instructions is, "Intensify that." The point is to find out how you do what you do. When you find that out, if you are not satisfied with what you do, you can begin to change it. You cannot change what you are doing until you know how you are doing it. It is for this reason that the question in Gestalt is always, How? and never, Why? *Why* you are doing it can be an excuse to continue it. Knowing *how* you are doing it gives you an option for change.

Demon Exercise 2: Body Armor Meditation

To the Guide:

I prefer to divide the group into couples for the body armor meditation. Part of the challenge of these exercises is to develop trust. For this reason I advise life-partners not to work with each other, but to allow themselves the challenge of contacting someone new. However, I do not insist on this.

While one person is meditating on her body posture, the other gives feedback. Many people are not in touch with what is going on in their bodies; consequently, outside feedback can be very helpful. The problem with doing it in couples is that people tend to get into discussions of what it means to have this leg turned out or this shoulder raised, and so on, which makes the process tedious and long. Since these side discussions are ways to avoid paying attention to the body meditation itself, I would discourage them. The feedback can be mostly physical. For instance, if the partner who is watching notices that the head is tilted one way or the other, rather than say, "Your head is tilted to the left," he might just reach down and gently tilt the head a little more in that direction. In this way the person can feel the tilt rather than talk about it.

If time is limited, you may want to guide the meditation for everyone at the same time. In this case you will have to be careful to give your instructions clearly enough for them to experience the deviations from within.

It is very easy to fall asleep during this work. This, too, is a form of resistance. I recommend that you have some device, such as touching the feet, for example, if you notice that someone is falling asleep, snoring, or clearly not following the process.

Remember, only that which the person's psyche is ready and willing to accept will become conscious. You may see tensions in a person's body that he or she is unwilling to own. Someone may even say, "People keep telling me I am rigid, and yet when I was lying on the floor, I found nothing wrong with my body; my body was absolutely perfect." Clearly, that person is resisting the process out of need. I wouldn't try to force anyone to acknowledge or intensify any more than he or she is ready and willing to do. Call attention to things that you see, but remember that people who are not ready to hear you will not hear you; it is that simple. You cannot push anyone further than his or her defense system will allow.

To the Journeyers:

In order to begin the meditation on the body armor, we are going to take some time experiencing the resistances evoked by the work on the Hero. Start by standing in the posture that you have developed for the Hero in the Fool's Dance. Hold the posture. Experience the Hero reaching toward the goal, toward the Miracle; envision the object of the quest in front of you so that you really get the feeling of that longing, that determination, that drive of the Hero. Hold the posture as long as you possibly can. Keep holding the posture, and as you hold it, think about all the reasons why you shouldn't or can't or won't achieve that goal: You're too fat, you're too old, you're a woman, you're a man . . . think of as many obstacles as you can that prevent you from reaching that goal. Keep thinking about them, all the while holding the posture. . . . After some time, feel the tensions building up in your body. Experience them. What is happening in your shoulders, for example? In your face? In your back? In your legs? Are you trembling anywhere? Hold the posture as long as you can and when you can't hold it any longer, let it go, shake out your body, and lie down on the floor.

To the Individual Journeyer:

I am giving you a special instruction because of the complexity of this particular exercise. After you have done the posture of the Hero and thought of all the reasons why you cannot accomplish your goal, lie down on the ground. Pay attention to whether your body is straight: that is to say, are your arms and legs parallel to your spinal column? Are the palms facing the floor and the feet tracking straight ahead or splayed out equidistant from the center? If they are not, intensify these deviations.

After you have explored the relationship to the center line of the body, pay attention to all of the bones of the body. Start at the head, the neck, the shoulders, arms and hands, the back, the pelvis, legs, and feet. Feel where you touch the floor and where you do not. In a fully relaxed body, there will be space behind the arch of the neck, at the small of the back (about a finger's width from the floor), under the knees and the ankles. Every other bone in the body should be touching the ground: that is to say, your hands, your wrists, your back. Your buttocks and your shoulder blades should be balanced equally on the ground. Experience all of that, and anywhere you have space between you and the ground, or any place you feel an imbalance between one side and the other, intensify the symptom. If you find that your arms are so rotated that you can't put your palms on the floor, turn them back so you feel what happens with your palms toward the floor. Feel if there is any space between your hands and your wrists and the floor. If there is, intensify that and then rotate your shoulders back to their original position. Intensify all of the deviations in your body. This will feel very strange to you, because it is an exaggeration of all of the muscular blocks within your body. By doing this you can feel the full extent of your body armor, which has been particularly evoked by the focus on the Hero.

Another way to do it is to put your body in the perfect position: that is, the spinal column is straight, the arms and the legs are under the shoulders and hips, parallel to the spine. The feet can be tracking straight ahead or splayed out to the sides, as long as they are splayed out equally. That will probably feel very strange. Hold it for a moment and then absolutely relax and feel where your body goes. Intensify all the deviations: in your shoulders, in your arms and hands, in your legs. This is your body fix. Go now to the section entitled "Soft Structures," below.

To the Group:

I am going to lead you in a meditation that proceeds step by step through all the major areas of the body. Any place you find the body is not touching the floor, intensify it. If the neck is arching, arch it more. Gradually, you are going to take on a posture that is an intensification of all the areas of the body that you find are blocked. By intensifying your body armor, you have a chance to take responsibility for it. Your system will only allow to come to consciousness the tensions you are ready to deal with. You may not become conscious of everything that is going on in your body, but your body will allow you to experience whatever is willing to open itself to your consciousness.

To the Guide:

Now you will lead the group through the meditation on body armor. First have them relax a bit, by gently rolling their heads back and forth, shaking out their hands and legs, and then finally settling down on the ground with their arms at their sides, their legs straight down, and their palms toward the floor.

Focus attention on the five cardinal lines of the body: the spinal column, the two arms, and the two legs, which should all be parallel. If they are not parallel, there may be a rotation in the shoulders or the hips, or there may be tension in the neck or the small of the back.

You will now go through a step-by-step process from the head to the feet, exploring how the body is lying on the ground in relationship to gravity. The only places that the body should not be touching the ground are the arch of the neck, a little bit in the small of the back (if it is touching the ground, that is fine, but there is an allowable arch in the small of the back), behind the knees, and behind the ankles. Otherwise, every bone should be touching the ground. If it isn't there is some tension. Go through a step-by-step process of examining the body to see if each bone is touching the ground, having them intensify each deviation they find. For example, if the wrists and palms are not touching the ground, have the person intensify that by making claws so the person can actually feel what he or she is doing unconsciously to makes this happen.

When you are detailing these parts of the body with the group, take it step by step in the sequence I will give. Let the intensification be cumulative. For example, when they find the deviation in the arms, intensify that, as well as whatever they found in their shoulders, neck, and head. After each intensification have them breathe and let it go. Part of the nature of the intensification and relaxation is to release some of the tension. Even though they are working to discover their Demon, they are at the same time releasing some of the tensions within their bodies. Emotions may surface. People may become angry or burst into tears. Allow for that expression, but do not let it become a distraction from the process. Since most tension in the body is an attempt to hold back unwanted feelings, emotions are frequently released as the tension is relaxed.

Head, Rotation

First, concentrate on the head. Pay attention to the way the head rests on the earth. If there is no rotation, the back of the head will be comfortably balanced on the ground. If it is rotated to one side, the nose, instead of pointing straight up toward the ceiling, will be pointing to the right or the left. The rotation is based on the ability to shake our heads "no." If it is rotated in one direction or the other, have the person intensify the direction of the rotation.

Head, Angle

If you drew a line from the top of the head through the nose down through the chin, that line should continue down through the center line of the body. Is the chin angled to one side? If the chin is angled to one side, have the person intensify it and add to that the rotation.

Neck

Most people hold tension in their neck. When lying on the ground without a cushion under the head, the planes of the face, that is, the forehead, the cheeks, and the chin, should be parallel to the floor. If the chin is higher than the forehead, there is clearly tension in the neck. If adjusting the head so that the planes of the face are parallel to the floor causes tension in the neck, the person has too great an arch in the neck. Intensify the arch of the neck if this is true, and add that to the angle and rotation of the head. By intensifying the deviation in the neck and head, you have a good opportunity to find out if the person is tightening the jaws, lips, and tongue. If this is so, have the person intensify all of that together, and then relax.

Shoulders

There are several things to look at in the shoulders. First of all, the blades should be touching the floor equally. They should be equidistant from the ears. People can generally feel whether or not they are lifting their shoulders up toward their ears. They might also be hunching them forward across their chest, or pushing them back so that their chest is sticking out. One shoulder may be up and one down. Pay attention to all the possibilities, and have them intensify the shoulder deviations, adding the tensions in the head and neck, and then relax.

Arms

The arms should be lying at the sides parallel to the spine, with the palms toward the floor. If they are rotated away so that the palms do not touch the ground, have the person turn the palms toward the ground to experience the space between the palms and wrists and the floor. The elbows should be rotated away the same distance from the center line so that they are pointing more or less toward the ground. The arms should not be broken at the elbows, but should create a straight line from the shoulders to the fingertips. Any deviations should be intensified.

Chest

Have the participants pay attention to their ribs as they breathe. The ribs are like fingers that are attached to the spinal column. They reach around and attach again in the front, except for the floating ribs at the bottom of the ribcage. As we breathe the fingers open with the inhalation to take more air in, and they close as the air is expelled. This is a very subtle movement. The ribs should move in all four directions, that is to say, the back and the front and both sides. Pay attention to whether all the ribs are moving as the person breathes. Have the person take deep breaths to discover if it is possible to get a satisfying feeling at the top of breath as in a yawn; or if, when reaching the fullness of breath, there is tension across the chest. Also notice whether the bottom of the chest is moving downward toward the floor. Many people hold air in the bottom of the chest, creating what is called a barrel chest. It is important to notice that. There should also be breath coming into the belly because the diaphragm is pulling downward. It is not as easy to intensify the deviations felt in the ribcage, but have them do what they can and add to that whatever other tensions they have found thus far.

Spinal Column

The spinal column is difficult to experience because we have to visualize it from within. Pay attention to whether the line of the spinal column (from the top of the head to the tailbone) is straight, or if there is an angle to one side. Also pay attention to the torsion of the spinal column. Is it twisted in one direction? If so, the buttocks and the shoulders will not be balanced equally on the ground; one buttock or shoulder will feel heavier than the other. The lighter one is pulling away from the floor; therefore, it carries the tension. The small of the back need not be touching the ground, but you shouldn't see a great space there. A person who places a hand flat on the floor and slides it under the small of the back should be able to feel the floor and the bone at the same time. If there is space between the hand and the backbone, there is an excessive arch in the small of the back. That and any other deviation should be intensified.

Pelvis

The exploration of the pelvis has been partly experienced with the rotation of the spine. However, have the participants pay attention to their buttocks: if one seems higher toward the ear than the other, have them intensify that.

Legs

One way to explore the legs is to have the participants bring their knees up so their feet are standing on the ground. In this way they can discover whether they have a tendency to clasp their knees together immediately upon raising their legs. Those who do carry tension in the inner thigh muscles. Have them intensify that tension by pressing their knees together.

Pay attention to how the feet rest on the ground. Are they tracking straight ahead? The toes should be resting lightly on the ground, not grasping or pulling away from it. Properly, the metatarsal arch pulls the center of the foot lightly away from the ground. Notice if, in this case, it seems to push down flat into the ground or to pull away from it in too excessive an arch. With the knees still bent, have them intensify whatever deviations they have found. Then have them straighten their legs, holding those tensions and adding to them the tensions in the rest of the body.

Soft Structures

Now that everyone has had a chance to experience the overall relationship of the bones to gravity and to the center line, the next step is to explore the soft structures of the body. The tensions there complete what I call "the body fix." This is the way we tried to fix ourselves in the process of growing up. In fact, we did fix ourselves in this way because this is how we were able to cope with situations in which we might otherwise not have survived. However, those situations are in the past. The "fix" is now obsolete, and we need to discover what we are ready to let go of.

We usually begin to fix ourselves by attempting to manipulate our own breath. This is one of the first manipulations babies learn in order to exert some control over themselves and also affect their parents. When the child suddenly starts turning blue, the parents come running. That manipulation influences the surrounding areas of the body. The diaphragm influences the stomach, the throat, and the tongue. It can even go so far as to influence the genitals and the rectum. These softer, more vulnerable parts of the body are affected by our earliest attempts to control ourselves. Frequently, the holding in the skeletal structure is related to the control exerted on these softer areas. The deviations of the skeletal structure are more obvious and so easier to discover. However, with the intensification of the skeletal structure, you will be able to feel more directly what you are controlling in the softer areas, that is to say, the genitals, the rectum, the abdomen, the stomach, the throat, the eyes, the face, the tongue.

Take on your whole body fix, from toe to topknot: start with feet, legs, pelvis, small of the back, angle and rotation of the spine, ribcage, shoulders, arms, hands, neck, angle and rotation of the head, jaws, lips, and tongue. Hold that intensely. As you do so, pay attention to the softer, more vulnerable areas. What do you feel in your genitals? Are you tightening them? If so, do that more. The same in the rectum. If you feel yourself sucking in the rectum, do that more. Are you tightening in the abdomen? The stomach? The throat? The tongue? Any parts of the face? The eyes? The eyebrows? The scalp? If any of those softer sections are being squeezed or tightened, do it more—hold it—feel it—then take a deep breath and with a loud sound, let it all go. Do this release with sound a couple of times. Then sink down into the earth and relax your body as much as possible.

If you are experiencing emotions, be with that for a while. Then meditate on the significance of this posture. What is the upper part of the body doing? What is the lower part of the body doing? What does the entire body seem to be expressing? Take some time to explore this. Then, when you feel ready, roll over on your left side before rising. (*Partners can massage or gently rock the person who is lying on the floor to alleviate any remaining tensions.*)

Demon Exercise 3: Battleground Drawing

To the Journeyers:

Take out a piece of paper. Recalling your body fix, draw a stick figure that indicates, very simply, what your legs are doing, what your arms are doing, whether your hands or toes are making claws, what your ribcage seems to be doing, how your head is situated on your neck—in other words, draw a stick figure of the overall structure of your body. Do as much as possible with simple straight lines. It is only for you; it will not be hung in the Louvre. It is a simple drawing to give you an idea of what you have done with your basic structure.

Next, recall where you found the greatest tensions when you were lying down. Take a color, let's say, the color green, and color on this stick figure the parts of your body where you found the greatest tension. If you have chronic pain, or if you felt pain while intensifying your body fix, take another color and indicate those areas. You may feel tension, for example, along the right side, between the eyes, and in the back of the neck. And you might find that you have pain in the center of the chest or in the loins. The pain and the tension may or may not be in the same place.

Then, if you simply could not feel anything when I was describing any of the parts of the body, or you felt at most a slight prickly feeling, then take a third color, maybe blue, and mark these " numb" areas. There are sometimes areas of the body where we have no feeling at all. I do not mean areas that feel comfortable, but those where you feel nothing at all. Frequently, people have a tendency to deaden themselves around the area of the pelvis.

It is important to get a sense of where you have maximum tension, maximum sensation, which we call pain, and lack of feeling, which we call numbness. Do a drawing of the body in this way and title the drawing, "The Battleground." This is the ground on which the battle rages between the part of you that wants to express and the part of you that is holding back, the battleground between the Heroic part that wants to go out and reach the goal, and the Demon-Saboteur that holds back and obstructs the path.

Demon Exercise 4: Point of View

To the Guide:

The process of allowing people to experience their point of view is not absolutely essential, but it is illuminating for people to discover how their body posture influences the way they perceive the world. I even include this exercise in the short weekend process, because I think it is valuable. If you do it, it is important to communicate the following information before you begin—the exercise can become so noisy that it is impossible to be heard while it is going on.

To the Journeyers:

Now that you have had a chance to experience how your skeleton relates to gravity lying down, we are going to discover how that body fix stands up, how it moves through space, and how you feel when you interact with other people from the extraordinary position of that body fix. This will help you discover how your body posture influences your point of view. The intellectual point of view is an actual reflection of the way the eyes perceive the world.

Having caricatured your own body fix through intensification, you will now experience how your eyes look at the world influenced by your body armor.

(*If you are in a group:* that world right now is the other people in the room. You may feel drawn to ask their help; you may be repulsed by them and want to turn away; you may want to hit out or grab at them. Simply allow yourself to experience your body fix in relationship to the others.)

As you contact your dominant feeling, try to find a word or a phrase that expresses it, such as, "Stay away," "Come closer," "Help me," or "You disgust me." That phrase will be an existential statement of the point of view you carry to the everyday world. You may not always experience it, but it is bound to color your way of looking at and meeting people and situations. It is the reflection of your body posture. As you change that posture, you will also change your point of view.

Stand up now and look down at the picture of your Battleground. Easily, without straining your body, spend a few moments finding the posture standing up. It may be slightly different from the way it was on the ground because your relationship to gravity is different. Your feet on the floor may be different. Feel what you have to do in order to stand in that posture. Then gradually take a deep breath and come back into the zero position of the Fool's Dance. To the count from 0 to 7, gradually, smoothly, move from your zero position to the posture of your Battleground. Move slowly from zero to zenith. Zenith is the posture of your Battleground at the point of highest intensity this side of pain. Count 0-1-2-3-4-5-6-7, zenith, hold, and then back to zero: 7-6-5-4-3-2-1-0, and shake out your body. This is the meditation to go from complete relaxation in the zero position, to zenith, and then back again.

The next phase of the meditation is to go once again from zero to zenith, and then at zenith to discover the rhythm of your breath. Is your breathing accent on the outbreath or on the inbreath? To discover this, make sounds with your breath, however you can. Breathe in the zenith position and let the sounds come out. Stay with those sounds for a while so you can get a sense of your breath rhythm, and then once again go backward from seven to zero and undo the body fix. So, 0-1-2-3-4-5-6-7, hold. Pay attention to breath. Sound. Intensify the sound. Experience what the feeling is in the sound. Then undo it, 7-6-5-4-3-2-1-0, and shake it out.

This time we're going to have a little fun! This is our fix, this is our trauma, this is our drama—why not enjoy it! We will go from zero to zenith, as we did before; we will add sound and begin to experience the feelings created by this fix. After a while, attempt to move around. You can open your eyes a little bit so as not to bump into anything or anyone. Discover what kind of movement you can make even though you are holding your legs and your feet in these strange positions. (*Individual journeyers might do the following exercise in front of a mirror.*)

In a Group:

Gradually, I am going to say, "Open your eyes and move around the room." Do so, but do not look at each other. Finally, I will give you the instruction to interact with each other. At this point stay with the sound, stay with the movement, but let your eyes open and look at each other. Experience the feelings that emerge. After a little while, search for the words that express these feelings. These words, when they come, will in effect incarnate your point of view.

Frequently, as they begin to look at each other, people burst into laughter. If that happens, intensify that laugh, intensify that smile, make it bigger, make it a grimace, and let that be part of your fix. Some people can never stop smiling; that is how their body armor expresses itself in the mouth.

Start from zero position. Relax your body, and move from zero to zenith in seven counts: 1-2-3-4-5-6-7, zenith, hold it; begin to add breath and sound, stay with that sound and with that breath. See what kinds of movements you can make. Begin to move around the room. Let your eyes come open but do not look at each other. Move around the room. As you are moving, experience what you feel.

In a Group:

Do not look at each other yet. Stay inside of yourself and experience this from within. Let the sound keep coming; do not stop making the sound. Now begin to look at each other. Be aware of your emotions as you look into each other's eyes. Let words come. Let the sound of your voice and the impulse of your movement transform itself into words. Interact with each other with these words. Do not go into dialogues and conversations, just interact with your phrases and continue moving around the room. (Do this for about five minutes.) Stop—7-6-5-4-3-2-1-0—and shake out your body.

To the Guide:

Take a little time to discuss the statements or phrases that people found, and help them discover the relationship to their everyday point of view.

The discussion of the point of view can help people clarify what the meaning of this is in their bodies and what they can do about it in their lives.

To the Journeyers:

If you found yourself saying "No," for example, you might ask yourself whether in your life you experience yourself negating other people or negating your relationships with other people. If you were saying "Help me," do you often feel needy in relationship to others? Spend a little time finding the relationship of your body posture to the way you are in the world and with other people. Coming to the point of view can be shocking if you discover that what you thought you were expressing and what you are actually communicating are in contradiction to each other. Someone, for example, may believe that she is saying "Love me," while what she is actually expressing is "Help me" or even "Stay away from me."

As this point of view becomes conscious, you can begin to change it. To someone who is unaware of this, life may seem a constant tragedy. But if, as you are walking into a new situation, you feel your body spontaneously taking on the body armor you have just discovered, then you can stop that and do something about it. You can change the way you move into a situation. You can take steps to change your point of view.

To the Guide:

This discussion may bring up material for the group. It is important, if you can, to allow some time for them to process it in small subgroups. But watch out that the whole of the time is not spent processing the individual material, or that you as the guide do not end up working with one person while the others wait. The purpose, ultimately, is to create the Demon. If someone gets into emotional process, allow it without making that person the star of the show. Sometimes people who have done a lot of Primal work or Bioenergetics feel that when they hit emotional pay dirt, they want to spend the rest of their time with it. It is important to allow time for that, but it is also important to keep things moving.

The process is a sequence. If possible, it is best to do the whole sequence from the body armor (which you have just done) all the way through to the creation of the Demon. If you end the day before the retroflected energy is released, the participants are likely not to sleep or to have a difficult night and to wake up with even more resistance. Proceeding from the body armor all the way through to the Demon allows them not only to experience how the energy is congested, but also to release the energy in the course of the day. I know some therapists prefer that group members hold onto their tensions through the night; but because of the dynamic nature of this particular process, it is better to complete it before sleeping.

REVERSING THE RETROFLECTION

To the Journeyers:

In the reach-stop exercise, the impulse behind the reaching was one of warmth and tenderness. But that impulse was stopped by the process of retroflection. Any undischarged energy held in the body too long becomes poisonous, and the process of self-victimization begins. Our internal controls imitate the way we are taught to control ourselves by our parents, teachers, and other supervisors. If we were mocked, we will tend to mock ourselves. If we were criticized, we will tend to criticize ourselves. If we were given the silent treatment, we will tend to close down on ourselves. As the cycle of control continues, the pattern intensifies, turning poisonous, almost murderous. We become victims of our own control.

We say, "I have got a headache," and never, "I am squeezing myself in my head right now," which is more accurate, despite how strange it sounds. It may be that I am stopping myself from thinking something that I don't want to allow expression, but the point is that I do it to myself. That is difficult for me to identify because originally the reaching-out impulse came from within and the stop came from someone outside. Then I started stopping myself. However, in the process of stopping myself, I continually projected this power outward: "Mother stopped me." It was necessary; it was necessary for my survival that I stopped myself. The pain (real or imagined) of being continually stopped by Mother was too much for me to bear. Be that as it may, I am identified not with the source of the control, but with its victim, the one who is in pain: "poor me." So I play the most popular game in town, the "poor me" game—"Poor me, nobody understands me; my husband ignores me, my wife nags me, the boss doesn't appreciate me, poor me!" Then "poor me" goes to another "poor me" who can say, "Oh, yes, poor you, your life is so hard"—and provide, not tea and sympathy, but coffee and contempt. That is why people do not want to stop the game. I can feel superior by saying "poor you" and giving you a little contempt. Later we can reverse the roles and you can give me a little contempt. We can call it friendship or compassion or other high-sounding names that have nothing to do with what is going on.

The more disindentified I am with this Controller, the more I project it outward, the more I need somebody else to play this monster so I can feel the poor, bereft, suffering victim of my life.

Retroflection is holding back something that wants to come out. In order to change that mechanism, we need to do what is known in gestalt as *reversing the retroflection*. Instead of doing it to myself, I do it to a cushion. Instead of choking back my need to speak up for myself forcefully, I choke the cushion. The same force that I use to restrict myself within, I now apply to the cushion, thereby reversing the flow of energy. Whatever you are doing to yourself you would like to be doing to somebody else, but it is too dangerous. The other person might stop loving you or fight back. (However, I am not advising reversing the retroflection on people, but only on cushions.)

In order to evolve the character of the Demon, we need to transfer the identification from the victim to the Controller. Instead of being at the result of the headache, we become the source, the headache-giver. Instead of being at the result of our twisted bodies, we become the body-twister. By reversing the retroflection on a grand scale, we find the material for the creation of the Demon.

If we were actors and we had a play to do, we would have to define the character of the Controller. The best actors find the character within themselves. The following series of exercises is designed to help us discover the role. (*The individual journeyer may be able to follow the next segment by substituting a cushion for a partner, but you may prefer to turn to Alternate Demon Exercise 7: Reversing the Retroflection: Short Form.*)

Now, what is that Controller controlling? Something that wants to come out. We will call that something the Spontaneous Child. The Controller is controlling our spontaneity. So in order to develop the character of the Controller, we must also develop the character of the Spontaneous Child.

This is both the simplest and the most complex phase of the workshop. This is the part people have the most trouble understanding. That is partly because the Demon wants to stay unconscious; if it becomes conscious, it won't be a Demon any more. It may work for you instead of against you. That is why we need to break this down very carefully, step by step. Be sure that you understand each phase before going on to the next.

Demon Exercise 5: Developing Scripts

Take a sheet of paper and draw a line to divide it in half. On one side you will develop the character of the Controller, and on the other, the character of the Spontaneous Child. Now divide each column into two segments. Under the Controller, label the two segments "Actions" and "Script." Under the Spontaneous Child, label the two segments "Reactions to Control" and "Spontaneous Impulses." You will work with one segment at a time, beginning with the segment titled "Actions" under the Controller. Draw two arrows facing each other, one from the Controller pointing toward the Spontaneous Child, and the other from the Spontaneous Child pointing toward the Controller. Under the Child's arrow, write "Reach" and under the Controller's arrow, write "Stop," to keep in mind the connection with the earlier exercise.

To the Guide:

Make sure that the participants understand each phase of the exercise. This means that you must understand it yourself.

1. Controller: Actions

To the Journeyers:

Find a space in the room, a cushion, and, if in a group, a partner. Begin the exercise by taking on your body fix, holding it intensely, and focusing on one segment, the head and neck segment. Feel what is going on there. Do not talk about it. Experience it.

As you begin to get a sense of what you are doing to yourself, grab a cushion and do the same thing to the cushion. Do to a cushion, physically, what you are doing to yourself. Add sound so you feel the emotional power in what you are doing. Imagine the cushion is your head. With your hands and arms, make the cushion feel the way your head feels. Make sounds as you do so. Intensify the sounds and let them becomes words. Speak to your head with the emotional force that you have discovered. The partner will write down the actions that you verbalize, such as, "I am crushing you. I am suffocating you. I am strangling you." Take the major areas of tension in your body and work each one through (head, chest, pelvis, legs). Find a word that describes what it is that you are doing to yourself in each place. It may be the same word. We frequently do the same thing to ourselves in different places. Search for words that have emotional connotation, like choking, suffocating, twisting, squeezing, pushing, blinding. Find such words to express each of the major tension areas in your body. This will give you a description of the physical actions of the Controller. Simplify it to five descriptive words.

In a Group:

After you have worked through the areas of tension, stand up and attempt to hold your partner's body in the position of your fix. This will not be easy. You will have to use your hands, arms, legs, everything to keep your partner in that position. You have become, momentarily, your Controller, and your partner has become you. Find a statement that expresses globally what you are doing to maintain your partner's body in this fix. Are you holding on? Are you crushing? Are you twisting? Find one statement that sums up the whole of what you are doing and express that.

Find the physical actions of the Controller and the words that express these. List these words under "Actions" in the "Controller" column.

2. Spontaneous Child: Responses

The next phase is the development of the character of the Spontaneous Child. The actions of the Controller—choking, holding, crushing—are retroflecting some energy that wants to come out. The Child has two kinds of actions. One is the original spontaneous action, which is generally pleasure-oriented—touching, singing, playing, dancing, making love. The second kind of action of this spontaneous part of ourselves, the Child, is the response to control.

How do you respond to control being exerted on you? Those are the responses of the Spontaneous Child. There are four or five possible responses to control. Do you give up? Do you fight back? Do you giggle? Do you make jokes? How do you respond to the way you are controlling yourself?

In a Group:

Just now, as the Controller, you did unto your partner what you do unto yourself. Now ask your partner to do that to you, and respond. You might do it several times, so that you can find out exactly what your responses are. Write them down under "Reactions to Control."

3. Spontaneous Child: Spontaneous Actions

In a Group:

Once again your partner controls you, holding you for a long time. When he releases you, explore what you are suddenly free to do—to run, to sing, to dance, to laugh, to make funny faces.

After playing with the possibilities physically, review the physical actions of the Controller and ask yourself, "What could I do if I weren't choking myself?" Or, "What would be possible if I weren't holding back my genitals?" Speculate on all the delightful possibilities you would be free to explore if you weren't controlling yourself. Discover what the Spontaneous Child could do if allowed to be completely free. Write these words down under the spontaneous impulses of the Spontaneous Child.

4. Controller: Script

On your paper one segment is still empty—the one titled "The Script" of the Controller. This is what the Controller says to the Spontaneous Child in order to stop the spontaneity.

Sit down with your partner now. Look at your spontaneous impulses and the way that you control them, and think about what you say to yourself in your head now to stop yourself from expressing those spontaneous actions. For example, if you want to express your anger to someone but you choke that back, what do you say in your head to choke off that impulse? Do you say, for example, "Oh, he won't listen to me anyway"? Do you say, "You're not important enough to say this to him"? Or "That's not nice"? Or "Be careful, don't make waves"? Generally these "shoulds" and "should nots" come from our childhood, but they live in us to this day and we say them to ourselves. The script of the Controller has to do with how you choke back your expression, how you stop your sexuality, how you twist yourself away from reaching out when you want to. What do you tell yourself to stop yourself from doing these things? Develop a script of about ten or fifteen statements. Since these characters are going to interact with each other, phrase the statements from the Controller to the Spontaneous Child as "you statements": for example, "You shouldn't do that, you don't have the right."

Demon Exercise 6: Controller/Spontaneous Child: Acting Out

To the Individual Journeyer:

The following exercises are designed for group interaction. I recommend that you read through this material for the information and then go directly to "Reversing the Retroflection: Short Form."

To the Guide:

During the last segment, the participants have been developing the scripts for the Controller and for the Spontaneous Child. The following exercise gives them a chance to experience both roles. In the exercise one person plays the Spontaneous Child of the other, while the person who is working plays her own Controller, controlling verbally and physically the one who is playing her Spontaneous Child.

People love their Spontaneous Child. They love not only to play it, but to see other people playing it. The tendency will be for them to want to play their own Spontaneous Child, and to let their partner play the monster who is controlling them, which is the way they experience it. However, that is not the point of this exercise. Frequently, I have to enunciate three or four times, "Remember, you are playing your own Controller, while the other person is playing you as your Spontaneous Child." Sometimes I suggest that they tell their partners the name that they were called as children. Playing the Controller gives them the possibility to discover what kind of energy they have to put out in order to control themselves.

In their scripts they have discovered the physical actions of the Controller. Is the Controller a choker, a strangler, a crusher, a twister, a pusher? What negative physical actions does the Controller act out on the body in order to suppress spontaneity? Now the Controller is going to play, as much as possible within the bounds of safety, those same actions on the person who is in the role of the Spontaneous Child. This means that a sense of trust must be developed between the people, and you have to be able to trust that the people are going to take care of themselves. Remind them of the no violence rule and the stop agreement: "Stop" means "Hands off, back away."

The exercise is a lot of fun and it is full of life. However, it is also very physical, so make sure that there are safety devices. A circle of cushions or mattresses can define where the game takes place so that the players do not bump against walls or break windows. They should remove any objects that might scratch, such as rings or watches, and their shoes (and their socks as well, if the floor is slippery).

If the group is larger than twelve people, divide it into two segments. One group sits on the outside and protects the space by holding up mattresses or cushions, while the others do their game in the center. This can be very helpful. It gives people a chance to see what is going on, and it is safer to have a smaller group interacting in the center. After all, you cannot really control the Spontaneous Child. It is really spontaneous and does whatever it wants to do. It plays, screams, yells, runs about, takes off its clothes, says whatever it wants to say, does whatever it wants to do. All Spontaneous Children are pretty much the same, so in playing another's, participants are pretty much playing their own. The Controller, then, has the enormous job of trying to contain this spontaneous energy.

Set up the exercise by having the couples sit down together for some time. The person who is going to work describes her Spontaneous Child. She also teaches her partner how the Child responds to control. It is this response to control that makes one Child different from another. Does the Child go dead? fight back? push? scream? freeze up? What does the Child do when it is being controlled? The people have discovered this in their scripts, and now the person who is playing the Spontaneous Child is going to act that out.

Give them a signal—a bell, or something that is loud enough for them to hear—and they begin. Allow them three to five minutes to act out. Then ring a second bell and call out, "Let the Controller begin to gain some control." That doesn't mean that the Controller suddenly takes absolute control; the Child gives in a bit. Let them play that out for another minute or two. Then sound a third bell and say, "Let the Controller gain control." Little by little, the Controller contains absolutely the Spontaneous Child. This will take some time; allow for that. Ring a fourth bell. At this point tell them to stop what they are doing and to stay in whatever postures they are in. Ask them to pay attention to that posture and breathe.

To the Group:

Pay attention to what you are feeling, in either role, how you feel about what you just had to do, or what you have just done. If you are the Controller, how do you feel about your Spontaneous Child? If you are the Child, what do you feel about being controlled like this? As the Child, think about the most effective means that your partner used in order to control you. What did you feel were the most effective modes of control?

To the Guide:

After they have had a chance to think about this, ring another bell and have them give each other feedback. When that is done, have them reverse roles. Always check between each session whether it was the right person playing the right role: the person who is working is playing the Controller; her partner is playing the Spontaneous Child. It is not just a parent and a child who are being played; both of them are full adults in size and force, but one is the Spontaneous Child part, the other is the Controller part of the same person. It is important not to confuse the Controller with Mother or Father. The exercise is not to play parent in relationship to a child, but for the person to play his or her own Controller, which may have shoulds and should nots that have come from all the controllers of childhood, not just the parents.

Demon Exercise 7: The Madhouse

To the Guide:

If participants were told in the first session that they were going to be doing this exercise, they probably would have left the group immediately! This exercise involves acting out shadow parts that most of us keep very well hidden, even from ourselves. The value of acting out the shadow in a safe place is that we don't have to act it out in our lives, or at least we can have some conscious control over it. As this kind of negative energy surfaces, we get a real sense of how we might unconsciously be treating members of our families, our spouses, or our children.

For the guide this is also delicate. You will be asking people to look at some of the most uncomfortable, secret aspects of themselves— and not only to look at them, but to enjoy playing them out. This makes it even more delicate, and at the same time, because of the humor, more possible. It is the guide's responsibility to give a sense of permission in this exercise as well as a sense of fun. "It's all right to bring these skeletons out of the closet because, after all, we've all got them and we're just playing." If the guide is uncomfortable, the group will feel it and the exercise will become oppressive. This exercise builds excitement for the Demon drawing. However, if you are really uncomfortable in leading it, don't do it. After the Spontaneous Child, you can go immediately to the Demon drawing.

The exercise is also very powerful and needs containment, because in it everyone is acting out his or her Controller gone mad. I define the Controller as that part of us that attempts to contain us, to control us, to hold us back from expressing ourselves. "Gone mad," this part now looks upon everyone else in the room as needing that same kind of control. For instance, if a person has a tendency to control his voice by choking back his need to express anger, then he might be "the angry choker" or "strangler," which means that he goes around the room strangling anyone who makes any noise whatsoever. Someone who tends to smother her sexuality will interpret any movement of the pelvis as sexual and attempt to smother anyone who is moving his or her pelvis, even to simply walk across the room. It is as if the Controller part has suddenly gone psychotic.

So give the group a chance to define their specialties. That means finding out their specialty of control, asking, What kind of a killer am I? And who is it that I kill? In their Controller script, are they stranglers, suffocaters, smotherers, twisters, castraters, molesters? What kind of killer are they, and who is it that they kill? For example, Jack the Ripper was always killing prostitutes—women who were sexual. So he was killing his own feminine sexual part. If they are stranglers, what are they strangling? Are they strangling people's expression? Are they strangling intimacy? Are they strangling the expression of rage? In the exercise they look on everybody in the room as doing the thing that needs to be controlled, and then they try to control them all. So to define the specialty, ask them to identify what they are doing and to whom.

Once again, remind them of the no violence and "stop" agreements. Require a third agreement to carry cushions or pillows, something on which they can act out the physical action of control while looking at the other person, so they are not physically touching each other. They are doing their "murdering" on the cushions while looking at each other. Now, the other person isn't going to fall over and drop dead because this happens. We think we are devastating each other, but this is not necessarily the case. The other people will just go on doing what they are doing. It gives everyone a chance to act out as fully as possible this crazy, psychotic part of themselves. If they want to experience the power of dramatizing the killer without looking at anyone, let them have a big cushion and go over in the corner and kill the cushion (without tearing it apart). That way they get a chance to experience the full physical and emotional dynamic of this Controller.

The objective of this whole series of exercises has been to transfer the identification from the victim to the victimizer. At this point, it is the victimizer gone mad. So they have moved from the one who says, "Oh, poor me, I am suffering!" to the one who makes them suffer.

To the Journeyers:

(*Everything I have said to the guide, above, I would essentially say to the group. Individual journeyers who have not gone to Alternate Demon Exercise 7 can do this exercise by writing a description of your psychotic Controller in your journal. Then write a statement as this Controller, telling who it is you control, how, and why. Brag about your work!*)

Everybody take a cushion and begin to mill around the room. Imagine that you are a killer, a strangler, a smotherer, a suffocater, or whatever, gone crazy. Say you're the Boston Strangler. You have just been taken in off the street by the police and brought to this hospital ward. Here you are in the day room. You are walking around in the room with all of these people. So hold on to your cushion and look around the room at all the people here. Realize how much they need to be controlled, because if you don't control them, they are going to destroy the world! So look around and select the ones that you think need the most control. You'll get to them in good time! How are you going to control them? What are you going to do? Be proud of your ability to contain the world, to make it a safe place for people like you to live in by destroying all the ones who are out of control. Be proud of that! Be proud of what you are doing to save humanity! Hitler, after all, worked very hard to save and perfect humanity, didn't he? When you feel ready, look for the first person who needs to be controlled, and start controlling them. Remember, no touching, no violence except to the cushion, and "Stop!" means hands off!

To the Guide:

Be very watchful that people do not get violent with each other, and intervene immediately if they do. Let them go for about five minutes. Immediately afterwards, gather the energy as quickly as possible into the Demon drawing.

Alternate Demon Exercise 7: Reversing the Retroflection, Short Form

To the Guide:

This is basically an abbreviated form of the above exercise. You will be taking the group through reversing the retroflection, expressing themselves on a cushion, and then gradually transforming that reversed retroflection into a Demon. They will dance out the Demons all together. In this exercise it is very important that those who have emerged as Demons not interact with the people who are still working on the reversal of the retroflection. They should interact only with others who have stood up and are dancing as Demons. It is also very important for you to be aware of how easy it is for people to slip back into the victim role. As soon as they begin to reverse the retroflection into the cushion, encourage them to stay in contact with that power and not fall back into feeling sorry for themselves. This often happens when they realize what they have been doing to themselves. However, the purpose of the exercise is to move through the victim into the Controller and gradually to transform the Controller into the Demon.

To do the exercise, have the participants take positions all around the room, each with a cushion in front of him or her. Even with a fairly large group, they can all do this together. Standing, they take on their body fix, experience it, become aware of what they are doing to themselves, do it more, and then when they feel ready to reverse it, they go down onto the floor and start doing to the cushion what they are doing to themselves. They make sounds with their voices and use their bodies to fully experience on the cushion the power of the reversal of the retroflected energy. The sounds may become emotional. Allow that. As they are doing this, turn on some rhythmic music. The music is their cue to gradually let their imagination transform the retroflected energy into a Demon. Encourage them to create their Demon spontaneously without thinking about it too much. Afterwards the Demon drawing will serve to complete and crystallize the image.

To the Journeyers:

If someone approached a gestalt therapist with a headache, for example, what you might observe is this: The therapist asks the client to pay attention to the headache. After a certain amount of time, the client is asked to describe the headache. The person might say, "I feel a band around my head, tightening and squeezing in from all directions." The client has created an image that can be enacted. The therapist then might place a cushion in front of the client and say, "This is your head. Do to the cushion what you are doing to your head." The client begins to squeeze the cushion. As the client squeezes the cushion, emotions frequently emerge. There is an energetic release as the client expresses herself by making sounds and saying to the cushion, "I am squeezing you! I am pushing you! You have to be perfect!" Frequently, this reversal of the retroflection relieves the headache. It is important that the person squeezing the cushion not crush it to her chest, because this retroflects the energy back in again. She must use her whole body to push the energy into the cushion and away from herself.

You are going to do the same thing, only you are going to do it from the point of view of your whole body fix instead of merely a headache. (*If you are alone, put on some rhythmic music.*) Stand with your cushion in front of you. Slowly take on your body fix . . . feel it . . . hold it . . . stay in it . . . After you have experienced it for a while, go down to the cushion on the floor and start doing to the cushion what you are doing to yourself: twisting, choking, strangling, suffocating. Whatever you are doing to yourself, do to the cushion. Intensify . . . do it more . . . Make sounds. Stay with the sounds. Keep doing this. Take time . . . Let the expression emerge as fully as possible as you reverse the retroflection on the cushion.

After you have done that for a while and you hear the rhythm of the music, let your movement take on the rhythm so that you are reversing the retroflection in rhythm. Little by little, let the music bring you up from the floor. Then, gradually, with your imagination create a monster. Move as that monster. Dance as that monster. Imagine the eyes of the monster, the claws, the teeth, the movement of the belly, the movement of the pelvis. Become your monster! Dance through the room! Look at the other monsters and interact with them. Dance a Demon dance!

CREATING THE DEMON

Demon Exercise 8. The Demon Drawing

To the Guide:

Describe the following exercise as quickly as possible and make sure that you cover all the points. Write the list of questions on a blackboard or post them on the wall. You want the group to take the energy from the madhouse exercise (or the Demon dance, above) directly into the drawing of the Demon. I generally do an example of it to encourage them and allow them as broad a range of "forbidden" material as possible.

━━━━━

To the Journeyers:

Everybody should have a sheet of paper and some colors. You will work in partners. One partner draws the most outrageous, scatological, horrible monster he can imagine, and speaks as the monster. The other sits in front of him asking questions, egging him on, encouraging him to make it even more horrible. This should be done as spontaneously as possible. You are creating out of your imagination the kind of Demon that might confront your Hero. The Demon emerges out of all the material you have been developing up to now, the more spontaneously the better. (*If you are working alone, put on some loud, lively music to encourage yourself to be as spontaneous as possible in drawing your Demon.*)

I would like you to begin by imagining that the parents are gone now. All we have here is a bunch of mischievous, spontaneous kids. And I want you to draw for yourself the most hideous, the most repulsive, the most ugly, the most monstrous Demon you can possibly imagine, while your partner helps you to do this. Imagine that you are the Demon. Talk like the Demon, make noises like the Demon, pretend to be the Demon, laugh like the Demon. And your partner encourages you to do so while you are drawing. Let your drawing help you. For instance, if you grab a color and you splash it on the page, your partner might say, "What's that?" The color is red and you might say, "This is the blood coming out of my nose!" Let it emerge spontaneously, whatever comes to you. Use the spontaneity of color and the flow of the Spontaneous Child to let yourself create a monster. In the process of the creation of this monster, your partner will help you by asking the following questions:

- What do you look like as the Demon?
- How do you deal with Heroes?
- What are your powers?
- What is your name?
- How were you born?

- Where do you live?
- What are you protecting?

Remember, the Demon stands at the gateway to the Land of Miracles and tries to stop the Hero from coming in. So how do you deal with heroes who want to get past you? What are your powers? Create a name for yourself. Create an imaginary birth. Where do you live? Create that environment. And, most important of all, what are you protecting? Create a symbol, an image, a picture of something that you as the Demon are protecting. Not abstractions, like happiness or sexuality, but something concrete, like a little egg in the center of your castle with a diamond ring in it. Something that the Demon cherishes. Don't worry about what it means. As the Demon, you are simply afraid that the Hero is going to take it away from you. (*Individual journeyers, write a first person autobiography of your Demon in your journal after you have finished the drawing.*)

Demon Exercise 9: The Demon Dance of Power

To the Guide:

The purpose of this particular aspect of the process is to give the participants a chance to act out in their bodies as fully as possible the Demon they have created with their imaginations. Just as the Heroes' Banquet was a way for them to express their Heroes in front of each other, the Demon Dance of Power is a way for them to express their Demons in front of each other.

As soon as they have finished their drawings, gather them together with some music, some rhythm. Let them build up an energy matrix of sound, stamping their feet, clapping their hands, creating rhythm together. Encourage them to dance out this monstrous image. When you feel the energy is built to a climax, go into the center or bring the rhythm down low enough so you can tell them what to do, and describe the Demon Dance of Power.

To The Group:

Okay, everybody, yesterday a whole group of Heroes came together here to brag and show off and pretend that they were so great that they made you want to vomit! It was ugly and ridiculous and stupid! They were all quite mad! Well, I called all of you Demons here together so that we can show off our power to each other. We're not going to let those Heroes get past us, are we?

In order to show off our power, each Demon, one at a time, will enter the center of the circle. Show us your body! Dance out your power! Act out whatever it is that you do to Heroes. Particularly, use the parts of your body that you accented when you drew this picture of yourself. Dance out your power! Show it off in a dance! When you feel that you have shown us your power, invite some other Demon to come into the center of the circle with you. Interact with each other. Compete with each other, outdo each other in showing off your magnificence and your power. Interact with each other, but do not touch each other. After a while the first Demon goes off and the second Demon continues dancing. She shows off her power, then invites another one into the center; they interact for a while, and then she goes off. Continue this until everyone has had a chance to do it.

The rest of the group is in a circle with musical instruments, encouraging them, laughing with them, shouting, giving whatever encouragement they can to go beyond themselves and celebrate this demonic energy. At the end, we will all dance together in a final celebration of our power.

To the Guide:

I generally allow time at the end for a period of free dance. If there is still more release that needs to take place, they can all do it at the same time, expressing themselves together. Some people may go off to the side and sit, but the dance may go on for an hour afterward because so much energy is released. Allow this to go on as long as you feel is comfortable, without forcing anyone to do more than he or she wants. When you feel they are ready, gather the group together. If you need some feedback, invite it, but the energy is not likely to be very verbal at this point. It is, however, very important to ground by doing a final chant as a closing of the day of the Demon. If the participants are not willing to do this, have everyone join hands and shout as loud as they can as an alternative to the chant. But then follow this with silence.

People have a tendency to stay up late this evening because of all the energy that has been released. You might call attention to the difference between the body fix in their zenith position and the release they experienced as they were dancing out the Demon: this is exactly the kind of physical freedom that they are holding back in the body armor. It is a good thing to point that out. You might also have them go back to the list of qualities they wrote up for themselves as Heroes; look at the qualities they had underlined as qualities they could not own. Nine times out of ten, they find that they have owned them all by now as Demons, because frequently the qualities that they are disowning in one aspect of themselves they will accept in the other.

To the Individual Journeyer:

Put on some loud, rhythmic music, and dance out your Demon similarly. Dance until you feel you have not only owned and enjoyed playing the monster, but until you can feel your energy beginning to wane. It is a good release. Make noise if you can. However, when you feel finished, sit down and spend some time reconnecting with the earth. Breathe. Touch the floor and chant a calming chant.

Alternate Demon Exercise 9: The Demon Run

The Demon Dance is one of the more powerful ways of bringing to life this demonic character in a safe, structured way. However, there are alternatives. If you arrive at the Demon when it is still daytime, and you are in a country setting, you can do what I call "the Demon Run."

Do the exercise in groups of three. One person is allowed to play her Demon, while the other two are like the good mother and the good father who allow her to act out her Demon as wildly as she likes without destroying the environment or hurting herself. It is wonderful to experience the physical release of energy in an outdoor environment. She might, of course, meet some other Demons who are running loose and interact with them. Again, maintain some sense of containment so they don't interact violently with each other. Have some protective devices and some control words.

The function of the two people accompanying the one doing the Demon Run is to remain permissive and protective, not controlling and coercive. It is very important that the one who is on the run has a sense that there is someone there who allows her to free herself. I recommend about a fifteen-minute run. Then suggest that the three come together and sit down and hold hands, chanting a few times among themselves to ground the energy. Suggest that they spend a few moments talking about what happened, and then select the next person to do his or her run. Continue until all three have had a chance to do it.

Alternate Exercise 9: "What's My Line" Demon Show

In this form the whole group acts as a panel. The Demon comes out and takes a seat or stands in the middle. Yourself, or someone in the group who is talented in such a way, plays host and questions the Demon as to his nature, what he does, the way he is, how he defends himself. The host suggests that the Demon show himself. The whole group can ask the Demon questions until the Demon expresses himself and gives as complete a picture as possible. This is slightly more theatrical and quite funny. It works very well in a place where the Demon Dance is not possible, or where people are more contained. The questions that come up and the nature of what goes on in the Demon Show can be very powerful in terms of people exposing hidden aspects of themselves, not only to the others but to themselves.

Ritual closing

To the Guide:

Everything up to now has been a technique to establish trust. The Demon Show, the Demon Run, and the Demon Dance would not be possible without it. Generally, by this time there has been a lot of release and the group has become very tightly formed. There may be people for whom it is too much. Remember, as in every other exercise, it is always possible to say no. It is very important for you as guide, as well as for the group members, not to ostracize a person who has said no. Accept that as part of his or her process. That way the person remains part of the whole.

CHAPTER 8
The Instrument of Power

*Y*ou have now had a chance to experience both the Hero and the Demon. As a result of this polarization and clarification, some level of integration may already be taking place. However, it is not complete, and you may also have a feeling of inner division. I remember an incident in which a woman came to me just before the confrontation and said, "I can't do the confrontation today because I feel too schizophrenic." That is precisely the right moment for the confrontation. It is this separation of the two opposing forces that we have been working to achieve.

You may experience some confusion about your identity in relation to these aspects. When people enact the Hero, they are pleased to find themselves able to identify with their heroic aspiration. However, when they come into contact with the power, the force, and the delicious sensuality of the Demon, they frequently say, "I much prefer identifying with the Demon!" Today you may fear that you have forsaken your Hero, and this inner division seems to demand a choice of either/or. Of course, it is that either/or that we want ultimately to dissolve so that you can experience both/and, and thus realize the completeness of your being.

I used to place the Instrument of Power at the end of the Hero process, because it belongs to the Hero. However, I found that people were becoming so identified with and so sympathetically moved by their demonic energy that they often began to feel about the Hero as the Demon does: "Poor fool, he thinks he's so powerful!" Therefore, in order to retrieve the identity with the Hero and to reestablish contact with the self-affirming, questing side, I moved the Instrument of Power to this position, just before the confrontation. As people find their Instruments of Power and come in contact again with the Spirit

Guide, something important happens. They seem to get clearer about every-thing. Things fall into place.

The Spirit Guide is the top point on the triangle. You have been deeply involved, first with the Hero and then with the Demon. Now suddenly you are put into that objective third position. The depth of the conflict be-tween Hero and Demon has become clearer, and this calls for some form of compassionate detachment. When you are on top of a mountain you can see the relationship between the lake and the house very differently from when you are walking on the circuitous path between. So it seems that a sense of objectivity comes with recontacting the Spirit Guide. The Spirit Guide can look into the two aspects of the personality and know what the healing is that needs to take place.

With the discovery of the Instrument of Power, the symbols can fall into place. There is a great sense of synchronicity that comes as people go out into nature looking for their Instruments of Power. The walk itself becomes magical. In creating the Hero and the Demon, you have been building up your internal fantasy world intensely. To take it out into nature is a way of making it bigger, of broadening it, and also of incorporating the greater world. A breath of fresh air enlivens it.

To the Guide:

Often, after the day of the Demon, people are up very late at night cel-ebrating, because they have released a good deal of their inner restriction. The stopper is out of the bottle and the genie doesn't want to go back in! So they may be a little tired this morning. This is another reason to place the Instru-ment of Power in this position, because it is an uplifting experience. When I am doing the process on a weekend, the Instrument of Power frequently comes on Sunday morning, a perfect time for a ritual celebration.

Very often during the period of the search for the Instrument of Power and the subsequent dedication, people become moved in a transpersonal way, as if they suddenly touched some mystical core of themselves. It is important to be aware of this, to acknowledge it and give it credence, because some may never before have reached that part of themselves. Since the journey is a jour-ney to the inner being, it is important to acknowledge it, accept it, and go on.

Ram Meditation, Day 4

FOOL'S DANCE

To the Journeyers:

Today you will add the image of the Battleground and the Demon. Generally, the Fool's Dance is done as a T'ai Chi movement, in which each posture has its own place and about equal time. However, when it comes to the Hero-Demon configuration, this changes. Between the Hero and the Demon is the Battleground, and the Battleground, of course, is all of the muscular tensions that you found in your body armor. Rather than making the Battleground an equal-time posture, I think of this as the resistance and constriction paralyzing the Hero. Then, out of that constriction, the Demon is born with all its power. It is important to clarify the difference between the Demon and the Battleground. The Battleground is all the crippling aspects of the conflict; the Demon is the power that cripples. The Battleground contracts and the Demon explodes. So when you have found the relationship of Hero-Battleground-Demon, try to experience the transition between the Hero and the Demon as the compression that ultimately explodes into the Demon. This is in contrast to the slow movements that characterize the rest of the postures.

To the Guide:

After they have done the Fool's Dance a couple of times on their own, to make sure that the postures are clear, take them through the story.

To the Journeyers:

Once upon a time there was a person named Me (*posture*), who went down a long flight of stairs to a room with four doors and opened the door marked "Home." This is the way I felt about the images behind that door (*posture*). The second door was called "Lifework." Upon opening that door, I felt this way about what I saw (*posture*). The third door was titled "Beloved." This is the way I felt about what I saw behind that door (*posture*). And the fourth door was called "Self," and this is the way I felt about the symbols of my self (*posture*). Upon closing the fourth door, I discovered a Throne of Miracles and I envisioned this Miracle (*posture*). Along came a Spirit Guide (*posture*), who led me to my own Heroic Self (*posture*). However, as I discovered my Hero, I could feel the tensions building in my body. My body became a veritable

Battleground of my own resistance (*posture*), which exploded into this Demon (*posture*).

POWER EXERCISE 1: FINDING THE INSTRUMENT OF POWER

To the Journeyers:

As the Hero approaches the Threshold of Adventure, she is given an Instrument of Power. An Instrument of Power is a physical object that symbolizes a power deeply embedded in the Hero, one which she is not in touch with at this particular point. It manifests a yet unknown aspect of the Heroic Self, some power that the Hero has not yet made conscious. So it needs to take the form of a physical object in order to bring it into awareness and make it substantial. The world of the Hero is the world that is known to the conscious mind. The object is a way of bringing this still hidden power into consciousness, just as a memento given by a loved one makes that loved one present every time it is glanced at.

Probably each of you has an Instrument of Power. It may be a jacket, something you wear around your neck, a ring, or something that someone has given to you: something that is important to you, that you want to be sure to have with you when you travel. It is only matter, and as matter it may not even be valuable. But you, and whoever gave it to you, put numinosity into it, put magic into it, and made it important. That is what an Instrument of Power is: a physical thing that has importance, that has magic, for you.

If the Hero is very idealistic and utopian, the Instrument of Power may have some element of earthiness about it. Frequently, it manifests the part of the psyche the person is out of touch with and that is most necessary to the unification of the Hero and the Demon. If the Hero is the head and the Demon is the body, the Instrument of Power generally has something to do with heart: because the heart is the pathway through which the two come together.

In some traditions a child, early on, goes out into the woods and finds a stone. He never shows that stone to anyone. He makes a little container for it and wears it around his neck until he reaches puberty. The stone becomes the child's soul stone; it is a physical manifestation of his soul. At the age of puberty, the child goes out into the woods and finds a place to bury the stone. No one else ever sees it. Then, any time in the course of his life when he needs some reaffirmation of his being, he goes out into the woods and digs up the soul stone and wears it round his neck while he is going through difficult times.

When the traumatic period is finished, he takes it back out to the woods and buries it again. That is his special, magical soul stone, a representation of his own inner core.

My Instrument of Power is my harp. Its natural capacities are also its magical powers. For instance, if the group is dissipated, I can pick up the harp and bring it together with a rhythm. So I can transform the space. The name of my Instrument of Power is Ammon-Ra. The magic of Ammon-Ra is that when I hold him to my chest, he enables me to take the rays of the sun through the crown of my head and transform them into magnetic vibrations that come out of my heart and pass through the harp. I trace these vibrations with my fingertips, creating music out of the rays of the sun. This music can change the environment, can unify Hero and Demon, and can heal. That is what my Spirit Guide told me. It is true that music can bring people together by making their hearts vibrate together. But this is *my* unifying power. I use the harp in order to do it, but the magic I put into the harp is my own. A child could take the harp and beat on it all day long and the group would never be unified. As a matter of fact, it would more likely do the opposite! So it isn't just the harp, it is the person who does it. The harp is just the instrument, the manifestation of the personal quality.

So on the one hand, the object is just stuff. But when a human being invests power into it, the object becomes magic. If the human being does not invest that power in it, it remains stuff. The object is a way of projecting our power. Of course, there can be a danger of separating oneself from one's power by projecting it into the object, saying, "That is doing it," as if I were to say, "It is my harp that unifies the group, and not my soul." That is a misunderstanding. But projection is a way we can come in contact with our powers. They are symbolized out there, and then we gradually own them.

In the mythical story, the Hero, who comes from a mundane existence of business to be taken care of, houses to be cleaned, and bills to be paid, needs some magical power in order to go beyond these everyday realities. The Hero comes from the land of the conscious, and the Demon of Resistance, from the land of the subconscious. The Demon has not only his own demonic nature, but the whole subconscious mind at his disposal. He may not know what it is or how to use it, but it is there. Therefore, in order to feel capable of dealing with the potential of the Demon, the Hero needs a magical device in order to balance the power.

To find your Instrument of Power, you are going to go for a walk in the environment. Let your Spirit Guide direct you. Do not decide in advance where you want to go. As you are walking along, participate in an ongoing fantasy with your Spirit Guide, imagining yourself being led. Somewhere along the way, an object will appear that is your Instrument of Power. It may be a blade of grass, a branch from a tree, a stone; some little object will attract your attention. Your Spirit Guide may even lead you to your own room and direct you to something that you already have.

When you find it, if you can, sit down in front of it and put the image of your Spirit Guide (your Tarot card) behind it. (*If you are working in the city, have the group return to the room to do this meditation.*) Take a few moments to close your eyes and meditate. Imagine that your Spirit Guide actually appears before you. Even if you do not see him or her as a visual image, imagine that your Spirit Guide arises there in front of you. Take a few moments to be in that presence. The Spirit Guide sees both Hero and Demon; the Spirit Guide knows all. Allow yourself to be in the presence of that knowledge.

Ask your Spirit Guide three questions: (1) What is the name of my Instrument of Power? (2) What are its magical powers? and (3) What are its practical uses? When I take this home with me from the journey into my real life, what practical use can I make of it? Listen to the answers.

Then imagine that your Spirit Guide gives you the Instrument of Power. At the same time, reach down in the real world and pick up the object and bring it back to this room.

Do not be surprised by what you find. One time when I was doing the Hero's Journey, we had a black belt karate expert in the group. He tended to fluctuate between heady spirituality and bodily gymnastics. Whenever we dealt with emotions, he was in trouble. It was a cold, winter Sunday morning, and I had instructed the group to go out into the city to find their Instruments of Power. Upon returning, he said, "I didn't find my Instrument of Power, but I have a funny story to tell you. I was walking through the park, and in the middle of the path I saw a fallen white bird. I knew that was my Instrument of Power! It was perfect! I rushed to pick it up, and when I got there I discovered that it was only a piece of Kleenex. I was very disappointed. However, I reached down to pick it up anyway, and underneath it was a pile of dog shit! Dog shit!" he laughed. "You know, my father used to say, 'If you step in dog shit, you have good luck for a day.' " He laughed again. As he turned to go away, I said, "And you didn't bring back your Instrument of Power?" "What do you mean, my Instrument of Power?" he asked. I said, "See how your judgment of what is and is not of value has prevented you from bringing back what your Spirit Guide led you to as an authentic Instrument of Power. I want you to use that dog shit as your Instrument of Power on the journey. It is probably the most important thing that you have to face up to. That piece of dog shit that you considered to be beneath you is not beneath you! You do not have to go back and pick up the actual dog shit, but imagine that you carry it in your hand as your very precious, very sacred Instrument of Power."

Later on, in the confrontation between the Hero and the Demon, he was completely stuck. The only thing he could think of to do was to take the dog shit and throw it in the face of the Demon. In that moment, the Demon suddenly experienced an illumination and they could look at one another with compassion, resolving the conflict between them.

This story has another level. Frequently, whatever you avoid in the group comes up to greet you in your everyday life as soon as you leave. Well, that is exactly what happened to this man. He rented out sports equipment. A man with whom he had contracted to lease out a good deal of his equipment for a special sports event suddenly lost his job; he'd been fired. Well, ordinarily, in such a situation Mr. Black Belt would snipe at his staff; he would release his anger with unpleasant little jibes at the people around him, but would never fully contact his authentic anger or the fear behind it. This time he remembered work he had avoided completely in the group, beating on cushions and releasing emotion. So instead of employing his habitual and ineffectual expression of anger, he went to the back room and started pounding on one of the football dummies, expressing his rage at the other man and his fear that he would not get his money. Suddenly, in the middle of his rage—as if the shit suddenly struck him—his eyes were opened and he could see with deep compassion what the other man, who had just lost his job, must be going through. After he had expressed himself, he immediately went to the telephone to call the man and tell him how sorry he was to hear that he had lost his job. As part of the conversation, the man said, "Oh, by the way, you don't have to worry about your money, that is all taken care of; the contract will be fulfilled."

So, don't be surprised at what your Instrument of Power might be, and don't turn your nose up at what it is! If something captures your attention and you think that couldn't possibly be it, that's it! Accept your Instrument of Power!

To the Guide:

Now you will send the group out to search for their Instruments of Power. Give them anywhere from a half-hour to an hour, whatever you feel is comfortable. Lead them off by telling them the story once more as they do the Fool's Dance, this time up to the Hero. At the end of this, they go out in silence, alone, led by their Spirit Guides, to find their Instruments of Power.

FOOL'S DANCE

To the Journeyers:

Once upon a time there was a person named Me (*posture*), who went down a long flight of stairs to a room with four doors and opened the door marked "Home." This is the way I felt about the images behind that door (*posture*). The second door was called "Lifework." Upon opening that door, I felt this way about what I saw (*posture*). The third door was titled "Beloved." This is the way I felt about what I saw behind that door (*posture*). And the fourth door was called "Self," and this is the way I felt about the symbols of my self (*posture*). Upon closing the fourth door, I discovered a Throne of Miracles and I envisioned this Miracle (*posture*). There appeared before me a Spirit Guide (*posture*) who led me to my own Heroic Self (*posture*). Stay in the feeling of the Hero and go out in silence to find your Instrument of Power.

POWER EXERCISE 2: RITUAL OF DEDICATION

Individual journeyers may wish to prepare an altar of dedication before going out to search for your Instrument of Power. In a group the guide prepares the space while the people are out.

Preparing the Space

To prepare the room as a sacred space, set up the altar in the center with the corners in the four directions: north, east, south, and west. In each of the four corners, place a symbol of the elemental energies, earth, air, fire, and water. I use the kabbalistic system, in which the north is symbolized by the element earth, for which I generally use scented oil. You could also have dirt itself, or fruits and vegetables—a beautiful display symbolizing the benefits of the element earth. The east is air, which I symbolize with incense or sage. The south is fire, for which I recommend a second candle. The west is water. I use a bowl of water with a flower or a plant sprig that people can use to sprinkle themselves and the altar. The group candle, the everlasting flame, is in the center. Add anything you wish to make the room and altar beautiful. Place the cushions in a circle around the altar, so that as the people enter with their Instruments of Power, they are coming into a sacred place. I also recommend that you have some music playing that encourages them not to gossip or chat, but to prepare themselves for the ritual of the consecration and dedication of the Instruments of Power.

Opening Celebration

I generally greet the group with harp music, using the phrase, "Praise God." This develops into a chant that climaxes with a big "Alleluia." The simple words "Praise God" gradually transform into "Praise God, Praise the Goddess; Praise the Lord, Praise the Lady; Praise the Father, Praise the Mother; Praise the Brother, Praise the Sister; Praise you, Praise me, Praise them, Praise us, Praise everyone, Praise the universe, Alleluia!" I then talk about what I mean when I say, "Praise God."

To the Journeyers:

In saying, "Praise God," I am talking about God's presence in everyone and everything. If you want to see the face of God, open your eyes and look around you: there is no place that you can look and not see the face of God. When I talk about praising God, I am also referring to that aspect of God that each of us carries within. The higher self, the spirit, or the inner light that we all carry is one of the cells in the whole body of God. We are not simply praising something outside of ourselves; we are praising something that is deep within. And it is all worthy of praise. By celebrating it, we open ourselves to the joy of being part of something that is huge and wonderful, beautiful and terrible, awesome and magnificent, each in its season, and all one with God.

It is also important to have fun doing it! Many so-called "primitive" cultures recognize the importance of being able to have fun in our sacred space. So much of Western spirituality is solemn, at least in my experience, and I think that takes away from the magnificence of it. When it is so serious and heavy, there is a tremendous urge to giggle. The Hopi Indians, aware of this urge, frequently provide a clown to inject an element of humor into their rituals, so that the participants can release themselves with laughter. Afterward, they can enter more profoundly into the depth of the ritual. So I think it is important to incorporate humor, joy, and fun, along with the solemnity and seriousness of any ritual. If some funny thing happens, embrace it! That is part of God, too!

Here in the room we have made the space sacred by creating an altar. It symbolizes a mini-universe. The candle is the center point, and our bodies create the outer periphery of the universe. As we place our Instruments of Power in the center, our symbols become the center of this universe and our bodies become the periphery; therefore, we compose the entire universe, as God composes the entire universe. We participate in creation by placing ourselves and our symbols into this sacred space. We will consecrate and dedicate our Instruments of Power. As I explained during the anointing of the Heroes, consecration is a way of making holy our quests. The Instrument of Power, given to us by our Spirit Guide, is another level of that consecration to a greater cause than our individual paths. It is simply a way of saying, "I am aware that I am part of a greater whole, and I consecrate myself and my gifts to that greater whole."

The four corners of the altar, north, east, south, and west, are dedicated to the four elemental energies of earth, air, fire, and water. If the element itself were to enter into our circle here in its raw, savage form, it would destroy us. The earth tumbling in from the north would overwhelm us with an avalanche. A hurricane would blow us all away. Fire would destroy us, and water would drown us. The pure elemental energies are too strong. So we ask the guardian spirits, the four Archangels who are said to stand guardian over the four elemental energies, to guide them and give us their beneficial aspects.

The Archangel at the doorway to the north is Ariel. Although Archangels are neither male nor female, I see Ariel as having a feminine form. Imagine a beautiful pregnant woman sunning herself in a garden of fruit and flowers, offering us the fruits of the earth. She is dressed in earth colors, browns and oranges. To the east is the Archangel Raphael, standing high on a windy hill with his yellow and blue robes whipping about him. His arms are outstretched as he gives us the healing element of air: cooling breezes, breath, inspiration and expiration. To the south is Michael. He is frequently depicted as standing in the center of the sun with golden robes, his flaming sword upraised. He destroys the demon of ignorance. It is the sword with which he drove Adam and Eve out of the Garden of Eden into the world to discover their humanity, and along the way his sword gives us light and warmth to illuminate our minds and our hearts, enabling us to make distinctions and to see relationships. To the west is Gabriel, whom I also see as a woman, with long flowing hair, wearing green and blue robes that cascade down her form like the waterfall behind which she stands. Her fingers reach through the water, offering us its cooling, thirst-quenching, cleansing benefits.

The candle in the center of the altar symbolizes the relationship of above and below. The human being stands in that place, manifesting both above and below, both spirit and matter. So the candle, which is the symbol of the group, becomes that human being, us. The Native American peoples frequently placed a bonfire at the center of their rituals, symbolizing the human spirit sending the smoke up as a prayer to the great mysterious one, while the ashes, falling down to the earth, symbolized the process of death and transformation.

Consecrating the Instruments of Power

In ancient times rituals were the province of priests and priestesses. That is still more or less true today. However, one aspect of the approaching new epoch is that we all can begin to take responsibility for that sacred position. We can create our own rituals to make the contact of the earth and the divine. You will create a brief ritual to invite the beneficial aspects of earth, air, fire, and water into the circle, our ritual universe, and also to bless your own Instrument of Power.

In a Group:

The four people who are seated just behind the four elements, go into the center and take the symbol of that element. Imagine that you are in the service of the Archangel who gives us the benefits of that element. The element of earth, for example, is symbolized by scented oil. Take it and anoint yourself and your Instrument of Power. Each of you will create a brief ritual and then pass the symbol to the left until it has made a complete circle of the group. When it returns to you, place it back on the altar. Thus, every member of the group has an opportunity to become a priest or priestess and invite, through the intercession of the Archangels, the four elemental energies into the circle. When all the elements are back in place, take your Instrument of Power and place it in the center of the circle, saying as you do so, "I place myself in the center of the circle."

To the Individual Journeyer:

Follow the same plan. Take time to create your altar, and find your own way to invite the four elemental energies into your circle and to recognize the above and below. You may want to walk around your altar to create the limits of its periphery, stopping at each of the four corners to create your ritual of blessing. Improvise. Trust your inspiration.

To the Guide:

I recommend that you have a method of timing this. For instance, have someone, or yourself, meditate on breathing slowly. At the end of each third breath, ring a bell, which is the cue for the person to pass on the symbol. People become absorbed by this ritual and sometimes they get carried away. If it takes too long, the ones at the end become irritated. Humor is to be encouraged, but irritation is to be discouraged, and too much time can dissipate the intensity of the ritual. So, find some way to contain it and give it limits.

This ritual has a richness about it, and by the time it is over the whole group is generally in a transcendent space. This is the time to introduce the next guided fantasy. This fantasy combines the dedication of the Instrument of Power with the preparation for the next stage of the journey, the confrontation of the Hero and the Demon.

Guided Fantasy: "The Golden Hero"

To the Journeyers:

Close your eyes, breathe into your belly, and recall the moment that you found your Instrument of Power. Bring that moment clearly into your memory. Imagine your Spirit Guide standing there in front of you. Allow yourself to experience fully the power and the beauty and the strength of that Spirit Guide—luminous, caring, standing there in front of you. Recall the three questions. Once again, ask the Spirit Guide the name of your Instrument of Power (*pause*), its magical properties—what power does this instrument have? (*pause*)—and its practical uses. Imagine your Spirit Guide reaching forward to present you with the Instrument of Power. You reach out to take it and, for a moment, your hands touch. Something is transmitted through that contact. You feel all the caring, all the warmth, all the wisdom of that Spirit Guide flowing into your hands. Then you take your Instrument of Power and your Spirit Guide points behind you. You turn around, and the scene transforms. You stand now in front of a beautiful Golden Mountain with the sun at its apex.

You take your Instrument of Power in hand and begin to climb the mountain of gold. As we climb, we chant . . .

To the Guide:

For the climbing of the Golden Mountain, I use a chanting meditation from the Arica school of Oscar Ichazo, a variation of the Rams. Rather than chanting the Rams as we have been doing every morning (three in the belly, three in the heart, and three in the head at different pitch levels), we begin at the lowest level. With each breath we go to the next pitch, climbing our body as the Golden Mountain, from the base in the belly, through the heart, to the pinnacle in the head. This tends to increase people's meditational state. As they are chanting, they might create little melodies, but they must continue to ascend. Each one does it in his or her own way. They don't wait for each other. The chanting gradually ascends until they reach their highest pitch. Recommend that people not go beyond where they comfortably can as they reach the highest level. They should not strain. Some may finish before the others. When you think they are all at the apex of their Golden Mountain, sound a bell so they know it is time to stop. Then begin the guided fantasy. (If you are not doing the Ram meditations, you might use an open "ah" sound.)

To the Journeyers:

Imagine that now you stand at the top of the Golden Mountain. The sun is directly overhead. You look around and you can see the entire countryside. Through that countryside winds your path, your way toward the magical land. But now you look upward toward the sun. You lift your Instrument of Power above your head and you call out in a loud voice: "I dedicate this, my Instrument of Power, to the accomplishment of my quest, to the realization of my Miracle, and to the illumination of my life!" At that moment a beam of sunlight touches the top of your Instrument of Power, filling it with golden light. And the light fills your hands, fills your arms, your shoulders, your chest, your heart, your breath; fills your stomach and abdomen, your whole body with golden light—and you stand there at the top of the mountain, a beacon of light. You have become the Golden Hero!

And now you look down, down at the countryside spread out in front of you. What kind of countryside is it? Somewhere in that landscape is a magical gateway, the miraculous entrance to another world, a threshold. It may open to a forest, to a lake or an ocean, a cave or a castle—your special threshold is waiting for you down there. So you take your Instrument of Power in hand, and you begin to walk down the mountain of gold. The Golden Hero on your way! Sun in your hair! The breeze blowing your clothes! The Golden Hero on your path! The birds and animals stare in astonishment as you pass. Never before have they seen anyone so beautiful as you, so powerful as you, the Golden Hero, on your way! The grasses part before you and all of nature looks on in wonder as you pass. The beauty, the glory of the Golden Hero, on your way!

You are descending the mountain. Your path winds through the land below. Look around you. Somewhere there is a magical portal—that threshold you must cross in order to accomplish your Miracle, to find the object of your quest—your Threshold of Adventure.

Imagine yourself now, standing in front of that threshold. You, the Golden Hero. However, you know that before you enter the Land of Miracles you must confront the guardian of the threshold—the Demon of your own Resistance, the guardian that stands there to prevent you from accomplishing what you choose to accomplish. So rather than wait for the Demon to sneak up behind you in some unguarded moment, you take your Instrument of Power in hand and loudly call out to the Demon by name, demanding that he or she come out now and confront you in front of the magical doorway.

Suddenly, the image of your Demon appears in front of you. It may not look exactly as it did yesterday; Demons can take many shapes, many forms, and many faces. But there, rising in front of you, is the shape of the Demon of your own Resistance. What does that Demon look like? Look into the eyes of the Demon. Look at your Demon! How powerful does that Demon look to you? How do you feel when you look into those eyes? The Demon looks back, staring at you, showing you all its power.

Now shift your perspective so that instead of you as the Hero looking at the Demon, your body takes on a change. Your face changes, and you become the Demon looking at that Hero who wants to pass through your doorway—who wants to go beyond you—who wants to take what you are protecting. Become that Demon! Experience that Demon looking at the Hero, the face, the body, the shoulders. How strong does that Hero look to you? Do you think that Hero can get by you? That Hero wants to take what you are protecting. Will you allow it? Make a Demon sound!

Let yourself breathe quietly again. However, instead of going back to the Hero, once more shift perspective. Now it is as if you were sitting in a theater looking at a movie screen. On one side is the Hero who stands facing the magical doorway, and that Hero is you. And standing confronting that Hero, preventing that Hero from entering into the magical place, is the Demon. That Demon is also you. There's the Hero. There's the Demon. There's the doorway. The scene is ready for the grand confrontation that must take place before you can cross the threshold and realize your Miracle.

Now let the movie screen in front of you recede into the darkness, becoming smaller and smaller, a point of light in the depth of the darkness, like a star at night. It is a hologram that contains the scene for you to call back when you are ready for the confrontation. All you have to do is close your eyes and see the point of light and bring the scene back into focus.

Now, in order to come back from the world of fantasy, let's chant the name of our Instrument of Power three times. That way the Instrument of Power can guide us from that place into this. The first time, as you chant the name, stay in the other world by remaining with your eyes closed. During the second chanting of the name, let your eyelids slowly open so that you are looking at your actual Instrument of Power there in front of you on the altar. And the third time, chant with your eyes fully open, looking at your Instrument of Power in the here and now.

POWER EXERCISE 3: SHARING THE STORY

To the Guide:

When the participants return from their inner vision, have them share in small groups or with partners the story of what happened to them as they were searching for their Instrument of Power. (*Individual journeyers, tell your story to your journal.*)

The next process is to be the Confrontation. Since you are going to need time to set up, I recommend that, during the break, after they finish sharing with each other, they organize themselves into groups of three or four for the confrontation. Say this only after they have had time to talk with each other. If you say it before, it will get them all excited about looking for partners for the confrontation before they have had a chance to share the information about the Instrument of Power.

FOOL'S DANCE

Find a posture that expresses the dedication of the Instrument of Power and add that posture to the end of your Fool's Dance. In large groups participants can do this in their subgroups and then go through the Fool's Dance to incorporate it.

CHAPTER 9
The Confrontation

*I*n one of his lectures, Joseph Campbell said that the difference between a schizophrenic episode and a spiritual awakening is that schizophrenics project their internal material outward and act it out on the stage of the world, whereas in a spiritual journey the same kind of material is enacted at deeper and deeper levels of the inner being. When the journeyer assumes the blindfold for the Confrontation, the journey deepens. I think of the Confrontation as the transformation from the Hero-candidate to the Initiate, the one who is about to take the initial step into the other world. In order to take that step, however, the journeyer has to go through the Confrontation with his or her resistance here at the threshold.

To the Individual Journeyer:

Study this chapter, and then use Alternate Form 1, below. Or, if you wish, write out your confrontation, as a dialogue, in your journal.

To the Guide:

In the afternoon session of the fourth day, the group divides up into subgroups of three or four. Each subgroup will work on its own, setting its own schedule, doing the Confrontations based on the form that you will give them. Generally, people have problems separating into groups. Sometimes the guide can help straighten that out, but I recommend that participants find their own way of dealing with the problem. It is my firm conviction that the groups tend to sort themselves out according to some sort of order. That is to say, people will radiate toward others of the same level. Those who are able to plunge deeply will find each other, while people who are going to work at a less emotional level will group together. Alternatively, however, I have recently begun letting chance sort out who works with whom. I write numbers on pieces of paper, put them in a hat, and let each person choose one at random. Participants can then look at what chance has given them as an additional bit to incorporate into their stories.

In an early version of the Hero's Journey, the Confrontation was quite theatrical. There were five people in a group. One person was the leading actor, another played the guide; the substitute played the role that the actor was not playing. The other two improvised a little musical background, giving the ambiance of a Chinese opera. This is very exciting. I recall an especially moving Hero's Journey in Germany in which we used this mode. The Hero, a woman, was a delicate, sweet, soulful innocent who wore a white dress and had as her Instrument of Power only a pair of Indian meditation bells. The Demon was a huge monster that stood at the gateway of a horrible battlefield, scarred with wounds of war. It was clearly Germany after World War II. The Demon shrieked at the Hero to go away. It was terribly moving to see that the Demon loved the Hero and didn't want her to have to confront the horrors and the realities of war. The woman who was playing the substitute looked so like the leading actress that it was as if twins were talking to each other. With the others playing music behind, it could have been televised as a play. Finally, the Hero, with her innocence and simplicity, began to ring the bells. She rang them for a long time—it must have been ten or fifteen minutes—and as she rang them, the Demon remembered that she used to play the piano before the war. This contact, by way of music and sound, brought the two together. The woman admitted later that she was the daughter of Nazis and had always experienced a deep conflict, in that she loved her father and her mother and hated what they stood for. She could not love her country because she so hated what it had done. This memory of the transcendent quality of music finally melted the Demon and allowed her to show her love to the Hero and let her know that her real concern was that she never have to face that kind of terror and devastation in her life. But the Hero needed to confront the truth. And the Demon, like Mother Germany, wept and opened her arms to the Hero, finally allowing her to come into the place of horror and heal it with her simplicity and with her love.

At that time I was using slightly more theatrical devices for the Confrontation. If you want to use such a device and have sufficient time for a group of five or six people to work together, it can be extraordinary. But I recommend that you work in groups of three or, at most, four.

It is important to realize that the additional members of the subgroups are there to intensify the inner atmosphere of the person working, not to be entertained. The work is not a performance for others, but an internal drama. Up until this point, even though there has been internal processing, the challenge has ultimately been to reveal. In both the Heroes' Banquet and the Demon Dance, part of the element of risk has been to show themselves as Hero, to show themselves as Demon in front of the others. But with the Confrontation, people put on blindfolds and the direction of the journey moves inward.

The Confrontations continue until the beginning of the first session the following afternoon. I recommend that the groups set their own time schedules within this period. That allows them an afternoon, an evening, and a morning session. If they need more time, they can work it out. I recommend that they begin and end each session with a moment of holding hands and chanting. This gives each individual session a feeling of completeness.

Once they have started working, you, as guide, simply go from group to group to oversee them. If you want to make suggestions, do so as unobtrusively as possible. Make suggestions to the guide and not to the person who is working, unless the guide asks you to do so or you feel that you have to do more than make a suggestion. Remember, the person working in the blindfold is in another reality, and your voice can be shocking. So it is very important, if you are going to intervene, to do so subtly.

It is a lovely, intriguing experience—far better than television!—to walk from one scene to another: to see in one room a magnificent, colorful drama taking place between highly articulate, archetypal personae, while in the next room Hero and Demon, with naked chests, are demolishing each other with fists and barbaric words. In another they confront each other while sipping tea, in yet another they pass business memos across a huge conference table. Each Confrontation reflects the nature of the person who is working and of the call that person has received.

To the Journeyers:

I like to think of myself as a safari guide. I have told you what kind of clothes to wear, what kind of mosquito repellent to use, what kind of film to load your cameras with, or perhaps what kind of ammunition to use in your rifle. We have spent some time getting ready for the journey. Then we all packed into the van and set out for the field. Maybe we stopped along the way and had a few drinks at the local bar, and then got back in the van. Now here we are at the edge of the jungle. That's where the wild things are! This is when I tip my hat, salute you, and say, "Goodbye, I'll see you later," because this is the time when you take full responsibility for your work. However, out of the richness of my experience as a safari guide, I would like to talk about Demons and Heroes and what sometimes can happen at the entrance to the Land of Miracles.

First of all, it is entirely possible that you may kill your Demon. If you do so, don't just leave your demon's body lying there at the Threshold of Adventure. I can assure you that the Demon will rise again and stalk you, because the Demon is as much a part of you as the Hero. Both of them are you, and you cannot kill your self. You can kill the self-destructive form the energy has taken, but not the energy itself. Remember, in this particular drama, it is an aspect of you that has taken on the name of Demon. You experienced through the Demon Dance the power and vitality and beauty of that part of yourself. So why would you want to kill it? Yes, destroy the negative impulse toward yourself, but transform the energy. However, you may need to experience your power to kill that which is killing you, and the Hero may kill the Demon. If you decide to do so, take your Instrument of Power and wave it over the body. The Demon will transform itself into something you can reincorporate: something you can eat, breathe, or drink. Take back the power of the Demon without the pain. Leave the pain at the cave mouth, not the Demon.

The worst of all possibilities is to avoid the Confrontation altogether or to do it all as a mental exercise. The more involved you are in your body, the better it is. Above all, do not try to plan the Confrontation. Let it happen by itself.

Any kind of relationship between the Hero and the Demon is possible. They can make an agreement or a contract; they can come together as friends or become one. You might discover after some time that they have something in common. Maybe they are both brave. Or maybe each wants something from the other. If they have something in common or want something from each other, you have terms for a contract, some sort of agreement that will be beneficial to both parties.

The Confrontation takes place until both parties are satisfied. If the Demon is not satisfied with the final moment, then you are not satisfied. It is very important to remember that. The Demon is not an enemy ultimately. The

Demon is a part of you that is maligned and needs to be satisfied, just as the Hero needs to be satisfied. Once upon a time, when I was doing the process in Ireland, a woman who had been working for a long time on her Confrontation came to me all smiles and said, "Well, I finished my Confrontation and I feel wonderful!" "What has happened to the Demon?" I asked, and she replied, "I have the Demon in a little green bottle that I carry with me." I asked, "How do you feel inside the bottle?" and she replied, "Oh, I can't stand it! I'm claustrophobic!" So I said, "Go back and continue the Confrontation until both parties are satisfied."

Sometimes, in the middle of the Confrontation, a childhood or some more recent biographical scene may appear. Do not avoid it. Go into the scene and act it out in the same way that you are acting out the Hero-Demon Confrontation. Play all the characters in the scene (yourself, mother, father, lover, and so on); express whatever needs to be expressed and, if possible, see if you can come to some sort of resolution. If resolution is not possible, at least experience the scene from all perspectives. When you finish that, come back to the threshold. One time a woman's Demon appeared as a huge spider suspended at the entrance to a cave. When she looked at the face of the spider, she realized it had her mother's face. This took her back to a scene in her childhood when her mother was forcing her to do something she didn't want to do. She went back and began exploring that scene. Suddenly, in the middle of the scene appeared her collie dog, who was her best friend as a child. She then took on the character of the collie dog and found, through the dog, the things she needed to express to her mother. After she expressed from the point of view of both the child and the dog all that she needed to express to her mother, she became her mother and experienced the impact of this expression as well as her mother's concerns for her health. When she returned to the cave mouth, she saw the spider as a minuscule creature she could carry with her on its thread as a helper for the rest of her journey. So, no matter what you do, always bring it back to the threshold.

You might consider that the Demon stands at the doorway to the subconscious. He has at his beck and call all of the magical forces and powers of the unconscious. It's almost as if he were holding a nuclear weapon as he stands there waiting for the Hero. For this reason, I have attempted to give the Hero as much help as possible. The Hero has the Instrument of Power and can call upon the Spirit Guide. The Hero also has all the other Heroes who gathered at the Heroes' Banquet. If you as Hero need help, all you have to do is call upon any of these resources and they can come to help you. However, since every character in the drama is an aspect of you, you simply take on that role, whether your Spirit Guide or another one of the Heroes, or take your Instrument of Power in your hand and give yourself the help that you need. The Confrontation is a form of Gestalt process, and in the Gestalt framework you play all the roles in your own drama.

Sometimes it is very effective to look deeply into the eyes of the Demon and try to discover what is beyond that terrible facade. Look deeply, you might be surprised by what you find. Behind every Demon is a hurt little child. Sometimes dramatic changes take place when that discovery is made. There can be as many resolutions of the Confrontation as there are people in the group. I never cease to be amazed by the genius of the creative unconscious.

THE CONFRONTATION

1. The first step is to contract the roles. The person who is going to do the work is the leading actor. This person contracts the other two or three people in the group to play the following roles:

Guide/Facilitator: The guide's function is to facilitate the Confrontation. As guide, you do not take over the power, nor are you responsible for the resolution. Rather, you are there to make suggestions and to keep track of the form of the Confrontation. It is important to remind the leading actor to make use as much as possible of the whole body so the drama does not just take place in the head. Suggest the use of sound from time to time, body posture, and change of roles from Hero to Demon. Keep the two roles communicating with each other. Any time a question is asked, suggest a change of roles to find out the answer. If the leading actor has been in one role for a long time and you are wondering what the other role thinks or feels about this, suggest a change of roles. It may be necessary from time to time to discuss the process with the leading actor, but don't enter into complicity with him. For example, if he says, "I don't like the way the Demon is looking at me," say, "Tell that to the Demon." This keeps him involved in the process. If you look on it as a play, you are like the director. You keep the interaction going and remind the Hero of his resources.

Substitute: The third role is the substitute. This is something that we do not usually do in Gestalt process, but I have found from my acting background that it can be very powerful in helping people experience their Confrontation more fully. The substitute plays the role opposite the one you, the leading actor, are playing. The substitute imitates you as much as possible. If you express yourself as the Demon and then change roles to respond as the Hero, the substitute will play the Demon, imitating you, so that you can hear the Demon from the Hero's point of view. Hearing the substitute imitate you intensifies the experience. Since you are wearing a blindfold, you do not see the substitute. You are in the world of the Hero and the Demon. But there is an actual presence in front of you. If there is some physical contact going on between the Hero and Demon, the substitute can act that out wherever possible. So if the Hero is taking the Demon's hand, you don't have to imagine that hand, you have a real one to touch.

Ordinarily, the substitute will respond any time there is a change of roles, unless the leading actor is so involved that he or she does not need the substitute. The substitute can repeat any of the lines that were said to him as the last role, but he does not create his own speech. The substitute is always a mirror, a reflection.

Protector/Support: If there are four people in the group, the fourth position could be the role of the protector or support. The leading actor is blindfolded, and needs to be protected against walking into walls or bumping into furniture. The protector keeps the leading actor safe from injury. If the leading actor needs to beat on a cushion, the protector provides one. If he or she wants to record the Confrontation on a cassette, the protector-support person could also take care of that.

The Leading Actor: The leading actor always makes the decision of whether or not to take the suggestion of the guide. If the guide is over-guiding, the leading actor can say that. You as leading actor take the responsibility for making sure that your drama is as full and complete as possible. It is very important to use your body as fully as possible. I encourage you to do the process standing up so you can move your whole body. You limit yourself when you do not move anything but your head and hands, and if you remain seated the tendency is to cut yourself off from the pelvis down. The Confrontation is done in a blindfold. You are not doing it for your group. You are doing it for yourself, and everyone on your team is there to help you intensify the inner experience of your drama. If they are doing something that is not appropriate for you, say so. As the leading actor, take responsibility for getting what you need.

2. Step number two is to put out your artworks and share them briefly, for ten or fifteen minutes. Do not spend the whole of your confrontation time talking about your artwork.

3. Put on your blindfold, get into zero position, and do your Fool's Dance, including the new posture of the dedication of the Instrument of Power. As you

are doing it, you tell your story. You do not have to say much, because they can see your postures. You just go through your Fool's Dance telling your story up to now. Then come back to zero and describe the scene at the threshold; describe what is happening with the Hero, what is happening with the Demon, and the threshold itself.

4. In the No theater of Japan there is a small bridge called "the flower walk," which the actor crosses to get from his dressing room to the stage. As the actor enters onto the bridge, he is the actor in the costume of the character. In his long, slow walk across the bridge, he takes on the being, the essence, the soul of the character that he is playing, so that by the time he takes his first step on stage, the actor is no longer there, only the character. The following exercise is based on that theatrical concept.

Begin in the zero position. As the guide counts seven beats with a rhythmic instrument, you take on the posture of the Hero. At the zenith, you are the Hero. Then the guide counts seven beats backwards and you return to zero. You repeat the same process from zero to seven, taking on the Demon position. Return to zero. Now you are going to do this a second time, adding sound at the zenith of each character in order to awaken the heart center. Do it a third time, transforming the tone of the sound into a declaration, "I am the Hero (*Name*)!" "I am the Demon (*Name*)!" With the declaration of identity, it is as if you have just finished the flower walk and stepped onto the stage. The character is there and you are ready for the Confrontation.

5. The guide counts you back to zero and asks in which role you would like to begin.

6. If you decide to start as the Hero, the substitute takes the position of the Demon and you begin. Remember, it is not a gossip session between you and your guide about Demons and Heroes; it is a Confrontation between the two. You do not talk *about* the Hero, you *are* the Hero. It is important for the guide to keep a keen ear, to be sure it does not become a story about something, but that it is a drama with all the characters participating in the here-and-now.

7. Continue the Confrontation until you reach a conclusion that is satisfactory to both parties.

8. At the end the leading actor will make a statement that sums up the conclusion. Keep the statement brief, if possible not more than ten words. (If, after hours of work, there seems to be no resolution possible, then simply state the impasse as it exists, for example, "I will never accept you, Demon."

In the reframing this becomes, "I will never accept myself." If that is your truth right now, it is more important to experience the truth than to experience a Hollywood ending. Also, there is another exercise following that may help.)

9. Reframe the statement of the conclusion in I, myself, here-and-now language. The entire process of the workshop until now has been to separate warring aspects of the personality in order to discover ultimately how they can be brought together in a new relationship. The Hero is you and the Demon is you. Reframing the statement clarifies the experience of the reintegration. For example, if the last statement is, "I can heal you, I can love you," from Hero to Demon, rephrased in I, myself language that might become, "I can heal myself, I can love myself." The word "can" is very helpful because it makes it a possibility in the here-and-now, whereas "will" demands a rigid program for the future.

10. Coming out of the drama is as important as the drama itself. The existential statement is your return to the here-and-now. As you remove your blindfold slowly, let your eyes gradually open and integrate the colors of the place where you are with the colors of the fantasy world. Take a moment to not only look at your partners, but to really see them. Then make your final statement to each member of your team. The statement becomes a mantram, a phrase that you can repeat over and over to yourself in your everyday life to recall this moment of transformation.

11. Terminate your contracts. During the Confrontation you contracted to be in a very special relationship with the members of your team. They have been in service to you as guide, substitute, and protector. It is necessary to terminate the contracts in order to return to an absolute peer relationship. The best formula is for each person to say, for example, "I am no longer your guide, I am Frank."

12. Give feedback to each other about how you felt, in your function as well as personally. Close by holding hands for a moment and chanting.

THE CONFRONTATION: ALTERNATE FORMS

Alternate Form 1

This is a short form of the Confrontation that can be used by individuals working alone or in weekend group work. Here, the Confrontation is done as a dance. In order to do this dance-Confrontation, it is necessary that the postures for the Hero and the Demon have a certain quality to them. The Hero must be reaching toward the goal, so that in the posture you feel this aspiration with your whole body. The posture of the Demon must be stopping that aspiration. It is good if you can work with a partner who can be protecting the space while you are going through the dance. Move back and forth between the two roles with the same meditation given in step 4 of the longer form, so you get into the feeling of the Hero and the feeling of the Demon. Then put on some music and dance out the Confrontation using words, sounds, and whatever else you need to fully experience it. The partner is there to bring cushions to beat on, to protect your space, and maybe even, like a shaman, to encourage you with a rhythm instrument. When the Confrontation has reached a satisfactory conclusion, sit down. When ready, share with your partner what you have discovered, formulating the final statement and translating it into the I, myself here-and-now framework.

While the more elaborate Confrontations are certainly subtler, deeper, and more literary, this dance-Confrontation can be very powerful. The integration of the Hero and the Demon can take place in the blinking of an eye, it doesn't actually need four hours!

Alternate Form 2

Another possible form is a follow-fantasy that can either end with the final statement at the end of the Confrontation or continue on through to the Reward. The participants work in dyads with the Workbook, which pretty much details the process. The leading actor puts on a blindfold, reclines on a mattress, and calls up the image of the Threshold of Adventure. She enters into the drama, allowing it to unfold in the eye of her mind and, from time to time, enters into the various characters. The other person facilitates, making suggestions by watching the Workbook. This is a little complicated because it calls for the facilitator to translate the material in the Workbook, which is not intended as a guide but as a response to the process. In this approach the guide also acts as a scribe, taking notes on the other's process. Or it is possible to record this entire segment of the journey on a cassette. This can be very helpful because so much transpires.

Other Forms

You may find some other form for the Confrontation based on your background and interests. The more spontaneous the Confrontation is, the better. Be sure the Hero and the Demon express everything they need to express to each other before they attempt to heal the relationship. Leaping to the resolution of the relationship before the roles have had a chance to express themselves is like putting a Band-Aid over a deep wound.

Also, remember to explore your resources. Consider how the Instrument of Power might help in resolving the Confrontation. The Spirit Guide sees the relationship between the Hero and the Demon with compassionate detachment and frequently presents the exact tool to unite them in the form of the Instrument of Power.

The Confrontation gives people a chance to work in depth. Thus far you have been preparing the ground for this moment. So make sure that you allow sufficient time to work it through as fully as possible. In a group the guide should always be available in case of problems.

CHAPTER 10
The Land of Miracles

Ram Meditation, Day 5

To prepare for your entrance into the Land of Miracles, it is valuable to clarify the final existential statement that you came to at the end of the Confrontation. Remember, the existential statement is expressed in these terms: the Hero is "I"; the Demon is "myself." The statement is expressed: "I . . . myself . . . here-and-now." Your statement should not be too long or complicated. If you experience a rush of emotion when the statement is simplified, you know it has touched the core.

To the Guide:

After the meditation and the passing of the flame, have each person say the final existential statement. You can help them to clarify their statements, but don't impose. If a participant has worked out a statement that is very precise, exactly what he or she wants, let that be. Clearly, that person has discovered his or her own meaning, and your way of expressing it may not be helpful.

Some people go through the Confrontation and neglect to come to an existential statement at the end. They are so relieved to have come to a conclusion that they don't seek out the statement that summarizes it. Help them do that now. The statement facilitates the crossing over from the fantasy world to the here-and-now. Besides, they can test the validity of the statement in their own being by expressing it before the whole group.

OPTIONAL EXERCISE: INTEGRATION OF HERO AND DEMON

If, in the process of the Confrontation, you have not come to a satisfactory conclusion—if you have been unable to integrate the Hero and the Demon—I recommend this process. It is a psychosynthesis exercise. Draw a triangle on a piece of paper and hang it on the wall. Put on some soft, rhythmic music and begin with some warmup exercises.

To the Guide:

Everyone can do this exercise. Some may find that they discover a higher level of integration than they were able to accomplish in the Confrontation. Others, however, may not want to do it, being satisfied with what they found for themselves. If everyone has come away from the Confrontation complete, I would not do this exercise. Do it only if there are people who are devastatingly incomplete. It is a way of bringing everyone to a comparable level of integration so that they can enter into the Land of Miracles. After the warmup exercises, give the following instructions.

To the Journeyers:

Face the triangle and let your body come to rest in the zero position. Look at one of the corners of the base of the triangle and recall your Hero, allowing your body to take on the posture of the Hero. Fully experience that posture. Move in the posture and recall the qualities of the Hero. What kind of person is the Hero? Dance this. Feel it in your body. As you are dancing, recall a time in your life when you felt this way. Let a scene emerge from your life in which you had this feeling. Experience this scene as fully as possible, with all your senses, all the while dancing in the posture of the Hero. Take a deep breath, exhale, and as you do so, come back to zero.

Now let your eyes crack open a bit and look at the other point at the base of the triangle. After a moment, close your eyes, go inside, and take on the body of the Demon. Feel the quality of the Demon in your back, in your arms, in your face, in your whole body. Move as the Demon. Experience the power and the vitality of the Demon. While dancing as the Demon, once again recall some scene from your life when you felt this way, when you felt like your Demon—that power or vitality or rage. Recall and relive that scene while continuing to dance in the body of the Demon. Then take a deep breath and let yourself dissolve down to zero.

Now as you listen to the music, simply dance back and forth between the postures of the Hero and the Demon and imagine yourself going up the two sides of the triangle toward its peak. As you are dancing, and your body takes on qualities of Hero and Demon, let the fragments of the scenes move through your mind. Keep moving up the sides of the triangle, flowing back and forth between Hero and Demon, between heroic scene and demonic scene, until you reach the top of the triangle. There let your body flow until you find a movement that synthesizes Hero and Demon. At the same time, allow a new scene to emerge that brings these two energies together at a new level. Feel what that is in your body. Feel what part used to be Demon, what part used to be Hero, and what the new element is, the new quality, the new experience. Allow a phrase: "I can," "I am" . . . Complete the phrase. Then take a deep breath, dissolve back down to zero, and sit down.

To the Guide:

Spend some time sharing, then put on some music and begin the Fool's Dance.

Fool's Dance

To the Journeyers:

Recall your Confrontation and dance through it briefly. Select three of the most important moments. Create postures for them. Then polish them into simple postures that you can add to your Fool's Dance. Finally, add a fourth posture that expresses your resolution. It can either be what you discovered with your triangle meditation just now, or the resolution with which you ended your Confrontation. As you take on that posture, say your final existential statement so that you can feel how the posture contains within it this statement of existence.

Now we will go through the Fool's Dance from the beginning. Zero-Me-Home-Lifework-Beloved-Self-Miracle-Spirit Guide-Hero-Battleground—*exploding into*—Demon-Instrument of Power-Confrontation 1-Confrontation 2-Confrontation 3-Resolution of the Confrontation. Do this several times and then sit down.

To the Individual Journeyer:

I recommend that you read through the following material, put on an hour-long tape of emotionally evocative but unfamiliar music, and, after doing the Fool's Dance, lie down and let your imagination go where it will. You might have another tape recorder near you to speak into in order to record your adventures. I recommend that you do this in a blindfold.

To the Guide:

Now you and the group are ready to enter the Land of Miracles.

I prefer to divide the Land of Miracles from the Supreme Ordeal because so much richness can be discovered in the follow fantasy of the individual. However, if time is short, the two can be combined.

If you do the Supreme Ordeal as a breath process, you must introduce it before going into the experience of the Land of Miracles. The cautions, the questions, and the suggestions concerning the breath process must then be included in the introductory talk.

Since the way you handle these two aspects of the process will depend on your situation, it will be necessary for you to study this and the following chapter completely before proceeding.

There are three possible ways to conclude the Land of Miracles experience:

1. Anima-Animus fantasy: Use this if you do not intend to go directly into the Supreme Ordeal.

2. Supreme Ordeal of Breath: Use this if you have had training and experience in guiding such breath processes.

3. Supreme Ordeal Guided Fantasy: Use this if you have not had training in the breath process or if you choose not to use it.

The participants will explore the Land of Miracles in dyads, with one person lying down and the other as guide. The guide will take notes and give suggestions from time to time, but will pretty much stay out of the way and allow the fantasy to unfold without too much intervention. Encourage people to participate as much as possible with whatever images they see in their Mysterium, interacting with them as they would in Gestalt process. Although they are lying down most of the time, some may prefer to sit up and talk to the characters in their Mysterium. They might even want to get up at the foot of the mattress and move a little bit. Sometimes people imagine themselves riding on horses or ducks, swimming, dancing, flying. Because they are lying down on the mattress, they are safe to do whatever they need to do. Encourage them to allow their bodies to follow the fantasy as fully as possible without interfering with each other or doing something that would be dangerous for themselves. One of the purposes of the guide is to protect the one who is working.

Select a series of different music tapes. They should have some variety, but should not be too well known so that people do not get distracted by familiar melodies. Then, with one or two cassette players, compose a sound collage of as many different kinds of music and sound as you can. Improvise, based on what you see happening in the room. However, do not drown them out with the sound.

If you prefer not to do this kind of freeform improvisation, find a single piece of music that provides a good background and let people follow their own paths. You can do it with no sound whatever as well.

Sometimes I walk through the room with incense or with a portable tape recorder, finding ways to create effects for people to incorporate into their Land of Miracles. Sounds made by other members of the group can also be part of their stories. If someone is shouting, that can be incorporated into the story rather than experienced as a distraction—it is all part of the Mysterium.

The first person will do it for about an hour. Then bring that person out and reverse the roles. It may be that one person works this afternoon and the other works in the evening, depending on the size of the group. If time is limited, go directly from the Mysterium into the Supreme Ordeal, so that the two processes are brought together. I much prefer to separate them, however, because this gives the people a chance to go more deeply into the spontaneous images that come in the Mysterium.

To begin the Mysterium, they are all in their places, with their partners to protect them.

To the Journeyers:

This is the place where anything is possible. There is a Land of Miracles deep within each one of us, within the deeper levels of the subconscious. As in dreams, anything is possible there. In the Land of Miracles, the most extraordinary beautiful visions can occur or hell can break loose. You may find yourself soaring through divine ecstasy or falling into the most horrible experience of your life. All of our potentials exist within each one of us. So it is hard to say what you are going to experience in that magical land.

In the Land of Miracles, the Hero may encounter some tests. That is why it might be hell at some point. If you encounter tests—if suddenly some Demon image appears—deal with it in the same way that you did at the entrance to the Mysterium. However, you will not be up and moving around. You will be lying down on a mattress. That is so you can let yourself soar. It is hard to fly when you are standing. When you are lying down, you can let yourself go into other extraordinary spaces.

Your Land of Miracles is what you make it. Once I worked with a woman who said of her Mysterium, "Nothing's happening, it's just blue." I asked, "What could be blue?" and she said, "The sky." "Look beneath you," I said, and she responded, "Oh my God, I'm flying!" And her Land of Miracles continued from there. As soon as she accepted what was happening as her Land of Miracles, it became miraculous. She was flying through the sky looking down on towns and rivers. But as long as she decided nothing was happening, nothing was. Your Land of Miracles is what you make it, and you make it what you accept it to be. If you accept that where you are is a magical land and begin to explore it, you might find some extraordinary things.

Put on your blindfold and spend a few moments describing to your partner your magical threshold . . . Those who are about to enter, stand up so you can do the Fool's Dance as preparation. We will do it once again as a story:

Once upon a time, there was a person named Me (*posture*). I walked down a long flight of stairs into a room with four doors, and opened the first door, marked "Home." This is the way I felt about what I experienced behind that door (*posture*). The second door was marked "Lifework." What I found behind that door made me feel this way (*posture*). The third door was to the room of the Beloved. Entering into that room made me feel this way (*posture*). The fourth door opened into the room of the Self. There I found images of myself that made me feel like this (*posture*). When I returned to the central room, I found a Throne of Miracles, and envisioned this Miracle (*posture*). Along came my Spirit Guide (*posture*), who led me on the path to the discovery of my own Heroic Self (*posture*). However, as I became a Hero, I felt all of my resistances contracting my body until my body became a veritable Battleground (*posture*), out of which exploded the Demon of my own Resistance (*posture*). Fortunately, my Spirit Guide gave me an Instrument of Power, which I dedicated to the fulfillment of my quest (*posture*). A fierce Confrontation took place between the Hero and the Demon. The first phase of the Confrontation was like this (*posture 1*). That was followed by the second phase which felt like this (*posture 2*), followed again by the third phase which felt like this (*posture 3*). The Confrontation resolved itself in this way (*posture*). And now I stand before the threshold of the Land of Miracles.

Now lie down on your mat, take a few deep breaths, and prepare in your imagination to enter into the magical place. Is there a door there? Can you see beyond the threshold? On the other side of that magical threshold things are very different from the way they are here. No one has ever been there before. You are the first. Take a step closer. If there is a door, reach out and push it open. Take another step until you are standing on the threshold itself. Sense the texture of the air. Let your foot slide forward and feel what is beneath you. Take your first step into the Land of Miracles. That breath you are taking right now is the first breath that has ever been breathed in this magical place. The sound of your footfall is unique in this magical place. The images that rise up around you, the feelings in your body and the taste in your mouth, the sounds that you hear, the odors that you smell, are all for the first time. It is like the birthday of creation, and you are there. Enter your Land of Miracles. Follow your path. Follow it wherever it leads you. This is a magical place. You can dance, you can fly, you can run, you can swim, you can crawl. You can mount some creature that will carry you to wherever you need to go. Follow your path. Take it where it leads you. Do this in silence for a while. Experience it without words for a while. Then when you are ready, staying in the fantasy, report something of what is happening to you to your partner so he or she can record it for you. If tests arise, confront them. Enter into your magical land and discover it for yourself.

To the Guide:

At the completion of this exercise, you may either go into the Anima-Animus fantasy, below (if you want to bring the group out of the Land of Miracles), or go on either to the Supreme Ordeal of Breath or the Supreme Ordeal guided fantasy, which are given in the following chapter.

Guided Fantasy: Anima-Animus

To the Guide:

The guided fantasy of the Anima-Animus is done at the end of the Mysterium fantasy, before the Supreme Ordeal. It is a nice way of ending the Mysterium fantasy; it brings people back into the here-and-now and it also keeps the miraculous unfolding.

It can be done either individually or with the group as a whole. If you find that a number of the participants are involved in tests, dealing with things that need to be finished, then it is impossible to do it for the group as a whole. If it is a small enough group, you can go to each individual. But if everyone has come to a kind of conclusion, you can lead everyone together. The same form can be used for both.

———

To the Journeyers:

Let go of words and follow the image you are dealing with right now to some conclusion. (*Allow time.*)

Partners, place your hand over the heart of the person lying down, and with your fingers do a slow opening gesture. You who are lying there, feel the opening of your heart. As your partner is doing the gesture, imagine that from your heart arises a kind of vapor, a kind of luminescent mist. Take a few breaths and feel that. Gradually, in front of you, this luminescent mist slowly takes a form and there appears before you what might be called your Divine Opposite. If you are a woman, it will be the form of a man; if you are a man, it will be the form of a woman. This form is your inner being, the best friend that you could possibly have. Your Divine Opposite. Let the vapor take on the face and the shape of that Divine Opposite. And if, by chance, the shape is not satisfactory to you, tell it to change; it is your best friend. That being can continue to change until he or she finds a form that is pleasant, agreeable, and satisfactory to you. Let that form emerge. Let that being look deeply and warmly into your eyes. That being has come from within you and is now manifest outside of you, looking lovingly at you; knowing you, knowing what you need; knowing about your life, about the issues that you are dealing with in your life. Imagine that being reaching out toward you to take you by the hand.

Take the hand of your Divine Opposite. At the same time, your real partner will take you by the hand and lead you on a journey. Imagine that it is your divine partner who is taking you by the hand, and with your eyes still covered, gradually rise and go with your partner. Your partner will guide you outdoors and sit you down in the environment and leave you. Be alone there for a while. Then gradually, when you feel ready, take off your blindfold and softly intermingle the lights of this reality with the Land of Miracles and look for a message there. Your partner has taken you to a place where you will find a message that will be very important in your life.

CHAPTER 11
The Supreme Ordeal

Ram Meditation, Day 6

FOOL'S DANCE

To the Journeyers:

Before you begin the Fool's Dance today, put on some music and simply review what happened for you in your Mysterium. Dance through it, recall what happened, what kind of images you perceived, what kinds of tests you may have confronted, how you traveled. Take some time dancing out your memory of your Mysterium until finally you find, once again, three postures that summarize for you the three most important moments in your Land of Miracles. (*Give people time to do this.*)

Now we will do the Fool's Dance once again. Zero-Me-Home-Lifework-Beloved-Self-Miracle-Spirit Guide-Hero-Battleground-Demon-Instrument of Power-Confrontation 1, Confrontation 2, Confrontation 3-Resolution-Mysterium 1-Mysterium 2-Mysterium 3. Do that several times until it is comfortable, and then sit down.

Today you confront the Supreme Ordeal of the entire journey. If you recall, at the beginning I said that after the person hears the call, the first level of resistance appears in relationship to the environment surrounding that person, that is to say, the family and friends, the living condition that militates against responding to the call. That is generally dealt with by having the encouragement of a friend who says, "Go ahead and take a chance with your life; answer this call." The second level of resistance we met at the entrance to the Land of Miracles in the confrontation with the Demon of Resistance. That's the inner protector that stops us from doing things we might want to do because it is afraid that we might ruin our reputations or be hurt in some other way. The Demon has reasons for stopping us from going on with our aspirations.

Now we are coming to the Supreme Ordeal. We can look on the Supreme Ordeal as the source of all that resistance, the most basic fear that is stimulated by this call, the image of the primordial terror that haunts us and frequently stops us from exploring and taking the risks to continue our evolution. For example, just as the Buddha, meditating beneath the Bo tree, was about to enter nirvana, a whole army of illusions—all the attachments that bind human beings to their sufferings—suddenly appeared before him, rushing at him, challenging him. This was his Supreme Ordeal, which he overcame by remaining in his Buddha nature in the face of these terrible things. So now you, too, must confront your Supreme Ordeal.

To the Guide:

In this formulation I allow an entire day for the Supreme Ordeal and call it Day 6. If more time is needed for the development of the Hero or the Demon, however, this day can combine the Supreme Ordeal with the Mysterium.

In the Supreme Ordeal, the Hero meets the deepest level of resistance to the call. It is a confrontation with the source of the fear, whatever the person's basic fear happens to be. Frequently, it is the fear of death. Formerly, I did the Supreme Ordeal as a separate process. After the Heroes had entered the Mysterium, they had a vision of their own death. This was followed by a four-day process in which they examined all the aspects of death and dying with the idea that on the evening of the third day they would die. On the morning of the fourth day they were resurrected back into the Land of Miracles, where they discovered their rewards. However, I have since separated the two processes and now call that the Death and Resurrection process.

To the Guide and to the Individual Journeyer:

Following are two approaches to the Supreme Ordeal, the breath approach and the guided fantasy approach. If you have not had experience or training in intensive breath work, either Reichian background, rebirthing, or Holotropic Breath work, I recommend that you use the guided fantasy.

The Breath Process

To the Journeyers:

The process that I have designed is in two parts. The first part is a guided fantasy that leads you into the Supreme Ordeal. This is followed by an hour-and-a-half to two-hour intensive meditation on breath with music. You will stay with the images of the Supreme Ordeal fantasy. However, I will guide you into a soft, relaxed, deep-breathing process that will become more and more intense as you suit the rhythm of your breath to the rhythm of the music. The breathing meditation will go on for about an hour and a half to two hours. You may experience many different things. You may have extraordinary transcendental visions, or experience what seem to be reincarnational memories. Perhaps you will experience your birth. Or it may be nothing more than two hours of breathing. The important thing is to let it happen and not to force yourself. It is a meditation on the rhythm of breath in relationship to music. You may experience the evidence of hyperventilation, such as numbness around the lips or contraction of the arms and hands. If you are too frightened by these effects, you can always slow your breathing or even stop the process. However, if you keep breathing with the rhythm, the blocks will dissolve and your body will soften again. The important thing is to adapt your breathing to the rhythm of the music and stay with that.

What are the two times in life when the struggle for breath is crucial? When you are born and when you die. Intense breathing meditation can recall these experiences, when your body was close to death or the experience of birth. This may be frightening. The function of the music is to help you breathe through even the most terrifying experiences.

You may find yourself becoming emotional. Express that emotion. The whole workshop has gradually led you to the place where you are able to allow the depths of your emotional expression. If you feel tension in your body, it may be that you have not resolved some emotional issue. By allowing expression, your body should finally relax so that you can feel totally present in the moment. So if emotion comes, allow it expression. When you are finished with that, come back to breath. The point is always to return to breath.

You are building up a charge, and at certain times that charge may need to release itself. This may manifest in little movements of the body, the previously mentioned paralysis, the trembling of your jaw, pounding, hitting, kicking—any number of different ways. Surrender to it all. Allow your body to do what it seems to want to do. The more you allow it to free itself, the more release you will experience as a result of the process. Muscular blocks in the system may become painful. You can ask the person who is working with you to employ some pressure there. Breathe to the pressure and let out sound. Generally, the block will dissolve and the breathing will soften again. You can ask your partner to put pressure any place that you feel pain or tightness and then breathe to that place. However, if your partner is putting too much pressure, just say stop. In that way you always have total control over what is going on.

When you oxygenate the system, sometimes you do not need to take a breath for a while. This is fine; don't. However, from time to time, the sitter will lean down and breathe softly into your ear to remind you to go back to breath. Do so when you are ready.

It is also possible, of course, that none of these things will happen. In the deep-breathing experience, anticipate nothing other than the process of breathing with music.

Considerations

If you have cardiac or kidney problems, do not push yourself. I recommend that you use what is called "circular breath," breathing more slowly and attempting to equilibrate the duration of the inbreath with the duration of the outbreath. Do not go beyond what is comfortable. If you are pregnant, I recommend that you also use the circular breath, because there is some question about what can happen to the placenta in a hyperventilation process, whether or not there is a stoppage of the blood supply to the infant. So do not go into hyperventilation.

Role of the Sitter

As sitter, your function is to protect your partner and his or her space, to provide whatever your partner needs, if necessary to remind your partner to continue breathing by breathing softly into his or her ear, and to give pressure when he or she asks for it to relieve tension or pain. It is a good idea to have the following available: some Kleenex tissue, a towel if your partner needs something to twist, cushions to hit, and a small glass of water to moisten your partner's lips. At the end of the process, your partner may want some physical contact. Do not give more than he or she asks for. In other words, do not take over; don't over-mother, and particularly, do not seduce the person you are working with. Think of yourself as a priest or priestess of breath, so if your partner wants contact, let the impulse come from your partner and not from you.

There is a Zen story about a man who wanted to be enlightened. He went to a Master and said, "I would like to be enlightened." And the Master said, "Fine, just go into the next room and breathe." He went into the next room and breathed for a long time. It was kind of boring. He just sat there breathing and breathing. But he felt better, he felt good. The breath got him a bit excited. After a couple of hours he came to the Master and said, "I feel good. Am I enlightened yet?" The Master said, "Just keep breathing."

So he went back and breathed some more. After a little while, his mouth began to prickle and his lips puckered involuntarily. His fingers felt paralyzed, with the thumb stuck to the middle finger. His arms contracted into what felt like chicken wings. And all the while he felt like he was covered with ants. What a very strange experience! The more he breathed, the more intense it got. Then suddenly, all the tension dissolved and he felt wonderful. He felt released. He jumped up and ran to the Master, wreathed in smiles, and said, "Master, I went through an extraordinary experience. Everything tightened up and I felt paralyzed, and now I feel wonderful! Am I enlightened yet?" The Master said, "Just go next door and keep breathing."

So he went back and continued with his breathing. He was filled with memories of his childhood. He remembered a time his mother tried to give him castor oil. He didn't want it, and she forced his mouth open and poured it down. He got angry at his mother and screamed. He beat up some cushions, imagining they were his father; he wept for his sister, his brother, and his friends. He reexperienced all the emotions of childhood, after which he felt absolutely wonderful, cleansed, released and exhausted. Drenched with sweat, he had lost pounds in the process. He thought, "Surely I am enlightened now!" He ran to the Master and said, "Master, I screamed, I yelled, I cried, I laughed, I was frightened, and now I feel wonderful. Am I enlightened yet?" The Master said, "Just keep breathing."

Once again he returned to breath. After a long, long time, he remembered being in his mother's womb, all soft and warm and slippery. He felt himself floating, until suddenly the edges of his universe pushed in on him. He had grown too big and was imprisoned in his mother's womb. The shocking implosion of contractions terrified him until he found his way out into freedom. Suddenly, he awakened to light and air, sound and gravity, everything that comes with the moment of birth. He felt reborn. "I must be enlightened now!" he thought. "I have been born again!" So he jumped up, as soon as he could stand, and went running to his Master. "Master, I have been reborn! I must be enlightened now!" The Master said, "Just go next door and keep breathing."

Once again he returned to his room of breath. This time he got angry and bored. The more he breathed, the more bored he got. After what seemed an eternity, he found himself riding a horse in the American Civil War as a Confederate soldier. He remembered dying. He went beyond that. He remembered being a slave in ancient Egypt, building the pyramid at Giza. He kept regressing farther and farther in his evolutionary development. He remembered being a wolf, a crab, a crustacean. He even remembered being an amoeba! He was so thrilled at having gone through the evolutionary process that he thought, "Now I know everything about what it is to be incarnated on the planet Earth." So he leapt up, all but flew to the Master, landed in front of him, and said, "Master, I must be enlightened now! I've gone through the whole evolution of all Earth species!" The Master looked in his eyes and said, "Just keep breathing."

So one more time he returned to his room. He breathed for three days and three nights. He felt really discouraged, and just as he was about to give up (perhaps he even did give up), the heavens opened, the clouds parted, and a ray of Alleluia sunlight filled the room. He saw Jesus and Mary, he saw Vishnu and Hanuman, Quetzalcoatl and Buddha, the gods and goddesses of ancient Greece, of Egypt, and of the Watusis. He saw every possible divine image imaginable waving at him, throwing flowers, and singing, Hosanna! Hosanna! Hosanna! He was absolutely enraptured! In the middle of the experience, he leapt up and ran to the Master, saying, "Master, gods and goddesses waving, welcoming, Hosanna! Alleluia! I am absolutely sure that I am enlightened now!" The Master looked at him for a long moment and smiled. Finally, the Master said, "Just keep breathing. This, too, will pass."

The point of this story is this: Don't get stuck in the manifestations; just keep breathing. That's the whole process, just keep breathing. Any or all of these images may make an appearance. The physical things, the birth memories, reincarnational memories, even animal and crustacean memories, all sorts of things may come. Just keep breathing and go through the process. The whole purpose of the breathing exercise is to purify through release all that stands in the way of your experience of transcendence, what might be called the state of grace. In order to reach that state you must go through all the levels of resistance, physical, emotional, and mental. So don't stop at the images, don't stop at the feelings, don't stop at the sensations, just keep breathing.

To the Guide:

Dr. Stanislav Grof has made a series of tapes that give musical shape to his Holotropic Breath process, and this process is similar to his. You might use these tapes, or do what I enjoy doing, which is to have two or more tape recorders on a mixer so that you can blend different kinds of music together to create your own score. The basic structure of the music is as follows: begin with something slow to ease into the deep breathing process, and then gradually introduce a rhythm. The rhythm should escalate little by little until it is quite intense. This continues for about three-quarters of an hour to an hour. Follow this by a fifteen-minute to a half-hour dramatic piece that builds to a climax, such as "Death and Transfiguration" by Richard Strauss, or Smetana's "The Moldau." After this, play some spiritual music that can lead them to an experience of peaceful transcendence, such as some of the sweet spiritual music of Vangelis in his suite "Heaven and Hell," the soft choir sounds of Peter Gabriel in "The Passion," or "The Lark Ascending," by Ralph Vaughan Williams. Then, after about a half-hour of this, play something familiar, such as the Pachelbel "Canon in D," to bring them back into the room.

In the construction of the musical program, I think in terms of the four levels of the birth process. The beginning is the cosmic union with the mother. The second, the intensive rhythmic phase, is the contractions. The third, the dramatic phase, is the birth itself, and the fourth phase is after the birth has taken place and the child is in the world. The final, familiar music is a way of bringing them back into the room.

FOOL'S DANCE

To the Journeyers:

Once again, I will lead you into the meditation with the Fool's Dance, as I did at the entrance to the Land of Miracles. One partner now puts on the blindfold, while the other is protecting.

Once upon a time there was a person named Me (*posture*). I walked down a long flight of stairs into a room with four doors. The first door was marked "Home," and this is what I felt when I discovered what was behind that door (*posture*). The second door was called "Lifework" (*posture*); the third, "Beloved" (*posture*); and the fourth, "Self" (*posture*). When I closed the door of the Self, I found a Throne of Miracles in the center of the room. I sat down and wished for this Miracle (*posture*). Along came a Spirit Guide (*posture*), who led me along the path to discover my own Heroic Self (*posture*). Becoming a Hero, I felt the tensions building in my body, turning it into a veritable Battleground (*posture*), out of which exploded my Demon of Resistance (*posture*). However, my Spirit Guide gave me an Instrument of Power, which I dedicated to the accomplishment of my quest (*posture*). A Confrontation took place between my Heroic Self and my Demonic Self: the first stage of the Confrontation felt like this (*posture*), the second phase like this (*posture*), and the third like this (*posture*). The Confrontation resolved itself in this way (*posture*). I entered into the Land of Miracles, and my path took me through various experiences. The first was like this (*posture*), the second like this (*posture*), and the third like this (*posture*).

GUIDED FANTASY: SUPREME ORDEAL OF BREATH

Now lie down on your mat, and take a few moments to be there in your Land of Miracles. Recall your Land of Miracles, the images, the pictures.

To the Guide:

If you are going directly into this fantasy from the Land of Miracles, introduce the Supreme Ordeal with these words: "Let go of words and just follow whatever image it is that you are dealing with right now to some conclusion, and let it finish." Give about five minutes for the completion of this image. Then continue as follows.

Imagine that you are on that path right now. The path begins to wind downward into the darkness until you come to the entrance to a cave. Over that cave you see written: "The Cave of the Supreme Ordeal." You enter into the darkness. It is cool, but safe. And there, somewhere in that cave, you discover a couch covered in black velvet. Lie down on the couch. It is dark, but it is safe. You are about to confront your Supreme Ordeal of Breath.

(*Sitters: Take your hand and place it high on the chest, just beneath the neck of your partner.*)

Take a few moments to breathe softly; if you are working with a partner, his or her hand is resting lightly on your chest at the base of the neck. Breathe to that hand. As you lie there breathing, above you a scene appears. It is the image of the most frightening scene you can possibly imagine, the thing that terrifies you the most. There it appears above you. Keep breathing and observe that scene. Take a few moments to communicate the scene to your partner. (*Pause.*) Now, breathing very slowly, imagine yourself entering into that scene, step by step, looking into each of the images that terrify you. Always keep breathing. Stay in the scene. Remember as you look at this frightening image that you have dealt with the Demon of your Resistance at the threshold; remember that you have your Instrument of Power and you have the support of your Spirit Guide. You have everything you need to be able to go through this Supreme Ordeal and complete it. With that in mind, continue to explore as deeply as possible this frightening image that you behold in front of you.

(*Sitters: With each breath let your hand gradually drift down the chest, downward toward the stomach, continue past the navel, down to just above the pubic bone. Little by little, with each breath, let your hand descend.*)

As you feel the hand descend, let your breath move downward as well, so that each breath becomes deeper, deeper, deeper, until finally you are breathing all the way down into your belly.

(*Sitters: When your hand reaches the abdomen, place the other hand high on the chest.*)

Initiates, let your breath fill the space between the two hands on your body. At the same time, let the hinge of your jaw relax. Let it relax until your jaw hangs open. When your throat is open, let it relax so that you are able to take in a maximum amount of air with a minimum of effort, filling the space between the two hands that warm your body. (*Allow time, five to ten minutes, then introduce rhythm into the music.*)

Gradually, notice the pulse in the music. Little by little, adapt your breathing to that rhythm. At first your breathing may overlap the rhythm, but slowly let it adapt itself. While observing the frightening images before you, let yourself enter into the Supreme Ordeal of Breath. Allow crisis, but do not push yourself. And continue breathing whatever happens. Surrender to your body, surrender to your breath. Allow sound, but always come back to breath. Surrender to the images, surrender to the feelings, surrender to the sensations, surrender to the music, and keep breathing . . .

In a Group: To End the Process

If you are still in process, allow yourself to continue breathing until you feel your body soften and relax. If you have completed the process, breathe normally and stay with the images you are observing. You have now completed your Supreme Ordeal. You have gone through it, it is finished. Now you can allow yourself to enjoy the images that are there for you. . . . And then, when you feel ready, make some contact with your partner. Gradually, return to the room and share with your partner what has happened for you in the process.

To the Guide:

You might have a sharing during the afternoon session, and then reverse the roles. Since this day is devoted entirely to the Supreme Ordeal, I recommend a quiet session in the evening. Have the participants do a drawing that expresses their Supreme Ordeal, or give them the evening free to draw and interact with each other. Tell them to create a posture for the Supreme Ordeal sometime before the morning session.

ALTERNATIVE SUPREME ORDEAL: GUIDED FANTASY

To the Guide:

If the Supreme Ordeal is being done as a separate process, have the participants choose partners. The person who is working does the Fool's Dance in a blindfold (as above) and then lies down on a mattress.

To the Journeyers:

Now you are on your path in your Land of Miracles. Follow that path and discover where it takes you. Let your body move with it. Just ahead you behold a small hill. As you approach it, you feel a kind of trepidation, because you know that you are approaching the hill of the Supreme Ordeal. On the other side of that hill is the most frightening scene you can imagine. Before you reach the top of that hill, take some time to breathe deeply, all the way down into your belly. And whatever happens, whatever you see, always keep breathing. Also, be aware of your resources: your Instrument of Power, the integrated Demon, and your Spirit Guide.

You reach the top of the hill. What do you behold? Look at the scene. Breathe. Be aware of how you feel. When you are ready, communicate the scene to your partner. (*Pause.*) Let go of words, because now it is time to enter into the scene. Step by step, approach the scene. Discover how you can confront these images. Confront everything that is there, and keep breathing.

Spend some time experiencing this Supreme Ordeal. Feel it in your body. Make sound. Confront whatever it is that you are afraid of. Take as long as you need to experience this Supreme Ordeal, and then, step by step, leave it. . . . Take a few moments to breathe and experience having accomplished this task. When you are ready, come back into the room, share the experience with a partner, and create a posture for the Fool's Dance that summarizes the Supreme Ordeal.

To the Guide:

Pennel Rock, who is presently leading Hero's Journey groups, gave me this suggestion for going more deeply into the Supreme Ordeal fantasy. Pennel forms the group into subgroups that act out each individual's Supreme Ordeal, allowing the individual to play out the various roles.

Ritual closing

CHAPTER 12
The Reward and the Return

To the Guide:

After the Supreme Ordeal, participants often feel that the journey has finished. Especially if it is done as breath work, they can enter deeply into emotional process and experience gratifying results. It is also true that in the Mysterium people have already received a series of gifts. So when you say, "Now we are about to approach the place of the Reward," they may say, "What do you mean? I've already got my reward; I feel completely satisfied." They may have received different messages and gifts, however, this is the Reward that gives meaning to the whole journey; it is also the path from the journey back to their everyday lives. Just as the Instrument of Power connects the Hero and the Demon, the Reward connects the internal world with the external world. It gives them a device whereby they can apply what they have learned on the inner stage to the issues of their everyday life. This final phase of the journey, from the Reward to the return to Homeground, is structured to prepare that path. So remind them that no matter what happens, they are still in the Mysterium until the end of the journey.

At this point in the process, I am concerned about an overabundance of images. The Reward fantasy contains the finding of the Reward, the departure of the Spirit Guide, the return to the room with four doors, and the decision about the concrete steps to be taken when they get home. This is followed by the meditation on the opening of the heart, the placing of the Reward in the heart, and the expansion of the heart field. Particularly when doing that meditation, you need to be aware of the receptivity of the group. In seven days participants are likely to be more open than in two days. You may need to modify the end of the heart meditation based on what you see happening in the faces of the group members.

As the heart opens to the world, the meditation takes on a spiritual-political character. At that point I focus on the hot spots of the world. You should know where these are so it can become a meditation on healing the troubled places on the planet. In the expansion out into the cosmos, it transforms into a strictly spiritual meditation, opening the consciousness as wide as possible. This last step I leave to your discretion and your diagnosis of the group.

Generally, this day ends with an early afternoon feedback session to complete the workshop. The Reward-Return process is a guided movement meditation preceded by the whole of the Fool's Dance, and it completes the mythic drama. For this final meditation, you might choose either a piece of music that you can use throughout or a series of pieces that you can play to highlight different features. Also, have some music ready for celebratory dancing at the end if it seems appropriate. Some groups end in silence.

Ram Meditation, Day 7

To the Journeyers:

The Reward is the summation, the lesson of the journey. It indicates in symbolic form what your journey has meant. It is the psyche's way of saying, "That is what it has all been about." Dr. William Arendson-Hein came to do the Hero's Journey with me when he was in his seventies. He was one of the first people to use LSD therapeutically and was a bit preoccupied with spiritual matters. For his Reward he received a stone. At first he was very disappointed. But the inside of the stone was crystal. He said that what he had to discover was the treasure of the earth, like the crystal in the stone. That was his reward! For years he had been investigating the treasures of the spirit, and now it was time for him to look into the treasure of the earth. He is an incredibly wise and loving man, and I was very moved by this revelation.

You too may find something that is a bit of a shock to you. It may not be the diamond of all wisdom. It may be a flower petal or a drop of water. It may be a very tiny thing. Accept what the psyche gives you. Whatever you receive, no matter how small—a blade of grass or the petal of a flower—accept it as the Grail of your particular journey. In the Parzival legend of Wolfram von Eschenbach, the Grail provides the nourishment that each one needs. Your Reward is the nourishment that your soul needs to make itself whole at this stage of your evolution. Receive it with reverence. If you recognize it to be the Grail, it is the Grail. If you reject the gift that is presented to you, then you are rejecting the purest message from your deepest self. The second choice can never be as clear and as pure as that first one. So appreciate what you are given as your gift. If you do, I can assure you that gift will serve you well.

When you began the journey and you sat on the Throne of Miracles, I could have said, as I used to, "Think of a Miracle, the most extraordinary Miracle you can imagine." I have since become convinced that your subconscious knows what you need far better than your conscious mind. However, it is difficult in the first session to allow the subconscious to pour into your consciousness without criticism and correction. By now, after several days of deep penetration and spontaneous pouring, the psyche can speak freely. It may reveal to you a longing unknown to your conscious mind. Frequently, the Reward illustrates not only that deepest longing, but, at the same time, the means to accomplish it. It is the completion of this journey and the call for your next journey, leading you to the manifestation of this Reward in your everyday life.

Your final task is to discover how to take what you have experienced in your journey into your ordinary life. Once you find your Reward, you will take it back to Homeground, into each of the four rooms, and there discover how it can heal those four aspects of your life.

When you have looked at this, you will be asked to think of a concrete step that you can take in each of those four areas to bring your Reward into manifestation: something simple and real. Let's say that you receive a magical palette that allows you to create your own vision of the world, painting the world as you like it. When you take your magical palette through the door marked "Home," you notice that the walls suddenly change color, the drapes are different, everything is much brighter than it was before. Well, a concrete step that you might take is to get a painter's book of colors and decide what color you'd like to paint the walls. Or call a painter and get an estimate. Or decide what color you would like to dye the drapes. You don't have to go out and rent a castle in Spain because you have decided you would like to change your apartment! Do something simple. Change the curtains on the kitchen door. That's a simple, concrete step. Once you've done that, you might decide to change the curtains over the kitchen sink. The simple, concrete step can lead you, step by step, moment by moment, to the fulfillment of your vision. But it can only lead you to the fulfillment of your vision if the step is simple. If you decide you are going to buy a Spanish castle, you will soon be saying to yourself, "Where did I get that idea?" and you'll go out for a pizza and forget all about it. If the first step is simple, it is likely that there will be more.

At the end of the Workbook, you will find a contract for you to make with yourself to take these concrete steps. It is a good idea to discuss this contract with somebody you can call if you are having trouble following through. Remember, in any journey the first level of resistance is environmental, and the way to get through that resistance is to have someone come along and say, "Go ahead, you can do it." If you are working in a group, you have a network of Heroes, of friends, of compatriots who can help each other in their souls' manifestation.

Now you will go through the whole Fool's Dance, including the posture you created for the Supreme Ordeal. The dance will lead directly into the meditation of the Reward. At one point you will sit down, as you did in the Homeground meditation. So you might want to have a cushion nearby so you can sit comfortably. Start at zero and I will tell it again like a story, only this time instead of simply taking the postures, allow yourself to dance through them freely.

RETURN EXERCISE 1: REWARD AND RETURN MOVEMENT MEDITATION

Once upon a time there was a person named Me. I went down a long flight of stairs into a room with four doors. The first door was marked "Home." I looked inside, and this is the way I felt about the images of Home. The second door was called "Lifework." This is the way I felt about the images of Lifework. The next door was called the room of the "Beloved," and this is the way I felt about the love in my life. The next door was marked "Self," and this is the way I felt about the symbols of the self that I found. As I closed the door marked "Self," I came back into the room with four doors, and in the center of the room I discovered a Throne of Miracles. I envisioned this Miracle. Along came a Spirit Guide who led me to find my own Heroic Self. As I became my Hero, I could feel all the tensions in my body, the restrictions that I put on myself. My body became a veritable Battleground, and out of this Battleground exploded the Demon of my own Resistance. Fortunately, my Spirit Guide gave me an Instrument of Power, which I dedicated to the accomplishment of my quest. A fierce Confrontation between the Hero and the Demon took place: the first phase was like this; the second like this; and the third like this. After a time the battle resolved itself in this way. I was able to cross the threshold into the Land of Miracles. In this magical land, I had many different experiences. Dance out your Land of Miracles. Let the three postures of your Land of Miracles flow into a dance. (*Pause.*) Finally, I came to the Supreme Ordeal [of Breath], and this was my experience.

Now you have completed your Supreme Ordeal and you are still in your Land of Miracles, following your path. Take some time to experience where you are. (*Pause.*) Just there, ahead of you, appears a temple gleaming in the sun. It is the place of the Reward. Go to the temple. Enter. Inside you will find a golden altar. A beam of sunlight is shining on it. On that altar is your Reward. Look for it. It's there. Take some time. (*Pause.*) When you are ready, pick up your Reward. Experience it, let it fill your being. Breathe it. Taste it with your whole body and soul, the Reward of your journey. Let yourself be with that Reward. Dance with it. (*Pause.*)

Imagine that as you savor your Reward, out of the beam of light your Spirit Guide appears, for the final time of your journey. That guardian spirit brought you here to this journey in the first place and has been guiding you throughout, finally bringing you here to the temple of the Reward. Holding the Reward in your hands, look into the eyes of your Spirit Guide and ask, "What is the meaning of this Reward?" And the guardian spirit will tell you. Ask your Spirit Guide, "How can this Reward illuminate my life?" and your Spirit Guide will show you a scene from the future in which this Reward has manifested itself in your life. Take some time to appreciate that scene. (*Pause.*)

Now it is time for your Spirit Guide to leave you. Look deeply into each other's eyes and experience what you feel for each other. Finally, your Spirit Guide says, "Goodbye for now. But any time you need me, all you have to do is call, because I am part of you." And with that the Spirit Guide embraces you and departs.

Lo and behold! Where the Spirit Guide stood, you now perceive a door. Go through that door. You will find that it leads you back to the original room with four doors from which you began the journey. Enter that room. Once again in the center you find the Throne of Miracles. Sit down on that throne holding your Reward in your hands. Ask yourself, "How does this Reward relate to the original Miracle I envisioned?" Is it the original Miracle, or is it perhaps something you can use to accomplish that Miracle? Take some time to meditate on the connection between this Reward and your original vision. (*Pause.*)

You look up from the throne and you notice that you are facing the door marked "Home." That door slowly swings open. Magically, your Reward lifts from your hands and floats through that door. Behold what happens to the images of home with the addition of this Reward.

Do the images change, become more colorful, or take on a new light? As you observe these changes, ask yourself, "What simple, concrete step can I take in my actual home that will manifest this reward there?" A simple, concrete step in the everyday world—a telephone call? A statement to your family? A new set of drapes? "What action can I take to manifest my reward in my home?" Imagine yourself taking that step. Even while seated, allow your body to take on a posture that suggests you taking that simple, concrete step in the everyday world to manifest your Reward. Are you willing to do that? Feel if your body is willing to take that step.

Once more, let the Reward come back from the room marked "Home" and return to your hands. Now imagine that the throne rotates so that you face the door marked "Lifework." The door opens. The Reward lifts and floats through the door to influence the images of Lifework. Behold what happens to these images with the manifestation of that Reward. (*Pause.*) What simple, real thing can you do in relationship to your work to manifest your Reward in that area of your life? Simple, real; nothing too big, something possible. Take on a posture that expresses that concrete step. Feel how your body responds to it; is your body willing to take that step? (*Pause.*)

Once more the Reward returns, the door closes, the throne rotates to face the room of the Beloved. Again, the door opens, the Reward rises from your hands and floats into that room. Behold what happens to images of love. (*Pause.*) Again, imagine a simple, concrete step that you can take in relationship to your love to manifest that Reward there. Visualize that step. Let your body take on a posture that suggests it, and feel whether your body will allow you to manifest this Reward in relationship to your love. (*Pause.*)

Once more, let your body come back to rest. As the Reward returns to your hands, the door closes, and the throne rotates to the fourth and final door, the room of the Self. The door opens. Once again the Reward lifts and enters into the room of the Self. Behold what happens to the symbols of the Self with the addition of this Reward. Once more ask yourself, "What simple, concrete step can I take to bring this Reward into manifestation in relationship to this most important aspect of my life, myself? Something especially for me." Let yourself take a posture that suggests something you can do only for you. Explore how your body feels when you do something for yourself, how you breathe when you give yourself this Reward. Are you willing to do that? (*Pause.*)

Once again, the Reward returns to your hands and you sit there on the Throne of Miracles. Soon you will leave this magical place and return to the everyday world. The Threshold of Adventure has become the Threshold of

Return, and as you cross it you must leave the magical powers behind. However, you take with you the gift of yourself and your experience.

Before leaving, spend a few moments meditating on the beat of your own heart. Imagine that your heart, like the petals of a rose, opens with each breath, with each pulse. Let the rose open, petal by petal, until finally it exposes its golden center. (*Pause.*) At the same time, the Reward in your hands becomes smaller and smaller, transparent and filled with light. It becomes a dewdrop of light. Place that dewdrop, like a diamond, in the golden center of the flower of your heart. (*Pause.*) Allow the petals of your heart to gently embrace the Reward. Let it fill your heart with its own special quality of light, cleansing and healing old wounds. The light extends beyond your heart, filling your whole chest with that special light, unique to you, cleansing, blessing, healing. Let it fill the whole of your body, radiating from the source at the center of your heart the unique blessing that is you.

You can let it extend even beyond your skin; let it expand outward, touching the other people in the group, blessing them with the Reward in your heart. Let it continue to expand downward into the earth, upward into the sky, and outward in all directions, blessing all the creatures that walk or crawl, that swim or fly in and out, above and through the dark and glorious body of Great Mother Earth.

Continue to let it expand. Let it bless the whole region that you are in. Let it expand to the country, blessing, healing with the Reward in your heart. Let it continue outward to the surrounding countries, to the continent, upward to the north, to the south, to the east and west, to the entire hemisphere that you are in, blessing, healing, particularly the troubled spots as well as familiar places. Let it keep expanding until it covers the whole of the planet Earth and all the creatures in it, blessing and healing, but always remembering that the blessing and healing originates from that Reward in your heart.

Why stop there? Let it go beyond, outward, to touch the moon, to touch Venus and Mars, the planets of the solar system, all the way upward toward the sun, and outward, outward, expanding yourself, your gift, your special quality to touch all the galaxies, the whole of the universe, and all the universes in the cosmos, letting that special Reward that is you extend to infinity. You are the source—you, the source of that blessing, reaching out to the whole of the cosmos, blessing every creature that exists. Share yourself, share yourself, share yourself with the whole of creation. (*Pause.*)

Just as you can expand yourself all the way out to the edges of the cosmos, so can you return. From infinity to the cosmos, through the universe, through the galaxies, the planets, this solar system, back to the planet Earth, to this hemisphere, this portion of the Earth, this place, this room, this group of people, this body. Bring it back all the way to that tiny point of light nestling in the golden center of your heart. There it stays for you to take with you when you go because it's you. You are your own special gift. There is no other like you in the whole of the universe.

Your Hero's Journey is finished. Your new journey is just about to begin.

> *You are free to fly!*
> *Free to live, free to die!*
> *You are free to be who you are.*
> *Who you are is free, that's who you really are!*

RETURN EXERCISE 2: FINAL ARTWORK

Make a drawing similar to the Homeground drawing. Now, however, the circle in the center is the Reward, and the images in the four rooms should suggest the transformation that has taken place and the concrete step that you are going to take in order to manifest the Reward.

RETURN EXERCISE 3: THE CONTRACT

Sit down with a partner (*the individual journeyer should sit down with a trusted friend*), and discuss what you discovered in your Reward. Using the form at the end of the Hero's Journey Workbook (see Appendix III), work out a contract with yourself, witnessed by your partner, as to what simple step you will take in each of the four areas of your life to manifest your Reward. Come to an agreement with your partner about how you can help to support each other in the accomplishment of these simple steps.

RETURN EXERCISE 4: COMPLETED FOOL'S DANCE

To the Guide:

To begin the sharing session in the afternoon, have the group members complete their Fool's Dance with the five final postures: Reward, Return

Home, Return Lifework, Return Beloved, Return Self, and the Transformed Me that completes the journey. The four Return postures can represent the concrete steps that they have decided to take or the transformations they experienced in each of the rooms. Leave it up to them. You might divide the group in half and tell the Fool's Dance story while one group performs for the other, and then reverse.

———

To the Journeyers:

Once upon a time there was a person named Me (*posture*). I went down a long flight of stairs into a room with four doors. The first door was marked "Home." I looked inside, and this is the way I felt about the images of Home (*posture*). The second door was called "Lifework." This is the way I felt about the images of Lifework (*posture*). The next door was called the room of the Beloved, and this is the way I felt about the love in my life (*posture*). The next door was marked Self, and this is the way I felt about the symbols of the Self that I found (*posture*).

As I closed the door marked Self, I came back into the room with four doors, and in the center of the room I discovered a Throne of Miracles. I envisioned this Miracle (*posture*). Along came a Spirit Guide (*posture*) who led me to find my own Heroic Self (*posture*). As I became my Hero, I could feel all the tensions in my body, the restrictions that I put upon myself. My body became a veritable Battleground (*posture*), and out of this Battleground exploded the Demon of my own Resistance (*posture*). Fortunately, my Spirit Guide gave me an Instrument of Power, which I dedicated to the accomplishment of my quest (*posture*). A fierce Confrontation between the Hero and the Demon took place: the first phase was like this (*posture*); the second like this (*posture*); and the third like this (*posture*). After a time the battle resolved itself in this way (*posture*). I was able to cross the threshold into the Land of Miracles. In this magical land I had many different experiences: Mysterium 1 (*posture*), Mysterium 2 (*posture*), Mysterium 3 (*posture*). Finally, I came to the Supreme Ordeal of Breath, and this was my experience (*posture*). Afterward, I found a Reward (*posture*). I took that Reward back to the room with four doors and this is what I experienced in relationship to Home (*posture*). My experience in relationship to Lifework was like this (*posture*). And this was my relationship to the Beloved (*posture*). And, finally, my relationship to Self (*posture*). I have now completed my journey, and this is the way I feel about myself now (*posture*). Return to zero.

RETURN EXERCISE 5: GROUP SHARING

To the Guide:

Allow people to talk about what has been important in their experience. It may be necessary to deal with separation anxieties, feelings about leaving each other, and the need to express resentment and appreciation.

To the Individual Journeyer:

In your journal, write a final statement that sums up the experience for you. What meaning do you find for yourself and your life out of this experience? How do you evaluate it?

To the Journeyers:

After an experience such as this, people often find themselves in a very exalted state. As we have been discovering in the course of the journey, every time we allow ourselves the pleasure of feeling good about ourselves, we tend immediately to oppress ourselves. The same process may take place now. Depression is an attempt of the organism to complete itself, to bring itself back to ground. Often we have the mistaken notion that the way to get back to ground is to go beneath ground into depression in order to finally establish the median between the two polarities. If, in a few days, you find yourself tending toward depression, do a bit of karma yoga—some physically active, simple task that you can complete and appreciate. The task you choose should be something you like to do: washing dishes, cleaning the house, or organizing your bedroom are all appropriate tasks if you enjoy them. Working in the garden is one of the best because it is working directly with the earth.

However, the depressive state need not necessarily be bad. From this position you can rest and integrate the work you have done. If that is the case, then use that time to rest and integrate rather than to punish yourself with self-criticism and self-destructive behavior.

Images from the process may return over the next six months to two years. Sometimes an image will disappear and then suddenly, in an unexpected moment, come back. I recommend that you allow this. Enter into the image to find out what the information arising from the deeper mind is, and what you need to integrate at this particular moment. Don't dismiss the images as silly, obsolete, or corny. Respect the symbol and let it speak to you. Whatever the psyche is doing, it is doing to some end; trust the process.

For me, the most positive ending of the journey is when people say, "I am excited to go back to my life to discover how I can apply these principles." Then I know that you have experienced the journey totally and are satisfied. You know what a journey is and you can experience returning to your everyday life as the next level of the journey.

Go, and may the peace that surpasses understanding overtake you on your way!

CLOSING RITUAL

To the Guide:

At the final moment, when all the discussion has taken place and people have had a chance to express themselves and closure has been made, bring the candle into the center of the group for a final ritual. Sit together holding hands. Look at the candle, close your eyes, and chant one more time as the final statement of the group. (For an alternate closure, see the final Ram Meditation.)

To the Journeyers:

To experience separation, hold hands strongly and then, in a very slow, meditative way, let the hands relax their grip. While this is happening, meditate on letting go of the experience, of each other, of the moment, of all contact. Finally, when the hands have separated, bring them together palm to palm, coming back into contact with yourself. Take a few moments to experience that contact with yourself and then open your eyes. All come together in the center to blow out the candle, and with the blowing out of the candle, the ritual is completed.

EPILOGUE:
The Return

*I*n this, the final chapter, I would like to remind you that the Hero's Journey does not really end. It goes through a cycle, concluding itself with the call to the next cycle . . . and so it goes, on and on. Recent events in my life have brought home to me forcefully the cyclical nature of the journey we are all on, and I would like to share these insights with you now.

During the course of writing this book, I lost two of my most precious relationships: my partner, Stanford Eugene Cates, to whom this book is dedicated, and my best friend, Janet Zuckerman; both died, one of AIDS and the other of cancer. In the same period of time, the Berlin Wall fell, the relationship between Russia and the United States changed dramatically, Bangladesh suffered terrible hurricanes and floods, the United States went to war in the Persian Gulf. The ecological disaster of the burning oil fields in Kuwait continues even now. Throughout these events I kept working on this book.

After Stanford's death, however, some sense of purpose seemed to go out of my life, as frequently happens with the death of a partner. In groups I began to present my heroic quest by saying, "For ten years I traveled with a fellow knight. We guided others across their thresholds all over the world. Then one day my companion contracted the plague and now he is gone, and I experience a hole in my heart. My quest is to find the Lacrima Christi, the healing crystal that can fill the hole in my heart."

Thankfully, as I worked on this book, my sense of purpose returned, and I feel that the completion of this book is my Lacrima Christi. Like the German woman whose Hero was the little girl ringing her bells at the threshold of the war-torn world, I am carrying the healing crystal that is the Hero's Journey into the midst of the devastated countryside. This book is an attempt to pass the crystal on so that others may look into it and perhaps divine something about the future of being human.

I was conceived on an August night in 1930 in Detroit, Michigan, just after the financial collapse of the American economy with the Great Depression. That was a time of desperation, and for my parents to conceive me on that hot summer night has always impressed me as an act of hope in a time of despair. Whether consciously or unconsciously, I am the incarnate expression of the hope and love between my parents and of my parents for the world. I have always felt that my being reflects that pledge to the future that my mother and father took through my conception.

This book expresses that hope, especially now, as we approach the third millennium. At every millennium people have had apocalyptic visions of the end of the earth, of hurricanes and earthquakes and volcanic eruptions, of plague and war and massive destruction. These events are happening all around us, as they have been from the beginning of time. This book is my act of affirmation of our continuity into the twenty-first century.

In 1941 Joseph Campbell looked at a picture of a temple guardian, a lion-like creature with a monstrous face protecting the threshold to the divine, and realized, in a flash, that all Hero myths, Western and Eastern, were alike. He spent five years developing that concept into his book *The Hero with a Thousand Faces*. The creative process out of which this book has grown started then. When I was working in the theater in the late 1960s, I became involved in agitation propaganda against the war in Vietnam. I decided to study the soldier-hero intensively, to discover what motivates the man of action. I turned to the legends of Cuchulain, the great soldier-hero of Ireland, as told by William Butler Yeats. Through this study I came in contact with Campbell's work, and *The Hero with a Thousand Faces* stayed with me from that moment on. I read it over and over again. It had a permanent influence on my work. Finally, in 1972, I met Joseph Campbell at Esalen. As I began to develop the concept of the Hero's Journey process, I would frequently talk with him about how to formulate the material.

One day, after I had been working with it for several years, Stanford said to me, "Many people are copying your process and some of them are doing it without crediting you. You ought to write a book." However, that seemed impossible because of my own constant journey. When Stanford developed AIDS, traveling became unbearable. It was a great good fortune for us that Laurance

Rockefeller awarded us a grant. This made it possible to stop journeying long enough to begin writing this book.

All the way through the writing, I thought, "This book will prove to everyone that I am the father of this process." However, as I come to the completion of it, I realize that this is so much mental static. The real reason for writing this book is beyond my ken. It has something to do with giving into the hands of as many people as possible the tools of inner vision, of self-discovery, and of the awareness of their own path in relationship to the evolution of humanity. I am not the only one who is presenting these tools, but I can make my contribution. So instead of establishing my authorship of the process, I offer this form of my own experience as a possibility of helping others.

In the course of my own journey, I have had to walk through the depths of my own inner hell. In order for me to be able to guide others through their hells, I had to experience my own. But having experienced it, I can say, "It is possible to walk through it." This book is one of the paths.

I have attended thousands of threshold Confrontations over the years, and I have seen many versions of hell. I have come to realize that there truly are monsters in the psyche—species monsters, national monsters, regional monsters, and most vicious of all, our own personal monsters. They do exist. However, I am also aware that the way to deal with them is not to run away from them, not to hide from them, not to pretend they are not there, and not to kill them, but to look them straight in the eye. This regard changes something. It is as if a veil drops and some deeper truth is revealed. And maybe even in the heart of that truth is treasure. At least so it would seem with the various monsters that I've encountered. Often one discovers that what appears as an apocalyptic war to end all wars is nothing more than a lovers' quarrel. Certainly, I found that to be true at the personal level of the inner monster. But what is a regional monster or a national monster or even a species monster, but a gestalt of individual monsters? And so it seems to me that the way to heal the great monster that is eating us up, eating our planet up, eating our brother and sister species up is to heal the individual monsters one by one. In my heroic vision, my partner from Pluto and I were to come together and bring the keys that would gestalt human consciousness. Those keys are a series of individual encounters of people with themselves, encounters in which they find out, by contact with an archetypal image such as the Hero's Journey, that they are not alone: that they are individuals, but not alone, and that the process of separation is an act of will, a decision, and therefore a decision that can be changed.

The Greek mythic epics were recorded at the time when the Western world was moving from matriarchy into patriarchy. All the gods and goddesses and heroes and heroines at that time were dealing with this transformation. Matriarchy had exhausted itself, had deteriorated and become decadent, demanding human sacrifice for its promulgation and continuation. Now, within this last century of the second millennium, it seems to me that we are witnessing the disintegration of patriarchy. And we wonder in despair how our species can possibly continue when all our structures are built on quicksand. Our financial, political, and social structures have been built in a hierarchical way with the leader on top. However, the base that bears the greatest weight has begun to submerge in the quicksand of pollution, nuclear meltdown, depersonalization, and separation.

So part of the end of the millennium is the end of patriarchy. We cannot go back to matriarchy; we have outgrown that; it no longer works. We can't try to polish up patriarchy with some magical brush, because it is clear that that doesn't work either. We cannot leave the world in the hands of Mother and Father anymore. We've got to take responsibility for it ourselves. And that to me is the time of the child, the son and daughter who have broken their toys and discovered what it is to be human while crawling around in the muck. It is time for us to stand up on our own two feet and look around, saying, "This world as we know it is ending! What are we going to do about it?" Not, "What are Mother and Father going to do about it?" but, "What are we, brother and sister, going to do about it?"

I think that this is the call of the human species now. That is what is behind the civil rights movement, the feminist movement, the gay movement. They are all movements toward equality, to prepare us to say, "We're in this together! You and I, brother, sister." As children of the new millennium, we are being called to take responsibility for our home.

The reward of the Hero's Journey presents the *new* thing, the sparkling new level of consciousness that the human being is about to enter. It is as if we have suddenly pierced a hole into another dimension and are able to see the first glimmering of the whole next phase of life. I think that now we as the human species are beginning to see the glimmer that expresses the next millennium of our existence. And it's not easy, because it calls for us to be able to stand up for ourselves, like the Hero who can say, "Yes!" and who can say, "No!" If our gorge rises against something we see going on in the world, we need to have the courage to challenge it. And if we see treasure, we need to seek it, to nurture it. That treasure, pouring up from the subconscious of the species right now, is the treasure of brotherhood and sisterhood, the treasure of the child.

So at the same time, this book is an act of hope for the future, an act of faith in the human species in a time of apocalyptic despair; it is also a prayer, not to God, but to the deepest part of ourselves, that we may awaken and open our eyes and recognize who we are.

APPENDIX I
Ram Meditations

R am is a Sanskrit word that is the first syllable in the name of Rama, an avatar of Vishnu in the Hindu pantheon. Ram is said to be the peace that comes after the burning out of impurities by the seed syllable, *Rang.* It is also said to evoke courage. Mahatma Gandhi, at the moment of his assassination, spoke the syllable Ram as his last mortal word. It is said that one who speaks the name Ram at the moment of death goes directly into the light and quits the wheel of karma, no longer returning to the cycle of birth and death. So the sound itself is powerful. Baba Hari Dass said that you don't have to know the meaning of the sound for it to work its power; "the drum doesn't say anything and the people dance."

The chanting of the Ram in three centers comes from Tantra. I became aware of it through my experiences with Oscar Ichazo's Arica system. The meditation serves several purposes: It unifies the group by focusing attention on the candle; it directs the attention of the group members inward; it aligns the body; it calms the mind; and it is also a teaching device.

The chanting puts people into a receptive, peaceful state, facilitating access to the creative process. The disturbances of normal life are gradually peeled away, revealing the inner landscape of the journey.

You may find that you become so involved in the chanting of the Rams that you lose track of how many you have chanted. A good way to keep track is to count the knuckles of your index finger with your thumb.

I use a pair of Indian meditation bells that have a strong and sensitive resonance. They are made from a number of different metallic alloys that create a particularly vibrant sound. They are said to drive away the process of thought in the mind so that you can hear the voice of God speaking through you. I use these to set a tone for the preparation for the guided meditation.

RAM MEDITATION, DAY ONE

To the Journeyers:

Sit comfortably on your pillow. Find a position that you can maintain for a period of time with your back straight. If that is a problem, prop up the pillows behind you so you can maintain that position comfortably. Focus your eyes on the candle.

Think for a moment of what is actually happening, the physical facts: the transformation of solid matter, the wax, into liquid and gas takes place at such a speed that the result of that metamorphosis is heat and light or fire. Both the cause and the result of that metamorphosis is the flame. Therefore the flame of the candle becomes the symbol of the group, that possibility for transformation. It becomes the eternal flame that burns day and night throughout the course of the workshop. It also represents the group's integrity, its wholeness.

Maintain your point of focus on the flame, but become aware of your peripheral vision, so that while holding the candle as your point of focus, you can also see the person to the left of you. This trick of awareness demands that you soften your gaze. Allow your peripheral awareness to move to the next person on your left, continuing around the circle, still holding the candle flame as your focus. Be aware of the person across the room from you, and continue circling. Now you are aware of the person to the right of you. Become aware of yourself as part of this circle of people. Allow your peripheral vision to continue circling the room, always experiencing yourself as part of that circle. As you do that, you may find that your eyelids grow heavy, and the room begins to change color and shape. Finally, your eyelids close. Enter within. Without changing your breath, become aware of it: how deeply, how quickly, how easily, or with what difficulty you breathe.

Now center your awareness in your belly. Imagine in the cradle of your pelvis a golden globe of light, of the same color and intensity as the candle flame. Allow your breath to deepen so as to fill that globe of light. As you inhale, the globe becomes larger and brighter. As you exhale, the globe becomes smaller and dimmer. Meditate on that. (*Pause.*)

We are going to chant the sound Ram to that globe of light in the belly. The purpose of the chant is to awaken that center, to make it vibrate with the sound. The belly center is the center of the body, the balance center, the center of movement and of stillness. The sound Ram contains within it the syllable Aum. We chant it softly and deeply, feeling it vibrate all the way down in the belly.

Exhale all the air from your lungs. Inhale through the nose. And chant: RAUM. (*Repeat three times.*) And then breathe naturally, and listen to the sound of the bells. (*Ring them three times.*)

Now, in the center of your chest, in the area of the heart, imagine a second globe of light, smaller than the first, more brilliant, that responds to both the rhythm of breath and the pulse of your heartbeat. Breathe to that center and allow yourself to become aware of both rhythms, breath and heartbeat. Once again, we chant the Ram three times to that center. This Ram is higher in pitch and stronger; it is sometimes called "the roar of the lion," the lion in the heart.

Exhale. Inhale through the nose. RAM. (*Repeat three times.*) Again, breathe naturally and listen to the sound of the bells. (*Ring three times.*)

Now bring your attention up to the center of your forehead, the area of the third eye. Imagine a tiny pinpoint of light about two inches into the skull. It is brilliant and unwavering, like a beacon at the top of a mountain. This is the mind center, the center of thought, image, and memory. The sound of the Ram here is high in pitch; it might even be nasal. Use a high head tone. Go only as high as you can comfortably. Don't force the sound. You may hear a kind of buzzing, as if your head were suddenly filled with bees. You may also feel a vibration in the sinuses, around the lips, and in the nasal cavity. This sound awakens that whole center, the upper area of the mind, of the head, of the third eye.

Exhale. Inhale through the nose. RAM. (*Repeat three times.*) Listen to the sound of the bells. (*Ring three times.*)

Be aware of those three globes. They are stacked one on top of the other—the tiniest at the top, the largest at the bottom—giving the structure substance and balance, like a pyramid of light. Imagine that a ray of light descends from the point of light in your head, downward through your face and neck, downward through your throat and upper chest, plunging into the globe of light in your heart and uniting and balancing heart and head. If you need to adjust your posture so that the line is straight, do so. Allow the line to continue downward, through your chest, through your stomach, till finally it enters the globe of light in your belly. In this way all three globes are balanced and unified. Sit for a moment meditating on the three globes of light balanced and unified, your back comfortably straight, like a pyramid of light. (*Pause.*) Bring your attention once again to the globe of light in your belly, and chant one single Ram there to ground and terminate the meditation.

Exhale. Inhale through the nose. RAM. (*Ring bells once.*)

Gradually, come back into the room. Yawn and stretch your body to release any tensions that might be there from holding one position for so long.

To the Guide:

If the opening session has taken place in the evening, there may not be time to do the entire three globes. In that case do only the globe in the belly, so that the group has had some chance to unify and enter into the alpha space before beginning the Homeground meditation. (If you do only one globe in the evening, then use the meditation just presented for Meditation 2, including the ending of the following meditation beginning with the line: "Allow the line of light to continue downward into the earth.")

Ritual of the Changing of the Vestal

RAM MEDITATION, DAY 2

To the Journeyers:

Bring your attention to the candle. Allow your body to relax, maintaining an upright position with your spine. Once again, become aware with your peripheral vision of the group as a whole, with yourself included. Follow the circle with your peripheral vision around to the left, across from you, to the right, through to yourself, and around again. As you do so, allow your eyelids to grow heavier with each outflow of breath, and finally allow them to close. Become aware of your own breath right now without changing it: How are you breathing? deeply? shallowly? quickly? slowly? (*Pause.*) Once more, place your awareness in your belly. Let your breath descend to that globe of light in the belly, allowing it to increase on the inhale and decrease on the exhale. We will chant the Ram three times in the belly.

Exhale. Inhale through the nose. RAM. (*Repeat three times.*) Breathe naturally and listen to the sound of the bells. (*Ring three times.*)

Direct your attention to the rhythmic center in the chest. Imagine there a globe of light that responds to the rhythm of breath and the pulse of your heart. (*Pause.*) Recall that the Ram in the heart is higher in pitch and fuller.

Exhale. Inhale through the nose. RAM. (*Repeat three times.*) Then breathe naturally. (*Ring bells three times.*)

Bring your attention to that point of light about two inches behind the center of the forehead, and chant the high-pitched Ram.

Exhale. Inhale. RAM (*three times*). (*Ring bells three times.*)

As you did yesterday, allow that line or ray of light to descend from the point of light in your head through the face and neck, downward through the center of the globe of light in your chest; continue downward to the center of the globe of light in your belly. Balance all three globes on top of each other, unified by that line of light.

Today allow that line of light to continue downward into the earth, to go beyond the limits of your body, through the cushion into the floor, attracted by the force of gravity deep down in the center of the earth. Allow that light to push itself through the crust of the earth, downward through hidden lakes and streams, through stone and granite, through deposits of fossil fuel, through all levels of sand and mud that compose the crust and the inner layers of our planet, attracted always toward that point which is the center of the earth. Allow it to push its way through all those levels until finally it reaches that molten core. There it situates itself in the point of the center of the earth. Imagine it like the long stem of a flower, reaching all the way down into the center of the Earth, and crowned by those three globes of light: the flower of human evolution at this moment. And if you can take another perspective, realize that all of us here sitting in a circle in this room touch at that point in the center of the earth, like a bouquet of flowers, separate yet in contact with each other and with the earth. Sit with that meditation for a moment. (*Pause.*)

Thus, with that line of light attached to the center of the earth, the earth itself becomes the fourth globe of light. And rather than chanting, listen to the sounds around us as the chant of that fourth globe of light, the planet earth, our home. Listen to the chant of the earth. (*Pause.*) Allowing that ray of light at the root to remain planted at the center of the earth, bring your attention back to the globe of light in your belly, and we will chant one Ram to close the meditation.

Exhale. Inhale. RAM. (*Ring bells once.*) And once again, with each in-breath, allow your eyelids to grow lighter, until finally they open and take in the light of the room and the candle and the awareness of the group. Then stretch out your body and make spontaneous sounds.

Ritual of the Changing of the Vestal

RAM MEDITATION, DAY 3

To the Journeyers:

Once again, sit in a circle with your back straight, focusing your attention on the flame. Hold the flame as your point of focus, and allow your peripheral vision to take in the rest of the group. Start to the left and continue around the circle, coming around to the right and passing through yourself as part of the circle of people. Continue to circle around. As you do so, let your eyelids grow heavy with each outbreath, until finally they close. Pay attention to breath. Simply note your own breath, where you find yourself breathing in your own body right now, without trying to change it, without judging it as good or bad, right or wrong, just simply paying attention to what is happening with your breath right now.

Then allow your awareness to descend to your belly. Once again, recall the globe of light there. The belly is the body center, the center that is connected with movement, with placement in space, with balance. While breathing into your belly, become aware of the whole of your body as a gestalt. As you focus your attention on the globe of light in your belly, let your inner peripheral awareness take in the rest of your body. Be aware of any sensations, any pressures. Be aware of your balance. Breathe to that globe of light in your belly. Chant the Ram three times in the belly.

Exhale. Inhale through the nose. RAM (*repeat three times*). (*Ring bells three times.*) Sit for a moment longer and be aware simply of your body. (*Pause.*)

Bring your awareness up into your chest, into the area of your heart in the middle of your chest. This center, the rhythmic center, is also the center of the emotions and feelings. As you breathe to the globe of light in your chest, be aware of your mood, what your internal atmosphere is right now. How does that influence the pulse of your heart and the rhythm of breath?

Exhale. Inhale. RAM (*repeat three times*). (*Ring bells three times.*) Sit silently, being aware of your emotions right now. (*Pause.*)

Bring your awareness to the point of light in your head. Be aware of any thoughts or images that preoccupy you at this moment.

Exhale. Inhale. RAM (*repeat three times*). (*Ring bells three times.*) Sit silently in the center of your thoughts. Imagine that you can concentrate yourself into that tiny pinpoint of light while all around you is a pool of your mindstuff. Thoughts and images rise to the top of the pool, then sink down again like fishes in water. Sit as witness in the center of your mind, observing the thoughts and images that rise and fall about you. (*Pause.*)

Once again, allow the ray or line of light to descend downward through the globe of light in your chest, downward through the belly, uniting and balancing head, heart, and belly—thoughts, feelings, and sensation. Let the beam of light quit your body, enter the earth, seeking its way into the very center of the earth, uniting you with the fourth globe of light. Listen to the sounds around you as the sound of the chant of the earth. (*Pause.*)

Now direct your attention to the ray of light that descends from the point in the center of the head all the way down to the center of the earth. Let it gradually transform into a kind of channel, a transparent channel that is filled with light, a channel that penetrates down to the center of the earth. Through that channel the light of your belly, of your heart, and of your head are replenished by the light of the earth. With each inhalation experience yourself filling your body, filling your heart, filling the light in your head with fresh, clean earth-light, nourishing you, healing you. As you exhale, imagine yourself releasing some of the light from your heart, your belly, and your head, downward through that channel to replenish and heal the earth as well. As you inhale you draw in nourishment from the earth; as you exhale you nourish the earth with your own inner light. Meditate on this. (*Pause.*)

Bring your attention once again to the globe of light in your belly. We will chant one more Ram to close the meditation. Exhale. Inhale. RAM. (*Ring bells once.*) Gradually let your eyelids grow lighter with each inbreath. Finally, they open; and as they do, look at the flame, become aware of the circle of people, and come back into the room and stretch.

Ritual of the Changing of the Vestal

RAM MEDITATION, DAY 4

To the Journeyers:

Once again, focus your attention on the candle. With your peripheral vision, follow the circle around the room. Include yourself as part of the circle. Allow your eyelids to grow heavy, and with each outbreath let them yearn to close, until finally they do. Bring your attention to your breath and your inner awareness. Gradually direct your attention to the globe of light in your belly. Feel its warmth, experience its brightness as you exhale and inhale, and it expands and contracts.

Exhale. Inhale. RAM (*three times*). (*Ring bells three times.*) Breathe naturally and experience the whole of your body from the periphery of your skin to the center of the globe of light in your belly, all of your body as one. (*Pause.*)

Bring your attention to the area of your heart in the center of your chest. Exhale. Inhale. RAM (*three times*). (*Ring bells three times.*) Become conscious of what your mood is, what the atmosphere of your being is today, however subtle the mood may be that you are experiencing. What do you feel about your relationship to this day, to the work, and to the people around you? Take a deep breath and let a sound come out that expresses what you feel. Stay with that feeling. (*Pause.*)

Then quit the center in your chest and bring your awareness to the point of light in your head. With your eyelids closed, direct your eyes upward, as if you could look into that light.

Exhale. Inhale. RAM (*three times*). (*Ring bells three times.*) Once again, sit in the center of that light and observe any thoughts or images that rise and fall around you, like fish swimming to the top of the pool, not identifying with anything, and yet aware of all. (*Pause.*)

Allow the ray of light to descend from the point of light in your head, through the center of the globe of light in your chest, through the globe of light in your belly, downward into the earth. Let it plunge like a root, finally attaching itself to that point that is the center of the earth. The earth then becomes the fourth globe of light. Listen to the sounds around you as the chant of the earth. (*Pause.*)

Allow that ray of light to transform itself into a channel through which you drink nourishment from the earth, replenishing all three globes. Focus your attention today on the globe of light in your belly. As you drink in the nourishment from the Great Mother, from the earth, allow that globe of light in the belly to transform into the bud of a huge yellow flower. And with each breath that yellow flower gradually opens. Let it open there in your belly, a golden yellow flower. As the flower opens, it fills your body with a golden light, all of your body, your torso, your arms, your head, your legs, seeking out any areas that need healing. And as that golden light fills your body all the way to your periphery, to your skin, it crystallizes as a kind of barrier so that none of your energy leaks out, nor can anything alien come in. Sit for a moment with the meditation on the open flower, your body filled with light, and the sealed periphery. Allow that flower to remain opened in your body so that the light can continue to heal you and protect you through the rest of the day, and we'll chant one Ram in the belly to close the meditation.

Exhale. Inhale. RAM. (*Bell.*) Gradually let your eyes open. Come back into the room and stretch.

Ritual of the Changing of the Vestal

RAM MEDITATION, DAY 5

To the Journeyers:

Today, in order to bring us back together, we are going to do the Rams a little differently. Rather than in the orderly fashion in which we have been doing them heretofore—three Rams in the belly, heart, and head followed by bells—we will do a "tune-up." We start by humming, so that we find the same basic tone. Then, in your own way and in your own rhythm, chant three Rams in the belly, three in the heart, and three in the head. The Rams are continuous. Don't wait for me or for the rest of the group. Afterward I will guide a meditation, and we will finish with one Ram in the belly.

Begin by looking at the candle flame. Allow your peripheral vision to take in the group as a whole, and experience yourself as part of that whole. Instead of making a circle of the group with your peripheral vision, be aware of the group as a whole while you hold the flame as your point of focus. Then, very gradually, allow your eyelids to close; with each outbreath allow your eyelids to grow heavier, until finally they close.

We will begin humming. In your own way, tune up all three centers. Exhale. Inhale. Hum. Rams in all three centers. (*At the conclusion of this, ring the bells seven times.*)

Once again, allow the ray of light to descend downward through the chest, downward through the belly in a straight line, integrating, bringing together, and balancing head, heart, and body; thoughts, feelings, and sensations; all three globes. Allow the line to descend downward into the earth, attracted by the forces of gravity to the liquid molten center. Listen to the sounds of the earth around you as the chant of the fourth globe of light, the earth.

To the Guide:

Allow three deep breaths for yourself as you listen to the sounds.

Once again, allow that ray of light to transform itself into a channel whereby the nourishment of the earth is brought up into the three globes. Recall the golden flower open in your belly, filling your body with healing light and sealing its periphery. (*Pause.*)

Today, focus your attention on the point of light in your head. That light gradually transforms itself into a lotus bud. With each inhalation the bud grows larger. Light fills it as the bud enlarges, filling gradually the whole of your head. Continue breathing as the petals of the lotus flower gradually begin to unfold. Petal by petal, the lotus opens. Imagine that the crown of your head opens, petal by delicate petal. The petals are like arms reaching toward the sun. And at the same time, the room is filled with a beautiful fragrance, the fragrance of your essential self. With the inbreath you drink in nourishment from the earth; and with the outbreath you fill the room with the fragrance of your soul's essence, from the petals of the lotus. Surround everyone in the room with that fragrance, healing and blessing them. And feel yourself healed and blessed with the fragrance from the essential self of the others. Finally, the lotus is fully opened. There in the center of it is that tiny pinpoint of light, a diamond glistening at the golden center of the lotus blossom. Sit with that image. (*Pause.*)

Light from the diamond in the center of the lotus radiates outward toward the cosmos, and the petals, like arms, reach out and gather the divine light into you, as well as the earth-light from beneath. . . . As you sit there with the lotus open on your crown, the light glistening in its center, recall the last moment of your confrontation between Hero and Demon. Bathe them in that healing frequency of light and the fragrance of the scent of your essence. Allow anything that needs healing to be further healed, further integrated in this light.

To the Guide:

If someone in the group has been ill or is suffering, you may allow at this point for a healing meditation, imagining that person or those people in the center of the circle, calling out their names. The group may also want to call out names of friends and family members who are ill.

Gradually, allow the petals of the lotus once again to enfold themselves to protect your crown and the light within. The bud closes and seals itself. Let the roots stay in the earth so that you can remain rooted in the earth. Allow the golden flower in your belly to remain open, healing your body with its light. We will chant one Ram to close. Exhale. Inhale. RAM. (*Bell.*)

Gradually, with each inbreath, let your eyelids grow light again, till finally they have opened and you come back into the circle and to the light. And then stretch.

Ritual of the Changing of the Vestal

RAM MEDITATION, DAY 6

To the Guide:

Use the same tune-up meditation given on Day 5. Allow for a little extra time at the end. Suggest that they might want to explore harmonies and melodies after the tune-up. When finished, ring the bells seven times.

To the Journeyers:

Recall the three globes of light and the line that integrates them with the earth, and listen to the chant of the earth. (*Pause.*)

Once again, allow the beam to turn into a channel and the nourishment from the earth to fill the yellow blossom in your belly, filling you with golden light. With each breath the lotus in your head opens, displaying the jewel in its center and filling the room with the fragrance of your essence. Let the lotus open completely, the petals reaching upward toward the sky above you, like arms calling something home. (*Pause.*)

Redirect your awareness now from that point of light toward the center of the earth. Let the light go beyond the center of the earth, pushing through the earth, against the force of gravity, until finally it comes out on the other side of the earth, wherever that may be. It enters into the night sky on the other side of the earth beneath you. Allow that beam to continue outward into the night sky, soaring past the moon, past the other planets in the solar system, penetrating deeply, deeply into space, beneath you. Let it go beyond the solar system into the other solar systems, and beyond the other solar systems to the edges of the universe. There it follows the curve of the universe in a huge arc, mounting behind you, up above you where it arcs downward to return to its source in the center of your head. The petals of the lotus, like arms, reach up to receive and welcome that beam of light back to its source, the diamond in the center of your head. Let it reintegrate and follow its path once again through you, through the earth, through the universe, and return home. The four globes of light are like a jewel on a huge ring of light that encircles the universe. Let your imagination follow that ring through the universe and back again. Experience the immensity.

Now, once again, allow the beam of light to separate itself from the jewel in the heart of the lotus, return upward into the sky, circle around behind, beneath, coming backward through the universe, backward through the other solar systems, backward from the furthest planets in this solar system, from the moon, through the night sky on the other side of the earth, through the crust of the earth, back into the center of the earth, and let it remain planted there for the rest of the day. Bring your attention back to your belly, and we will chant one Ram to close.

Exhale. Inhale. RAM. (*Bell.*) Gradually, with each inbreath let your eyelids grow lighter, until finally they open to the flame, to the group, to the room.

Ritual of the Changing of the Vestal

RAM MEDITATION, DAY 7

To the Journeyers:

Because of the richness of the imagery in the Reward fantasy, we are going to do a very simple meditation this morning. It's called a free Ram. We will start with a humming sound that transforms into the sound of the Ram. Then just begin chanting Rams at random, with the idea of tuning up all three centers, but in any order you wish. You may wish to start in the heart, then go up to the head, and down to the belly. You may go in any direction you wish, but always there will be a kind of harmony because of the fact that we are all singing together. It may sound a bit like the music of the movie *2001*, with all these different tune-ups going on at the same time. After you have tuned up all three centers, explore chanting the Ram in any way you like, creating little melodies, harmonies, even rhythms. Create a morning song without words. It will continue until everybody is finished, and then I will ring the bell. RAMS. (*Bells seven times. Allow a silent meditation of five to ten minutes.*)

Bring your attention back to your belly and we will chant one Ram to close.

Exhale. Inhale. RAM. (*Bell.*)

Gradually, with each inbreath let your eyelids grow lighter until finally they open to the flame, to the group, to the room. And stretch.

Ritual of the Changing of the Vestal

ALTERNATE RAM MEDITATION, DAY 7

To the Guide:

Chant the Rams as above. Follow with this meditation.

To the Journeyers:

Once again, allow the beam of light to descend from the point of light in your head, through your heart, through your belly, balancing, aligning, and uniting the three globes of light that are your individual body, and then entering into the earth, plunging down to the center of the earth, the fourth globe of light. Listen to the sounds of the earth. (*Pause.*) Allow the beam of light to transform itself into a channel, taking in nourishment. Recall the golden flower in your belly filling your body with healing light. Once again, allow the lotus to unfold, exposing the jewel in its golden center: inhaling, taking in nourishment; exhaling, scenting the air with the fragrance of your own essence. Once again, pushing down through the center of the earth, the beam of light continues until it exits the earth on the other side, goes downward into the night sky, past the moon, the planets of the solar system, past the other solar systems, out to the edges of the universe, where it arcs beneath you, around behind you, tracing the edges of the universe. It descends from above and reunites with the point of light in your head. All three globes are united with each other, with the earth, and with the universe.

Then take your right hand and place it palm up toward the person to the right of you. Place your left palm in the upturned hand of the person on the left of you, so you are making contact with the people on either side of you. Spend a moment aware of that contact. (*Pause.*)

Imagine that with your right hand you can receive the energy of the person on the right of you, allow it to pass through your arm, through your body, through your left arm, and give it to the person on the left of you. Take in from the right, let it pass through you, and let go to the left. Relax your arms as much as possible. Let all the tension in your body disappear. Let your body become an open window so that the energy from the rest of the group can blow through you. Nobody there, just energy in movement, all those huge rings of light rotating in a kind of carousel of light. The energy blowing through you, cleansing you, healing you. Let that energy move faster and faster, faster and faster, so that the rings of light that extend all the way out to the edges of the universe are rotating faster than the speed of light. There is no time for you to tense up against them. Just allow them to blow through you, until finally they all merge into one huge sunburst of light that reaches out to the four corners of the universe. And the source of that light is here in this room, from the point of the candle to the edges of the universe, one huge sunburst of light. In that way you are united with your own three centers, with the earth, with the universe, and with each other, in light. The light moves so quickly it is almost as if it were not moving at all. Dissolve into that one huge sunburst of light. (*Pause.*)

Now, little by little, the light begins to slow down. It begins to differentiate itself again into the individual circles, slower and slower. Finally, your own circle of light finds your body again. Take hold of the hands on either side of you, firmly, as if to say goodbye for now. And then gradually let your hands relax, separate from the people on either side of you, little by little, letting go. Finally, bring your own hands together to make contact with yourself. Let the ring of light separate from the top of your head, go upward, backward, down around, through the universe, through the solar systems, through the planets, backward from the other side of the earth, through the crust into the earth, to the center of the earth. At the same time, let the lotus close quietly to protect the diamond at its center. Allow the golden flower to remain open in your belly. Take a deep breath, and we will chant one Ram to close. RAM. (*Bell.*)

APPENDIX II
Daily Structure

I. SEVEN-DAY STRUCTURE

Day One

- Homeground and the Call
- Begin with a luncheon meal, the first session scheduled to start at 3 o'clock.

Preparation
    Music to bring people together, including the song "Why Not?"
    Introduction
        History of the process
        The plot of the story
        Technical details of the process
            how it works
            agreements
Meditation to establish ritual (Rams)
Homeground
    Guided fantasy
    Homeground drawing
    Begin Workbook
Art Museum Exercise
Choosing the Spirit Guide
Sharing (either with the whole group or in subgroups)
Closing meditation

Day Two: The Hero

Ritual opening (see Appendix I, Ram meditation, Day Two)
Talk about the Hero
Begin Fool's Dance
Images of Heroes
    Childhood Hero
    Movie Star
    Animal
    Adventurer
    Important person
    Lover
    God/Goddess
Owning: triads with mirrors
Support process
Hero fantasy
Coat of arms
Costumes
Heroes' Banquet
Heroic presentations
Anointing
Passing the loving cup
Party-dance
Ritual closing

Day Three: The Demon

Ritual opening
Talk about the Demon and body armor
Fool's Dance
Body armor meditation and intensification
Drawing the Battleground
Point of view
Developing scripts for Controller-Spontaneous Child
Spontaneous Child dramatization
Madhouse exercise
Demon drawing
Demon Dance of Power
Ritual closing

Day Four: The Instrument of Power

Ritual opening
Fool's Dance
Finding the Instrument of Power
    Explanation
    Walk with the Spirit Guide
Dedication of the Instruments of Power
    Ritual
    Guided fantasy: "Threshold of Adventure"
Confrontation
    Discussion
    Divide into teams. Teams are independent and work together till Day Five afternoon. Each group does its own ritual closing of the day.

Day Five: Confrontation and Mysterium

Teams continue working together until afternoon session.
Ritual opening
Sharing
Fool's Dance
Crossing the Threshold
    Discussion
    Guided fantasy through Threshold
    Follow fantasy
    Guided fantasy: "Divine Opposite"
Group sharing
Ritual closing

Day Six: The Supreme Ordeal

Ritual opening
Fool's Dance
Supreme Ordeal [of Breath]
    Talk
    Considerations
    Breathing process [or guided fantasy]
Sharing
Ritual closing

Day Seven: Reward and Return

Ritual opening
Talk about Reward and Return
Reward fantasy
Reward and Return artwork
Finish Fool's Dance
Sharing
Final ritual closing

II. WEEKEND STRUCTURE

Friday evening

Music
Introduction
    History of process
    Story of plot
    Technical details of process
        How it works
        Agreements
Homeground
    Guided fantasy
    Drawing
    Begin Workbooks
    Choosing Spirit Guides
    Set up dates for sharing
Closing meditation

Saturday: 10 A.M. to 10 P.M.

Ritual opening
Fool's Dance
Images of Heroes
    Childhood Hero
    Movie star
    Animal

      Important Person
      God/Goddess
Owning triads
Abbreviated support process
Hero fantasy
Coats of arms
Heroes' Banquet
Heroic presentations
Anointing and loving cup
Party/Dance
Ritual closing

Sunday: 10 A.M. to 10 P.M.

Ritual opening
Fool's Dance
Demon: abbreviated version
    Talk about body armor
    Body armor meditation
    Reversing retroflection
    Demon Dance
    Demon drawing
Confrontation-Dance
Guided meditation into Mysterium, Reward, Return
Sharing
Ritual closing

APPENDIX III
The Hero's Journey Workbook[1]

This Picture Summed up the Experience of Homeground

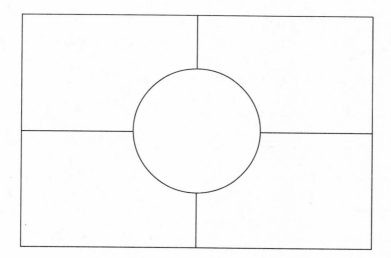

HOMEGROUND

Once upon a time there was a person named (your name)_____

_____

who fell asleep and had a most peculiar dream.

(Your name) _____
found herself/himself walking down a stairway that led deep into the center of
the Earth. At the bottom of that stairway was a room with four huge doors, and
on each door was written a word. She/he went across the room to the door with

the word "Home" written on it, and found _____

_____

_____

_____

_____

_____ .

She/he felt _____

_____ about what she/he saw.

The next door was entitled "Lifework." Behind that door she/he found

_____

_____

_____

_____

_____

which made her/him feel _____

_____

_____ .

The third door had the word "Beloved" written on it, and behind that

door was _____

_____

_____

_____

_____

_____

_____ .

When (your name) _____

came out of that door, she/he realized that she/he felt very _____

_____

_____ .

       Finally, (your name) _____

came to the door named "Self," opened it, went inside, and found _____

_____

_____

_____

_____ ,

all of which evoked feelings of _____

_____

_____

_____

_____ .

THE CALL

Returning to the central room, (your name) _____
realized that she/he had just seen a picture of her/his life. She/he became
pensive, and wondered how she/he felt about it all, and how, given a chance,
she/he would want to change it.

Just then, to (your name) _____'s
great surprise, there appeared before her/him a magnificent golden throne
with huge gold letters on the back that said, "Throne of Miracles." (Your

name) _____ knew that if
she/he sat on this throne, any miracle that she/he visualized would come to

her/him. As (your name) _____
sat on the throne, she/he realized that she/he would have to be really honest
with herself/himself about the images behind the four doors. Were they real

images, or were they ideal images? She/he decided that they were_____
_____ (the truth of

the matter being _____

_____

_____

_____

_____

_____).

Now (your name) _____

was ready to make a wish. She/he visualized _____

_____

_____

_____

_____

_____

_____

_____

_____

_____ ,

which would change her/his life by _____

_____

_____

_____

_____

_____ .

     As she/he got up from the throne and started to ascend the stairway again, she/he realized, "My journey has begun."

     When (your name) _____
awoke, she/he didn't believe that such a miracle was possible.

     "That could never happen to me, I'm too _____

_____

_____. And besides,

I have to think about _____

_____

_____

_____

_____

_____

_____ . . . and I
don't know if I believe in this stuff anyway."

    The Hero (Hero's name) _____

    However, the next night, as (your name) _____

_____ slept, the call to the miraculous was
stronger than the call to the mundane. She/he was visited by images of heroes,
gods and goddesses, animals, and friends—images that evoked heroic qualities that she/he had forgotten existed.

    She/he saw the animal _____

_____

_____ , which stimulated qualities of

_____ .

The childhood hero _____

_____ evoked

_____

_____ . The

god/goddess _____

_____

reminded her/him of her/his_____

_____

_____ .

She/he found that she/he could say, "I am _____

_____

_____

_____

_____

_____

_____ ;

but she/he had difficulty saying, "I am _____

_____

_____

_____

_____ .

Suddenly, there appeared before her/him a tribe of helpers and

friends who offered their support. (Your name) _____

_____ asked the tribe to encourage

her/his feelings of _____

and responded to their aid by _____

_____

_____

_____

_____ .

That made her/him feel _____

_____

_____

_____

_____

_____ .

Although (your name) _____

had fallen asleep at home in her/his bed, she/he awakened in a sunlit

meadow. Looking around, she/he saw that the meadow was _____

_____

_____

_____

_____

_____

_____ . She/he could hear the sounds of

_____

_____

_____

_____ , and smell

_____

_____

_____

_____ .

Under her/his feet, the ground was _____

_____

_____

_____

_____ .

(Your name) _____
found a path winding through the meadow. On the path was a signpost that
said:

To the House
of
The Hero!

(Describe the path:) _____

_____

_____

_____

_____

_____

_____

_____ .

Finally, she/he found the house. The house was _____

_____

_____

_____

_____ , and was in a setting of

_____

_____

_____

_____ .

She/he went up to the door and knocked and waited. After a few

moments, she/he heard footsteps inside. The footsteps sounded _____

_____

_____ , and she/he felt

_____

_____

_____ .

Slowly, the door swung open. And there, standing before her/him,
framed in the doorway, stood her/his own heroic self. (Describe):

_____

_____

_____

_____

_____

_____

_____

_____

_____

_____

_____ .

For a long moment, they looked into each other's eyes, and then together, they walked through the house. The inside of the house was _____

_____

_____

_____

_____ .

Finally, they came to the Hero's favorite room. It was the _____

_____ room, and it looked

_____

_____

_____

_____

_____

_____ . The two of them sat down together to have a chat.

"What is your secret name?" asked (your name) _____

_____ .

"_____

_____ ," responded the Hero.
"What is your quest?"

The Hero replied, "_____

_____

_____

_____

_____

_____

_____ ."

"What do you want from me?" (your name)_____

_____ asked.

The Hero looked deeply into (your name)_____

_____'s eyes and said,

"_____

_____

_____

_____

_____

_____

_____ ."

They talked a little longer about _____

_____

_____

_____

_____

_____

_____.

(Your name) _____

found that she/he was feeling _____

_____

_____

_____.

Soon it was time to leave, so they walked together to the door.

The room was flooded with sunlight as the Hero, (Hero's name)_____

_____, opened the door. The two looked deeply into each other's eyes again and reached out to share a farewell embrace.

Suddenly, a miraculous thing happened. As the two selves, the heroic and the mundane, stood heart to heart, their breath became one, their hearts beat with a single rhythm, the pores of their bodies opened, and they merged

into one presence. This is how the person (your name) _____

_____ became the

Hero (Hero's name) _____

_____ , standing in her/his doorway, looking out at
the path of adventure she/he was about to follow.

    Feelings of _____

_____

_____

and _____

_____

_____ surged through the
newly united self as she/he stepped out into the brilliant sunshine.

    A few moments later, off to the left, she/he heard the sounds of pound-
ing hooves and saw a rider on a white horse coming toward her/him. The rider
bore a message that said, "You are cordially invited to the first annual Confer-

ence of Heroes, to be held on this day, _____ ,

in _____

_____."

    So the Hero (Hero's name) _____

_____ , in order to establish herself/himself at the conference,
designed this coat of arms:

The Conference of Heroes was extraordinary. (Hero's name) _____

_____ found that she/he was not alone
in her/his quest for the miraculous. There were, after all, others in the world
like herself/himself, other Heroes willing to support her/him in accomplishing
her/his heroic quest.

Among those present were the Heroes _____

_____

_____

_____

_____

_____

_____ .

She/he was most impressed by _____

_____

_____

_____

_____ ; and she/he found

_____

_____

_____ the most dissimilar to herself/himself.

She/he appeared at the conference dressed in _____

_____

_____

_____ and proclaimed, "I am (Hero's name)

_____ .

"My powers are _____

_____

_____

_____

_____ .

"My quest is _____

_____

_____

_____ ."

And she/he availed herself/himself of their cooperation by asking

them to _____

_____

_____

_____

_____ .

Afterward, she/he felt _____

_____

_____

_____

_____

_____ .

    She/he realized that in her/his mundane life, she/he relates to groups

of people similarly, in that _____

_____

_____

_____ . And yet there was

something quite different: _____

_____

_____

_____

_____

_____

_____ .

THE PREMONITION

    That night, as (your name) _____
was sleeping, she/he had a strange dream. She/he dreamed that a battle was
going on, and that it was taking place in her/his own body. Awareness of muscle aches and tensions showed all the ways that the Hero was being blocked
from expression. She/he could actually visualize the internal stresses and
strains of the battle. An image emerged that looked like this:

BATTLEFIELD

A strange and frightening figure began to present itself—the figure of a vic-timizer who tortured its victims by _____

_____

_____

_____

_____

_____ .

     Somehow, the Hero (Hero's name)_____

_____ knew that this was someone she/he would have to deal with. It was the vague shadow of the Demon

(Demon's name)_____ .

THE DEMON (DEMON'S NAME)_____

     This is the story of the Demon (Demon's name) _____

_____ .

The Demon was (describe): _____

_____

_____

_____

_____

_____

_____

_____ .

(Demon's name) _____

_____ deals with Heroes by

_____

_____

_____

_____

_____ .

(Demon's name) _____

_____ defends herself/himself by

_____

_____

_____

_____

_____

_____ .

Her/his lair is _____

_____

_____

_____

_____ .

She/he was born by _____

_____

_____

_____ .

She/he is protecting _____

_____

_____

_____

_____ .

THE DEMON (DEMON'S NAME) _____

THE INSTRUMENT OF POWER

This is how the Hero (Hero's name) _____

_____ acquired the Instrument of Power,

_____

_____

_____

_____

_____

_____

_____ .

The Hero (Hero's name) _____

_____ took her/his magical Instrument into the
conference room and laid it on the altar as the other Heroes had done. They

fell into deep meditation and once again (Hero's name) _____

_____ found herself/himself in

_____

_____

_____ , where he/she had

found the Instrument of Power. Recalling the scene, she/he saw _____

_____

_____

_____

_____

_____ .

    The scene changed magically and (Hero's name) _____

_____ saw her/his Spirit Guide. (Describe Guide:)

_____

_____

_____

_____

_____

_____

_____

_____ .

    (Hero's name) _____

_____ asked her/his Guide, "What is the name of
my Instrument of Power?"

    "_____

_____," answered the Guide.

    "What are its powers?"

    "_____

_____

_____

_____

_____

_____

_____."

      "How can I use it in my daily life?"

      " _____

_____

_____

_____

_____

_____."

      (Hero's name) _____

_____ was filled with a sense of

_____ ,

as she/he presented _____

_____

_____ to the other Heroes. She/he

was impressed with the other power objects, especially _____

_____

_____

_____ of the Hero (Hero's name)

_____

(Describe:) _____

_____

_____

_____

_____

_____

_____

_____ .

THE CONFRONTATION

Many a story could be told of the adventures of the Hero (Hero's

name) _____ .

Many a minstrel could strum his lute to chant these extraordinary tales. But
the strangest of all is the legendary confrontation at the magical doorway with

the fearsome Demon guardian (Demon's name) _____

_____ .

In the morning after the premonition dream, the Hero (Hero's name)

_____

shook off the lingering strangeness and began to stride along the pathway of

deep adventure. The sky was_____

_____ ; the road was

_____ ;

and everywhere the Hero looked _____

_____

_____

_____

_____

_____

_____

_____

_____

_____

_____ .

Finally, she/he came to the top of a hill. The country stretched out beneath her/him, and there, just ahead, was the magical threshold she/he knew was

meant for her/him. It looked _____

_____

_____

_____

_____

_____

_____ .

And so, with her/his faithful Instrument of Power _____

_____

in her/his hand, a song in her/his heart, the Hero _____

_____

_____

toward the entrance.

    Suddenly, (describe the entire confrontation:) _____

_____

_____

_____

_____

_____

_____

_____

_____

_____

_____

_____ .

THE MYSTERIUM

The great Confrontation was over. As the Hero (Hero's name) _____

_____ looked around, she/he saw

_____

_____

_____

_____

_____

_____ .

There before her/him stood the entrance to the Land of Miracles.

(Describe:) _____

234   Appendix III

_____

_____

_____

_____

_____

_____

_____

_____

_____ .

She/he stepped forward _____

_____

_____ and entered. She/he felt

_____

_____ as she/he realized that this was the first time anyone had stepped across this threshold; that each breath was new; that each form and shape that greeted her/him was "the first time"; and that each new taste, smell, touch was totally and miraculously her/his own.

(Describe in detail:) _____

_____

_____

_____

_____

_____

_____

_____

_____

_____

_____

_____

_____

_____

_____

_____

_____

_____ .

Armed with the magical power of (Instrument's name) _____

_____ ,

protected by the Spirit Guide (Guide's name) _____

_____ ,

and confident of her/his newly recovered powers, the Hero (Hero's name)_____

_____

proceeded into the depths of her/his Mysterium and encountered these trials:

_____

_____

_____

_____

_____

_____

_____

_____

_____

_____

_____

_____

_____

_____

_____

_____

_____

_____

_____

_____.

THE SUPREME ORDEAL

Finally, the Hero (Hero's name) _____

_____ came upon the Supreme Ordeal.

This is the way it happened: _____

_____

_____

_____

_____

_____

_____

_____

_____

_____

_____

_____

_____

_____

_____

_____

_____

_____ .

THE REWARD

Finally, the great goal was near at hand. The Hero (Hero's name) _____

_____

approached the place of the Reward. She/he saw_____

_____

_____

_____

_____

_____

_____

_____

_____

_____.

She/he stood before her/his Reward and felt _____

_____

_____

_____

_____

_____

_____

_____.

She/he asked these questions:
"What is the meaning of my Reward?"
"What is its special power?"
"How can it serve me in my life?"

And this is what happened: _____

_____

_____

_____

_____

_____

_____

_____

_____

_____

_____

_____

_____

_____ .

THE RETURN

Once again the Hero (Hero's name) _____

_____ found herself/himself
climbing down the long stairway into the room with four doors, only now she/he
was rich in the knowledge and experience of her/his miraculous journey.

She/he sat on the Throne of Miracles, holding her/his Reward in
her/his hand.

"How does this Reward reflect my original wish?"_____

_____

_____

_____

_____

_____

_____

_____

_____

_____

_____ .

That made her/him feel _____

_____

_____

_____

_____

_____ .

Then she/he called out to the door marked "Home," and sent the

Reward into that room. "How does my Reward illuminate my home?" _____

_____

_____

_____

_____

_____

_____

_____

_____

_____ .

"What simple step can I take to encourage the process?"_____

_____

_____

_____

_____

_____

_____ .

Then she/he called out, "Open!" to the door marked "Lifework." In that room the Reward _____

_____

_____

_____

_____

_____

_____ .

The simple step she/he could take was _____

_____

_____

_____

_____

_____

_____

_____ .

In the room marked "Beloved," the Reward _____

_____

_____

_____

_____

_____

_____ .

And she/he imagined herself/himself _____

_____

_____

_____

_____

_____

_____ .

Finally, she/he sent the Reward into the room marked "Self": _____

_____

_____

_____

_____

_____

_____

_____

_____

_____ .

And she/he knew that what she/he could do to facilitate the process was

_____

_____

_____

_____

_____

_____

_____

_____ .

All of this made her/him feel _____

_____

_____

_____

_____

_____

_____

_____

_____

_____ .

     At that moment the Hero (Hero's name) _____

_____ awoke once again to find,
not Hero, not Demon, not magician, not god, but simply the person she/he had
always been . . . yet somehow different because of the miraculous journey

she/he had just finished. " _____

_____

_____

_____

_____

_____

_____

_____

_____

_____

_____

_____

_____

_____

_____

_____

_____

_____

_____

_____

_____

_____

_____

_____

_____ ," is what she/he said.

The End

CONTRACTS

"A journey of a thousand miles begins with one single step."
—Laotse

Now that you have taken your inner journey, it is time to prepare the way back to the world you left behind. You may want to make some changes. You may see things differently. You may find that your Demon self is still sabotaging you, out of habit. The following "single-step" contracts may help you facilitate whatever changes you may want to make.

Before you verbalize the contracts, however, ask yourself the following questions and answer them as honestly and thoroughly as you can:

1. How would the quality of my life be changed?

2. What specific things would need changing?

3. What am I willing to do to effect change?

4. How would others perceive these changes?

5. How might I sabotage myself?

6. What can I do to prevent that sabotage?

I, (your name) _____

_____ contract with myself to

_____

_____

on (today's date) _____ at (time)

_____ . I realize I could sabotage myself by

_____

_____

_____

_____

_____ ,

and will _____

_____

_____

_____

_____

in order to give myself extra support. I know this may mean _____

_____

_____

_____

_____

_____

_____ , and I am willing to take

responsibility by _____

_____

_____

_____

_____

_____

_____

_____

_____

_____

_____

_____

_____

_____

_____

_____

_____ .

If I need a little help, I can always _____

_____

_____

_____

_____

_____

_____

_____

_____

_____ .

Signed, (your name) _____ .

Witnessed (name of witness) _____ .